The Eastasia Edge

THE EASTASIA EDGE

Roy Hofheinz, Jr.

Kent E. Calder

Basic Books, Inc., Publishers

NEW YORK

Library of Congress Cataloging in Publication Data

Hofheinz, Roy, 1935–
    The Eastasia edge.

    Includes bibliographical references and index.
    1.   East Asia—Economic conditions.   2.   Asia, South-
eastern—Economic conditions.   3.   East Asia—Foreign
economic relations.   4.   Asia, Southeastern—Foreign
economic relations.   I.   Calder, Kent E.   II.   Title.
HC460.5.H63   330.95'0428   81–68409
ISBN 0–465–01776–2 (cloth) AACR2
ISBN 0–465–01777–0 (paper)

Contents

Part IV
THE OUTSIDE WORLD

APPENDICES

Foreword

THREE DECADES AGO, George Orwell, in his now classic political novel *1984,* described a world divided against itself and at war. Three great regions—Oceania (the Americas and the British Isles), Eurasia (Europe and Russia), and Eastasia (China, Korea, Japan, and Southeast Asia)—struggled against one another for the remaining territories and resources of the world. Though these regions professed different philosophies, their similar political systems allowed each region to wage war without alarming its people, no matter which other region was the enemy of the moment.

Most readers of Orwell, who died in 1950, are familiar with his fantastic description of the society of Oceania, the homeland of Winston Smith and his girlfriend Julia. We remember the distortions of the language Newspeak ("War is Peace"), the atrocities of the Thought Police empowered to control the minds of citizens, the eternal vigilance of Big Brother and the Party. We tend to forget that the excuse for all these affronts to human dignity was the intense competition between Oceania and its enemies, first Eurasia and then, suddenly and without warning, Eastasia.

We have adopted the term Eastasia from Orwell's book because it prophetically described the coalescence of the Chinese-culture area of the western Pacific, which so profoundly challenges the West today. In many respects Orwell's account is out-of-date or quite wrong. In particular, he underestimated the extent of economic interdependence among the world's regions. He described an Eastasian political philosophy ("Death Worship") which has no clear counterpart in current times, though one can see its origins in the Japanese kamikaze practice of self-immolation in war. He did not foresee that thermonuclear weapons would modify the conflict between the superpowers and compel them to rely on proxies. And of course his nightmare about the political degeneracy of Western society and the spread of totalitarianism from Russia to America and Britain has mercifully not yet come to pass. But Orwell's geopolitical fantasy of a world divided across the Pacific into regional power blocs continues to arouse anxiety.

In another respect, too, Orwell seems to have been right. He observed correctly that the behavior of nations is a product of their political arrangements. He understood that foreign policy is an extension of domestic policy and that economic competition and military defense are both responses—not mutually exclusive—to the same imperative of survival. We argue here that Eastasia survives, and indeed thrives, because of its political integrity—or, rather, the political integrity of each of its nations. Some would call the political systems of Eastasia Orwellian in that they often make demands on their subjects that many Westerners could not tolerate. But we must remember that these very demands—and the positive response of Eastasians to them—underlie the striking performance of the Eastasian economies today.

There is, to be sure, a slight resemblance between modern Eastasia and the Oceania of Orwell's nightmare. In the personality cult of Mao Zedong or Kim Il-sung, we see shades of the slavish worship which Orwell personified in Big Brother. Chinese "thought reform" for intellectuals, particularly intense in the 1950s, might have made Party representatives in Oceania proud. Even the regimentation of certain Japanese factories, where workers run on the job, wear identical uniforms, and attend interminable inspirational meetings, bears resemblance to Orwell's description of Oceania's mobilization for war.

For all the provocative parallels, the analogy to Orwell produces only a caricature of Eastasia, not a full or reliable picture. Still, in the extremes of the Orwellian image, we begin to glimpse the peculiar strength and resilience of social systems sharply at variance with our own. That Eastasians can tolerate high levels of nonsense while performing reliably under pressure shows the strength of their loyalty to government and institutions. This loyalty lies at the heart of what we call the "Eastasia Edge."

We argue that Eastasia has an advantage over us in the way it is organized and motivated—that its political system, broadly conceived, gives it an "edge" in crucial areas of economic competition. But as with any sharp, finely honed blade, there is also built-in weakness. The samurai sword of Eastasian strength could well be cracked against the jagged rock of raw-material shortages, Western protectionism, or even internal political disarray. We must never forget that Eastasian fortunes (and hence the nature of our competition) are subject to dramatic and unpredictable change. Yet judging from the record of the past, the drive to overcome will be unrelenting, as Eastasians overcompensate for their lack of resources, their overpopulation, their backwardness. Like a driven runner consumed with a sense of destiny mixed with lingering fears of failure, Eastasia plunges on—with a motive force all the more powerful for the uncertainties of the final lap.

We started this book after discovering in a seminar we taught at Harvard that few observers realized that Eastasia had taken the advantage over us. It is a joint effort in the fullest sense, drawing on our different areas of expertise. Calder contributed most heavily to the portraits of Japan, South Korea, and Singapore. Chapters 6, 10, 11, 12, 14, and 16 are the product of his efforts. Hofheinz worked most on China, Hong Kong, and North Korea. Chapters 1, 3, 7, 8, 9, and 13 came first from his typewriter. The authors drafted several remaining chapters jointly. Each has benefited greatly from criticisms and suggestions by the other, so that the work as a whole is one of thoroughgoing and equal partnership.

We owe many debts, first of all to the businesspeople, diplomats, and students in our seminar, and to the Fairbank Center for East Asian Research and the Japan Institute at Harvard which housed and supported us at the beginning of our work. Patricia Morikawa, David Sagal, Greg Ornatowski, Kenje Ogata, Stephen Pollock, Jim Tyson, and especially Jim Altschul and Vicki Woodruff assisted us energetically in preparing our material. We take full responsibility for the assertions of opinion and fact found herein.

Palm Desert, California
Cambridge, Massachusetts
July 1981

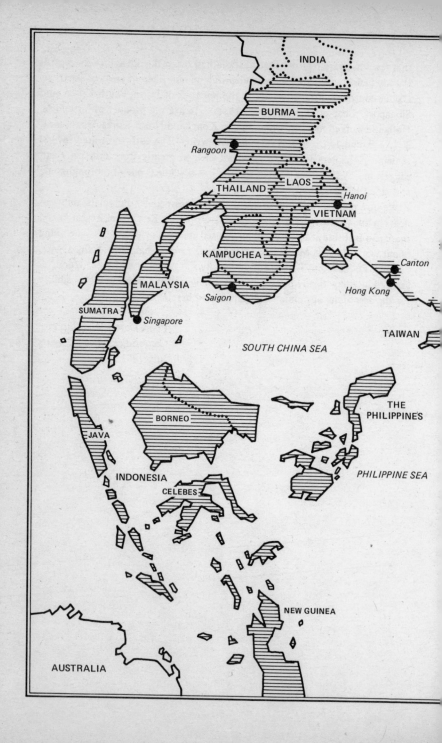

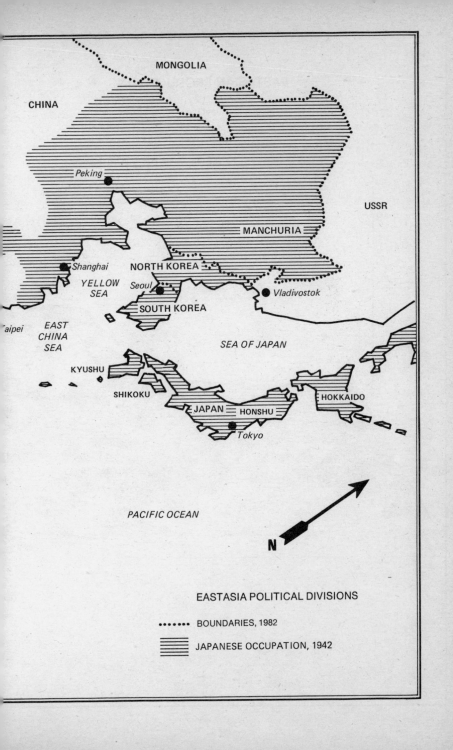

MONGOLIA

CHINA

Peking

USSR

MANCHURIA

Shanghai

YELLOW
SEA

NORTH KOREA

Seoul

Vladivostok

SOUTH KOREA

Taipei

EAST
CHINA
SEA

SEA OF JAPAN

KYUSHU

SHIKOKU

HOKKAIDO

JAPAN   HONSHU

Tokyo

N

PACIFIC OCEAN

EASTASIA POLITICAL DIVISIONS

••••••   BOUNDARIES, 1982

▭▭▭   JAPANESE OCCUPATION, 1942

EASTASIAN PRODUCTIVITY

Industrial Output per Capita, 1980

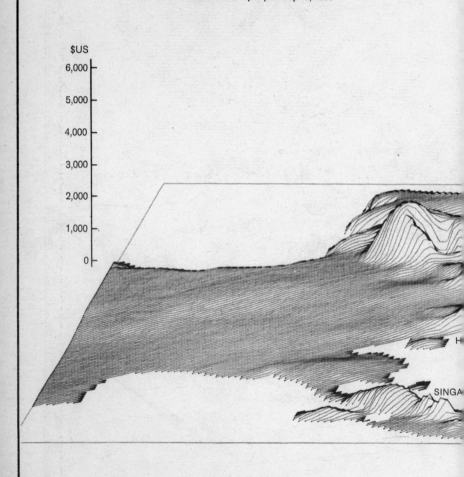

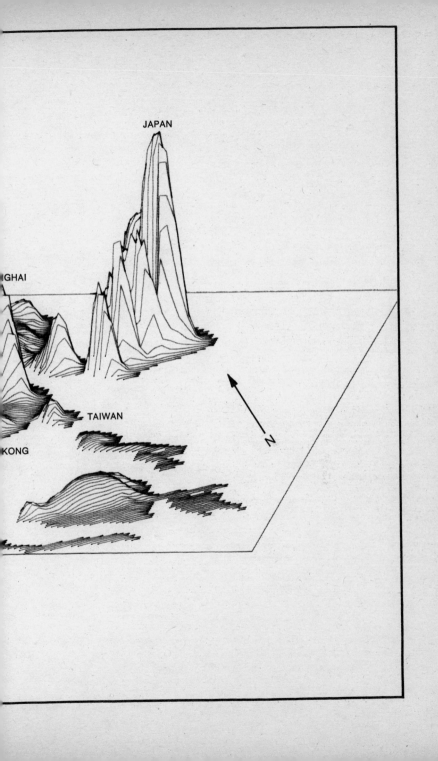

Part I

THREAT

1

Challenge from Eastasia

AMERICANS have never been afraid of threats. The problem has always been to see them clearly. We tend to magnify military threats and to discount other challenges. Our war-making power is the strongest in the world, but our defenses against unarmed aggression and competition are weak. Nowhere is this failing more obvious than in our inability to understand the contemporary challenge coming from Eastasia.

In the last forty years the United States has fought three wars on Asian soil —one victoriously against the Japanese, one indifferently against the Chinese in Korea, and one disastrously against the Vietnamese. Over a quarter million Americans have died, with countless dollars spent, in defending one Asian nation against another, in blocking the spread of alien ideologies, in ensuring the freedom of the Asian seas. We have struggled to bring Japan, Korea, and China into the world of international trade, even extending large credits and foreign assistance to restore our former enemies to prosperity. Yet despite this impressive commitment to defending our strategic interests, we remain remarkably unaware of the threat coming from Asia.

The reason for this oversight is that the threat is for the moment primarily economic. The United States now depends more on Eastasia economically than it does on Western Europe. Since 1975, the value of combined U.S. transpacific trade has exceeded that of all U.S. transatlantic commerce.[1] Our imports from Eastasia exceed our exports by nearly three to two.[2] Japanese autos, well-built and fuel-efficient, have captured one quarter of the market in the United States, the home of automotive mass production.[3] The threat is aimed not only at the United States but also at Western Europe, where Koreans and Taiwanese have now taken major portions of the British home market for textiles, and where Japanese have penetrated deeply into the West German steel market. Clearly, few sectors in the traditional developed economies are immune to Eastasian inroads.

Asian nations have begun to compete head-on with us in industries of the future as well as those of the past. In 1979, for example, Eastasia produced more than twice as many integrated circuits as Western Europe, and the gap was widening.[4] Eastasia provided nearly 10 percent of U.S. consumption of integrated circuits, the building blocks of all modern electronic devices from television sets to computers, and nearly 70 percent in such key product lines as 64-K random-access memories.[5] Leading U.S. businesses like IBM now depend more and more on advanced components purchased from such Asian firms as Hitachi and Nippon Electric.

Technology and the Future

A look at the future will quickly shatter complacency. Asian companies are now starting to dominate such advanced technologies as automation, telecommunications, and data processing. Installations of industrial robots, for example, will grow from $375 million in 1980 to more than $2 billion in 1990, and the Japan Industrial Robot Association projects that its members will account for 70 percent of this new worldwide market.[6] "Seeing and feeling" robots are being developed that will permit whole factories to operate without a single laborer. According to experts at the Draper Laboratories in Cambridge, Mass., Japan already leads the United States in this field by three years, and the Japanese Ministry of International Trade and Industry is planning to develop a prototype unmanned factory by 1985.[7]

In telecommunications the wave of the future is the use of tiny optical fibers to transmit millions of messages in microwave and satellite relays to replace expensive ground cables, and in sophisticated switching devices to permit connections between computers and communications lines. In each of these cutting-edge technologies, as well as in the development of microelectronic devices to handle them, Asian firms are springing into the lead. Nippon Electric (NEC) already has half the world market for microwave relay ground stations and has teamed up with Japan's international telecommunications monopoly Kokusai Denshin Denwa (KDD) to push into the optical fiber market. NEC, along with Fujitsu, has specialized in selling the critical interfaces that permit computers to talk over telephone lines, and now dominates this field in which U.S. firms are limited by antitrust regulations.

In the future, Eastasian countries also expect to be highly competitive in the aircraft industry. Through separate joint ventures with Boeing (fuselage) and Rolls Royce (jet engines), and through the production under license in Japan of the F-15 supersonic fighter, Japanese firms by the late 1980s will know how to produce sophisticated aircraft. Asian entry into this market, traditionally dominated by the United States, is certain.[8]

The high noon of European and American industrial supremacy has passed, bringing to an end the brief period of a few hundred years in which Asia, especially the eastern part of Asia, did not dominate the world. China, which invented gunpowder and movable type while Europe was still in the Dark Ages, and Japan, which pioneered in commercial organization many centuries ago, appear to be reemerging as the world's dominant economic force. Yet we Americans, by and large, remain convinced that the U.S.-centered order in Eastasia established by General Douglas MacArthur in the late 1940s remains unchanged—perhaps even enhanced by the strategic maneuverings in China of Richard Nixon, Henry Kissinger, and Zbigniew Brzezinski. Perceiving our interests and strategic position largely in military terms, we fail to sense the silent economic changes, as unambiguous in their implications as earthquakes are for the shape of continents, which have altered the map of the world more fundamentally than did the conflicts in Korea and Vietnam or perhaps World War II itself.

The growing economic might of Eastasia has already had a strong impact on the rest of the world. Consumers in the developed countries recognize Japanese brands as well as their own. Whereas before 1960 the word "Japanese" often meant cheap, low-quality merchandise, Western consumers now often prefer Japanese products to those of their own countries. The rapid sales growth of Sony television sets, Toyota autos, and Honda motorcycles came as much from improved quality as from lower prices. Japanese products have penetrated not only the developed world, generating large trade surpluses in the late 1970s, but also the less-developed, particularly the nations bordering the Pacific Ocean.

Wherever Japan's competitive advantage has faded, with increasing costs in the home islands, the "little Japans" have often stepped into the breach. Tatung color television sets from Taiwan, Hyundai Pony autos from South Korea, and electronic watches in bewildering variety from Hong Kong are now pushing aside Panasonics, Datsuns, and Seikos from their "traditional" markets. While Eastasian countries compete fiercely and openly with one another, their combined impact on the rest of the world is staggering.

TABLE 1–1
How Eastasia Outpaces its Neighbors:
Real Annualized per Capita Economic Growth
in Asia, 1960–78

EASTASIA	
ROK	9.9
Hong Kong	9.0
Republic of China	6.2
Singapore	6.0
Japan	6.0
DPRK	5.4
China	4.9
OTHER ASIA	
Pakistan	4.8
Thailand	4.1
Malaysia	3.4
Sri Lanka	3.4
Indonesia	3.1
Philippines	2.9
India	1.5
Vietnam	0.6
Nepal	0.5
Laos	0.4
Burma	−0.1
Kampuchea	−0.8

SOURCE: Donald Wise, ed., *Asia Yearbook 1980* (Hong Kong: Far Eastern Economic Review, 1980), p. 10.
NOTE: Throughout this book in the tables and figures, the following abbreviations are used: DPRK (Democratic People's Republic of Korea); GDR (German Democratic Republic); HK (Hong Kong); PRC (People's Republic of China); ROC (Republic of China); and ROK (Republic of Korea).

Eastasia's presence is felt elsewhere than in the market for consumer goods, however. Eastasians have purchased the largest hotel in Los Angeles and extensive portions of Waikiki in Hawaii. Eastasians have become preferred customers for many traditional American items from antiques to beefsteaks since Eastasian currencies rose in value during the late 1970s. The world banking system felt the effect of massive capital accumulation by Eastasian financial institutions, as the "Asiadollar" market centered on Singapore swelled with deficit U.S. currency. By 1980, fifteen of the fifty largest banks in the world were Eastasian. Eastasian companies have joined the ranks of the "multinational corporations" that dominate world trading. South Korea had as many companies on *Fortune* magazine's prestigious list of the 500 largest non-American multinational corporations in 1979 as did Italy, a particularly striking fact since no Korean firm had appeared on the list only six years previously.[9]

The Dynamics of Growth

If the current situation were the end of it, Eastasia would be no more than a manageable irritation, not a major threat to our well-being. But the fact is that Eastasia's impact continues to grow at a rapid rate. The seven countries of Eastasia in 1977 contained 26 percent of the world's population on only 8 percent of its land, and produced more than 14 percent of the world's economic product.[10] But Eastasia during the prior seventeen years contributed more than 22 percent of the *growth* in the world's product.[11] Of these seven countries only China grew at less than 5 percent a year over the 1960–78 period in product per capita, as table 1–1 makes clear. No country elsewhere in Asia grew faster than China. Among the Communist nations, with the exception of Romania (with its petroleum resources and freewheeling economy) the most rapidly growing countries are the Eastasian states of the People's Republic of China and the Democratic People's Republic of Korea, as table 1–2 shows. Industrial Eastasia is well on the way to becoming a highly prosperous and potentially well-integrated regional economy, one already racing past the North American and European economies in size and dynamism.

Even such dynamic growth would not be so disturbing were it quietly contained and insulated from the rest of the world. A rich, self-sufficient Eastasia that drew little on outside resources and made few demands on distant markets and economies would be a great blessing. But of all the regions of the world, contemporary Eastasia is the one most dependent upon long-distance international trade for its livelihood. Several of the smaller nations have a trade

TABLE 1–2

The Eastasia Edge in the Communist World:
Annual Growth Rate of GNP, 1960–77,
Centralized Economies

Romania	8.5%
China	**5.1**
DPRK	**5.1**
Bulgaria	4.4
Albania	4.3
Poland	4.1
USSR	3.7
GDR	3.2
Hungary	2.9
Czechoslovakia	2.6
Mongolia	0.8
Cuba	−0.4

SOURCE: World Bank, *World Development Indicators,* June 1979, p.10–11.

volume greater than their total national product. Japan's international trade account, $214 billion in 1979, dwarfs the entire economies of many nations.[12] Without imports and exports the entrepôt states of Singapore and Hong Kong would be little more than the fishing villages they once were. The island of Taiwan alone exports more than Spain, Austria, Denmark, Brazil, South Africa, Indonesia, Nigeria, Libya, or Venezuela and ranked sixteenth in the world in total exports in 1978, up from twenty-fifth in 1977.[13] South Korea was fifteenth in 1978.[14] Even the People's Republic of China, for many years closed to interchange with the outside world, has now opened its doors to foreign trade and investment, to the point of encouraging export-processing zones and joint-venture investments on Chinese soil.[15] In Eastasia, export business has become a way of life, and future growth will depend in many cases on increasing exports, regardless of their effect on the economies of the rest of the world.

Japan Is Not Alone

It would be a great mistake to single out Japan as our sole adversary in the coming economic struggle. Japan was indeed the first of the Eastasian nations to rise and compete directly with the West. It adopted Occidental military, economic, and political strategies to compete with the rest of the world. By 1910, Imperial Japan had already created a powerful modern military force, had defeated two giant neighbors, China and Russia, and had dispatched its military to seize Taiwan and Korea. Since its defeat in World War II, Japan has led the resurgence of Eastasia, becoming the leading edge of the region's economy. As table 1–3 shows, Japan's economy in 1977 accounted for more than two-thirds of the total regional product.

Nevertheless, some recent developments have drawn attention to the other nations of the region as potential trading partners and adversaries. A third of the region's trade with the rest of the world in 1978 came from nations other than Japan, up from a quarter only six years earlier. Japan has less than a tenth of Eastasia's territory and population, and an even smaller proportion of the region's natural resources. Other countries have contributed nearly a third of the economic growth of Eastasia, and their relative importance is increasing.

Particularly arresting is the prospect of a mature China. While still largely a poor country, China has grown faster than the other giants of Asia, India,

FIGURE 1-1

The Narrowing Gap: Gross National Product per Capita, 1950–80

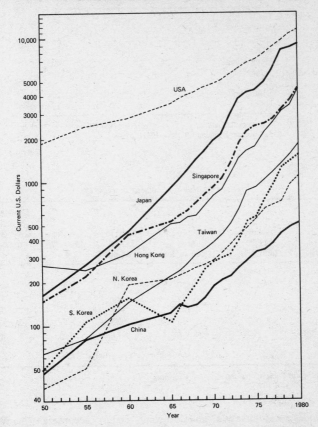

NOTE: Data represents annual Gross National Product in native currencies divided by year-end population and by the year-end exchange rate for the U.S. dollar. The basic data sources are as follows:

1950–1977 (except China, Taiwan, and North Korea) from World Bank, *World Tables* (Baltimore: Johns Hopkins, 1977, 1980).

1978–1980 (Except China, Hong Kong, Taiwan, and North Korea) from International Monetary Fund, *International Financial Statistics* (Washington: International Monetary Fund, June, 1981). China from National Foreign Assessment Center, *China: A Statistical Compendium* (Washington, D.C.: Central Intelligence Agency, July, 1979) and *China Business Review,* July–August 1981. Taiwan from Council for Economic Planning and Development, *Taiwan Statistical Data Book* (Taipei: Executive Yuan, 1979).

North Korea from Joseph Sang-hoon Chung, *The North Korean Economy: Structure and Development* (Stanford: Hoover Institution, 1974); and National Foreign Assessment Center, *Korea: The Economic Race Between North and South* (Washington D.C.: Central Intelligence Agency, January, 1978). 1980 figures for Taiwan, Hong Kong and North Korea were derived from data given in Far Eastern Economic Review *Asia Yearbook,* 1981.

TABLE 1–3

Total Foreign Trade as a Percentage of GNP, 1980

Japan	26
DPRK	20
ROK	54
ROC	83
Hong Kong	160
Singapore	189
China	5
United States	16
USSR	16

SOURCE: Donald Wise, ed., *Asia Yearbook 1981* (Hong Kong: Far Eastern Economic Review, 1981), p. 10.

TABLE 1–4

The Anatomy of Eastasia in Figures

Country	Population, 1977 (millions)	Area (1,000 sq. km)	GNP in U.S. $ (billions)	Growth 1960–77 (%)	Contribution to regional GNP growth, 1960–77 (%)
Japan	113.2	372	642	7.7	68.4
China	885.6	9670	345	5.1	24.3
ROK	36.0	99	30	7.4	3.0
DPRK	16.7	121	11	5.1	0.8
ROC	16.8	36	20	6.2	1.7
Hong Kong	4.5	1	11	6.5	1.0
Singapore	2.3	1	7	7.5	0.7
TOTAL	1,075.1	1,597	1,066	6.8	100.0

SOURCE: World Bank, *World Development Indicators,* June 1979, pp. 10–11.

and Indonesia and ranks as a "middle income" country according to the World Bank. The poorest of the Eastasian countries in per capita income, China still produces a third of the gross product of the region and has more people than any other nation on earth. China's urban population alone, now numbering over 100 million, is greater than that of all Japan. If China's natural and human resources could be merged with Japan's skills and economic power, the combination would be insurmountable.

The smaller nations of Eastasia may be tiny in comparison with China and Japan, but they are respectable performers in their own right. Korea, the largest, has a combined north-south population of over 50 million. With twice the people of our most populous state, California, Korea is roughly the size of Italy, France, or Great Britain. Taiwan, or the Republic of China as it prefers to be called, has over 17 million people, more than inhabit eight European countries and forty-eight American states. Even Hong Kong and Singapore, which are mere city-states with no hinterland, are large cities by world standards: their combined population of 7 million exceeds that of fifty-five other nations.

But what is most significant about these smaller Eastasian states (which the Japanese call "little Japans" and the Chinese "tiger cubs" or "little dragons") is not their size or their wealth. It is the dynamic example they hold out to the rest of Asia. Singapore has the highest per capita income ($4,150 in 1979) of all the Asian nations outside Japan.[16] Hong Kong, with a population 98 percent Chinese, has rapidly become a major manufacturing center after many years as a mere trading port. Taiwan, under a different political and economic system from its sister provinces in China, has rapidly outpaced them to become China's most affluent province. Just as little England showed great America the way to world power, so are these smaller nations showing their giant motherland, China, the path to the future. Meanwhile, they provide a lively zone of free markets and international trade which has become the backbone of the Eastasian economic system.

A New Generation

The Japanese militarists of the 1930s maintained a dream that propelled them into aggression against the European and American powers. They called this dream the "Greater East Asian Co-Prosperity Sphere." At its largest extent (see front endpaper map) this empire coincided roughly with the area of the world we call Eastasia. Japanese soldiers occupied Korea, much of China, Hong Kong, Taiwan, Singapore, and a number of important Southeast Asian capital cities with substantial Chinese ethnic populations. The victims of this aggressive expansionism resisted nobly, and Japan's current economic offensive into the region has suffered somewhat from their bitter memories.

The Japanese militarists, however, were interested in empire not because they wished to dominate Eastasia politically, but because they recognized Japan's urgent need for raw materials and markets in an increasingly sharp competition with the West. The striking fact is that, since World War II, Japan has essentially achieved its goals of growth to world power status and of dominance of western Pacific markets without firing a shot. Eastasia today is a zone of co-prosperity nearly as comfortable and extensive as the Japanese general staff of 1943 could have wished.

This transformation of Eastasia into a highly productive zone occurred because the several nations of the region undertook national strategies similar to Japan's, with the same patriotism and determination as that which compelled the Japanese patriots in the 1940s. Today's Eastasian leaders are a far cry from the jingoists who planned the simultaneous attacks on Pearl Harbor and Singapore. They are more pacific: even once-militant China's rulers have backed off from their aggressive stance in order to build their nation. Having learned the lesson of the destructiveness of war, they are more economically oriented. And they are more technically proficient, with years of experience at playing our game—that of diplomacy and technological competition.

What separates them from their predecessors is that in the intervening years the work and the sacrifice of generations has begun to pay off. They have begun to enjoy that edge over the rest of the world which Eastasian leaders for centuries thought was theirs. And seizing the opportunity from us at each turn, they have begun to turn their weaknesses to advantage. We must begin to explore the nature of their advantage, and how they acquired it.

The Edge—Does It Matter?

One might still ask whether it makes any difference that we have lost the edge to Eastasia in trade, manufacturing, and various subjective psychocultural dimensions. The answer is not yet clear, but there is every indication that we will suffer as a country unless we recognize the deeper implications of our continuing slide in world markets. If we do not meet the challenge of the Eastasia Edge, the list of disastrous consequences may be long indeed.

Most evident is the grim reality that our economic prosperity depends on keeping abreast of Eastasia. If the American dollar were to decline again, as appears entirely possible, our energy import costs could well rise, and our foreign buying power diminish. As our productivity begins to lag further behind, inflation will be more and more difficult to control. Eastasian dominance of assembly and processing industries like auto and precision machinery will cause continued decline in our industrial heartland, especially in older, already decaying urban centers from New York to Chicago. Declining profits will make investment in new plants difficult, thus rendering our industry even less competitive. Declining competitiveness will cause us to lose out in expanding markets, as we already have in the Middle East and Southeast Asia. America will be a less attractive investment target than Eastasia, where growth ensures a satisfactory long-run return; capital will thus flow out of the United States, making revitalization even more difficult. Failure to recognize and respond to the challenge will set in motion a vicious economic circle. Even if our multinationals prosper by moving abroad, those of us who remain at home will surely suffer.

Our social well-being also depends directly on a successful response. Low competitiveness leads to rising unemployment—nearly 15 percent in Detroit during 1980–81 because of Japanese auto inroads in the United States market. It intensifies dissatisfaction in society, increases the welfare burden, skews the distribution of income, and increases political disaffection among the urban poor. In other words, it aggravates the deepening social ills of what economist Lester Thurow has called the "zero-sum society".[17]

Failure to come to grips with the Eastasia Edge could also fundamentally affect this nation's attitudes toward the outside world. Increasing foreign ownership of American assets, including controlling interests in major corporations, may produce dramatic changes in our attitudes toward foreign investment. Controls on foreign acquisitions may increase resentment abroad, but their absence could well generate domestic xenophobia.

Another disastrous decade could produce a major redistribution of power within the United States. Large agricultural interests, which may gain leverage as our major source of foreign exchange, will likely grow at the expense of industrial and commercial interests. The differential impact of Eastasian competition may benefit some regions of the United States at the expense of others, resulting in large population movements away from centers of heavy industry (concentrated in the Northeast and Midwest) toward centers of trade and distribution. Indeed, such a development is already occurring. Over time we may come to think of ourselves as the agricultural hinterland to the Eastasian industrial centers, a mere appendage to the world economic heartland as it shifts westward across the Pacific Basin.

Ignorance of the edge which Eastasia holds over us may even threaten our national security, no matter how many Trident submarines or B-1 bombers we build over the ensuing decades. Failures of industrial and technical leadership may impair our ability to match Soviet weapons production. An unsound industrial base could make it impossible for us to build up our military strength without serious inflation, further weakening our industry. Lines of supply of essential finished goods, components, and raw materials may become increasingly vulnerable, as we come to depend on Eastasia for such items as spare parts and industrial supplies to run our national security establishment. Moreover, Eastasia may become increasingly independent from the United States diplomatically, with a declining interest in preserving American power abroad. While America is unlikely to face military challenge from Eastasia in the near future, we must count on a steady erosion of our ability to defend ourselves against attack from other directions if we do not come to grips with the Eastasia Edge.

Not all of these disasters are certain to strike. But at least some of them have already happened, or will most certainly happen regardless of how we tackle the challenge before us. What is clear is that some response is needed, and that first response should be to seek understanding. We should seek partnership as well, and use their strength to help build our own. The temptation is strong to lash out against our trade partners, to throw up barriers to deeper contacts, and to launch crash programs to catch up by copying our competitors. But if we do not understand how Eastasia got the edge on us and how we can use that edge to our own advantage, even our most purposeful efforts will be like building on sand. When our potential adversaries come from a world so different from our own, so deeply ingrown, so ancient in its historical roots, to ignore the *why* of their recent performance is foolish indeed.

2

Perceiving the Edge

THE competitive edge that Eastasia maintains is not a simple advantage. It would be easier if this were the case. If there were a "secret" to economic performance, if this edge entailed a single strength that we might turn into a weakness, if a single nation represented the entire challenge instead of an entire region of the world, then our response might be simple and the threat short-lived. Unfortunately, the more we delve into the phenomenon of Eastasia's competitive edge, the more complex it appears, and the more deeply rooted are our problems in dealing with it.

Many Americans have only recently become aware of the erosion of United States leadership, as our newspaper reporters, academics, and politicians bring the matter forcefully before us. Declining trade balances, a flood of well-made, low-priced imports, loss of control of major business enterprises to foreign interests, the decline of large sectors of our manufacturing industry—all these have riveted our attention on the rapid rise of Eastasian competition. Now hardly a day goes by without a congressional hearing, a series of editorials, or a television network special on "how the Japanese are beating us" at the economic game. Like so many blind men trying to guess the size of an elephant, we grasp at the problem unknowingly, perceiving only bits and pieces at a time. The time has come to see it whole.

Little symbolizes the challenge from Eastasia more than the flood of Japanese autos that poured into our ports during 1980 at a rate of 5,200 a day, well over double the level of five years earlier.[1] As a U.S. Department of Transportation study showed in early 1981, Japanese manufacturers can land Datsuns or Subarus at American ports for less than 80 percent of Detroit's cost for comparable American cars.[2] Each new design effort by our automakers is

15

matched and bettered by our competitors, even before it can be introduced.

Industry defenders often assert that this Japanese edge is a product of cheap labor costs, of price-cutting attacks aimed at increasing Japan's American market share, of "dumping," and of Japanese overproduction. When each of these excuses is shown to be groundless, new explanations are thrown forward: Japan's managers are master strategists who understand our markets better than we do, know how to motivate their workers, and think ahead further than ours can. Alternatively, Japanese workers are said to be more dedicated to their jobs, harder working, and more committed to the success of their employers than our own workers. Examined critically, often these explanations also prove false.

Japan's successes in auto exports derive not from any single competitive edge but from a complex of advantages. Ever since Prime Minister Ito Hirobumi declared in the 1880s that "iron is the nation," Japan has seen competitiveness in steel as a national priority and currently has eight of the world's ten largest blast furnaces. From the mills they feed comes cold-rolled sheet steel nearly 25 percent cheaper than that of Pittsburgh.[3] Japanese quality —seen in better interiors and details, fuel consumption figures, and electronic extras—makes a deep impression on American consumers. Design is a way of life in Japan, a country where the cosmetic touch is apparent in every storefront. Electronics, including the microcircuitry that makes Japanese cars fuel-efficient, is a national pastime. Government standards encourage the maintenance of high-quality products up and down the production chain. Every Japanese automobile, in this sense, is the product of a nation, not just of an efficient factory.

A Japanese auto factory is a wonder to behold. Steel, integrated circuits, and other building blocks are molded into parts and delivered to production lines only minutes before assembly by hundreds of specialized suppliers. Sparks fly as each of a bevy of industrial robots, named after the latest Tokyo movie idols, completes 256 simultaneous spot welds. A handful of workers, looking more like technicians, watch the machinery whirl and occasionally stop the line to correct slight quality flaws. Observers compare the clean, well-lit premises to department stores or hospitals rather than to factories. It seems to many that the secret lies in the internal organization of such industrial plants.

But consider some additional facts. Robots, or automated assembling machines, are a product of the Japanese government's farsighted policy of rapid tax depreciation on installed automatons—which explains why Japan has more than half the world's supply of such equipment. Quality control in the factory is in the hands of Japanese —workers, not managers—who are remarkable for their attention to detail. Pride of workmanship, loyalty to the enterprise, willingness to sacrifice short-term goals—all these virtues of auto workers in Japan contribute further to the competitiveness of their product. These workers, in turn, are not products of their factories' efforts at personnel management, but of schools that stress achievement and families that demand performance from their children. They are the first to recognize, as often we do not, that their output is the result of an entire economic system, which together is more than the sum of its parts.

Half a world away sprawls another example of Eastasian dynamism. Jutting half a mile into the blue Persian Gulf at the Saudi Arabian port of Jubail is a massive docking facility—the largest of its kind in the world—for crude oil supertankers. Steel, which is $50 to $100 a ton cheaper than even Japan's, flowed from a Korean mill larger than any in the United States to create this project in 1979. The steel was carried to Saudi Arabia in Korean-built bottoms. Cement, poured into armor rocks and stabits to form nearly five miles of causeways, came from Korea in the same fashion. Thousands of South Korean workers were imported to build everything from slipways to mosques. The Jubail complex is one of the most massive civil engineering feats in the world and has put the South Korean firm of Hyundai on the map as one of the world's great construction companies, on a par with (but often cheaper than) leaders such as Brown and Root or Morrison Knudsen. With its capability of berthing four 300,000-ton supertankers simultaneously, it has changed trading patterns in the Persian Gulf. Not coincidentally, it has helped oil-poor South Korea to survive the energy crisis of the 1980s by providing over a billion dollars of construction income to offset increased oil bills.

How was this massive feat accomplished despite the harsh desert environment and the fierce competition for oil dollars? The answer lies not simply in the aggressive salesmanship of Hyundai representatives or the toughness of Korean construction workers, although these were advantages. It also must include the strong support, through inexpensive credit and diplomatic leverage, of the South Korean government, which was not afraid to weigh in on behalf of its economic representatives abroad. And the answer must include the global reach of South Korean industrial and trading interests, with their strategic understanding of the need to control supply, transportation, and construction simultaneously. Here again, as in the case of the Japanese auto factory, the success derives from the system, not from its parts.

Three thousand miles northwest of Jubail lies another, less happy monument to the cutting power of the Eastasia Edge. It is the half-shuttered town of Biel in Switzerland, once the heart of the world's watchmaking industry. Biel and the towns of the surrounding Jura mountains have seen their population of watchmakers fall from 89,500 to less than 47,000 in one decade, as the sales of Eastasian electronic watches have soared around the globe.[4] Once a mark of prestige and the undisputed market leader, the Swiss watch is now but a poor second in sales to the rapidly proliferating Eastasian products. How did this disaster come to pass?

The answer lies in the quicker responsiveness of the Eastasian economies to market opportunity. In the early 1970s many engineers, in Europe as well as in Japan, recognized the potential of microelectronics in watchmaking. The integrated circuit, the liquid crystal display, the quartz crystal diode—devices that revolutionized the industry—remained obscure to Swiss management, as the Société Générale de l'Horlogèrie Suisse, the holding company for watch-component manufacturers, jealously protected its traditional technology. Executives with little sense of technical developments made decisions without communications from the production floor.

In Japan, on the other hand, the fledgling watch industry remained sensitive to new ideas from its engineers. The dialogue both among firms and between managers and workers, which is typical in Eastasia, brought these new ideas to light and into the testing stage long before Europe moved. Moreover, the production designers could rely on a semiconductor industry twice as productive as that of Europe and with a cost position to match. Along with these advantages of responsiveness and better sourcing of components, Japanese watchmakers could draw heavily on the skills of assemblers in other Eastasian countries, notably Taiwan, South Korea, and especially Hong Kong, where they found a large work force eager to put its hands to use. Once again the success came from the system, this time a regional system, and not from the individual firms or managers or laborers.

These three examples—Japanese automobiles, Korean heavy construction, and Eastasian watches—demonstrate the importance of thinking about the Eastasia Edge as a whole. They suggest that we are dealing not with a single brilliant idea, aggressive firm, or talented country, but with a large, complex, and forcefully developing part of the world. They also suggest that behind the "edge" lies a set of behavior patterns common throughout the region yet very different from our own.

Some Faulty Perceptions

Of course, the Eastasia Edge has not gone unnoticed over the past few years. Indeed, it was fashionable in the early years of Eastasian growth to ridicule the efforts of Japanese by calling their political leaders "traveling transistor salesmen," and to speak of "cheap Japanese products" as though they could never match the quality of our own more expensive ones. Even today the term "Chinese copy" is standard in the electronics industry for a shabby attempt to reproduce a sophisticated item by using inferior technology. This attitude gave rise to the perception of Eastasian success as the result of "cheap labor" —Orientals who worked in sweathouses for a pittance. However true this argument might have been in the 1950s or even 1960s, it is no longer convincing.

While it is true that the income of the average Eastasian (particularly when a billion Chinese are included) is dramatically lower than in America, the edge which Eastasia holds depends less and less on wage differentials in industry. In Japan, our biggest competitor, per capita income exceeded that of the United States briefly in late 1978, and will decisively move beyond us by the mid-1980s. Wages in Singapore, already well over $4,000 in 1979, may exceed those in Great Britain within two years.[5] The poorest nation in capitalist Eastasia—namely South Korea—has a per capita income eight times that of less competitive India, and nearly fifteen times that of Bangladesh.[6] Except in the People's Republic of China, Eastasian labor in general is becoming more and more expensive, yet Eastasian industry is becoming simultaneously more competitive with our own.

What is more important is that unit labor costs—wages divided by the number of units of a product manufactured—have been declining rapidly in recent years. Between 1977 and 1980, Japan's unit labor costs declined 5.5 percent, while those in every major Western industrial nation were rising.[7] Thanks to rising labor productivity, Singapore's unit labor costs were lower in 1979 than in 1973, despite the "shock" of increased oil prices.[8] Eastasian countries have indeed experienced rising wage bills in recent years, thus refuting the simplistic "cheap labor" theory. But these higher costs have been more than overcome by savings in the production process. Therein lies the challenge to the outside world.

Another faulty perception is what we might, with due respect to James C. Abegglen of the Boston Consulting Group, call "Eastasia, Inc." In 1970, Abegglen argued that the Japanese political economy was "organized like a giant conglomerate, with government filling the function of corporate headquarters."[9] He coined the expression "Japan, Inc." in order to stress Japan's cohesiveness and the government's role in coordinating private corporations. Others have applied the same notion to government-business relations in Korea, Singapore, and elsewhere in Eastasia. There is even a body of literature that is beginning to treat China as a case of "Eastasia, Inc."[10]

The problems with such a conception are many. Eastasian governments, as we shall see, often are at odds with major sectors of their economies. For example, when Japan's powerful Ministry of International Trade and Industry (MITI) tried to force mergers on automobile and computer builders in the late 1960s and early 1970s, it failed miserably. South Korean efforts to reorganize the electric power sector during 1980–81 similarly stumbled. Many Eastasian firms, including Toyota, Matsushita, Samsung, and Formosa Plastics, interact little with their national governments and are often at odds with the state on specific issues. Even in totally Communist and theoretically centralized China, cases of regional and entrepreneurial defiance—or at least independence—of central authority abound. Governments have a fascinating relationship with businesses in Eastasia, but it is not the relationship of a "general staff" or even a "board of directors" to a conglomerate.

Moreover, despite the prevailing perception in the United States, Eastasian governments do not intervene massively in their societies. By international standards, government revenues are remarkably low as a proportion of national product. Except in the Communist societies, where all managers are bureaucrats, government officials represent only a small portion of the working population—only 17.1 per thousand in Japan in 1980, as opposed to 22.5 in the United States, 20.2 in Britain, and 85.4 in France.[11] Even in Communist China the central or "state" bureaucracy, as distinct from the relatively autarkic regional and economic bureaucracy, represents a similarly small proportion of the larger society. We propose to use the term "leanness" to describe this ability of Eastasian countries to rule massive economies with small governments. This pattern calls into question the concept of "Eastasia, Inc."

Observers of Eastasia often make the opposite mistake by assuming that corporate practice alone accounts for economic success. According to this view, for example, China's industrial growth results from communal decision making, profit-sharing schemes, or mass exhortation of laborers to produce more.[12] Japan's phenomenal success gets explained by such managerial techniques as "quality circles," cross-training programs, or lifetime employment. Our business schools now compete eagerly to teach students Japanese organizational behavior, as though these "secrets" could easily be put to use in American corporate life.

One problem with this assumption immediately strikes the eye. Corporate behavior varies widely within Eastasia, from that of the tiny, backyard factory in Hong Kong to the most technologically sophisticated giants of Japan. Even in Japan, corporate management varies enormously from firm to firm. For every firm that uses a "Theory Z" or the "Panasonic system" to increase its productivity, there may be ten others that use different methods. That a managerial maverick like Matsushita Kōnosuke should be treated in America as typical of Japanese business practice in his management of Matsushita Electric suggests how far we have to go in our understanding of the Eastasian scene.[13]

Although this corporatist interpretation is a useful antidote to overstatements of the role of government, it too remains incomplete. Japanese and other Eastasian firms function within a very different political environment from that of the West. Certain corporations can take long-term risks (such as lifetime employment) because they know that government stands behind them —providing long-term credits, export market information, and favorable tax treatment for promising industries. National governments, and not local governments or companies, build harbors, roads, railways, and other facilities that firms would otherwise have to build themselves or raise local support for.[14] After serious economic setbacks, such the as oil-price hikes of the 1970s, governments step in to subsidize and help restructure entire industries, thus giving many companies the leeway to develop creative internal practices. Without the support of government (which still remains aloof from control and direction of the firm), the striking innovativeness of Eastasian companies would be less apparent.

A third mistaken interpretation of Eastasian success is that it fundamentally derives from some presumed mental or spiritual advantage that Eastasians have over us. Those who marveled in the 1960s at the "New China" emerging during the Great Proletarian Cultural Revolution often noted the spiritual nature of the transformation. Chairman Mao insisted that ordinary people could become true revolutionaries by increasing production—so long as they were bold, compassionate, evenhanded, and above all unselfish. These same characteristics also made them admirable servants of the party and the state. China's new leaders after Mao's death now acknowledge that the spiritual exhortations of the 1960s caused a severe economic crisis from which the country is just beginning to recover.

The current Japanese counterpart to this spiritualist view, borrowing the name of the ancient Samurai ethic, might be called the Bushido theory. Japan's economic performance, according to the theory, results from personal or cultural values lacking in the outside world: powerful loyalties to superiors, unstinting attention to results, and above all valor in the combat of competition. Disciples of Bushido, like the Western Maoists, tend to be highly pessimistic about the West's ability to match Eastasia. Implicit in their worship of the spiritual side of Eastasian life is the assumption that it could never take deep root in America.

The problem with such views is that, while they grasp a major element of reality, they remain incomplete. They fail, for example, to explain the ebb and flow of performance over time—why Japan faltered in the 1930s, China in the 1960s, or South Korea briefly in the early 1980s. They fail to account for differences between systems sharing similar "spiritual" traits, such as Maoist China and the North Korea of Kim Il-sung. And they fail particularly to explain why spiritual energies are directed to economic goals rather than to unproductive ends like military expansion (in Japan in the 1940s) or radical redistribution schemes (in China in the mid-1960s). No matter how deep-seated the motivation, how well it is channeled is often the key to whether it increases or decreases a nation's wealth.

The Eastasian Synergy—Through the Looking Glass

What these three faulty interpretations—statist, corporatist, and spiritualist—all fail to do is to examine the problem as a whole. It is the combination of these elements that has produced the Eastasia Edge. The countries of the region have longer recorded histories, larger and denser populations, and more collective experience of commerce and statecraft than the rest of the world combined. They are complex nations whose parts are intricately related. Each of their successes—in technology, exports, energy, and rural development—must be studied from this holistic viewpoint to determine how the parts interact. Engineers have a word for such a combination that produces more together than separately—synergy. Our problem is to understand the workings of the synergistic Eastasian systems as a whole, including their political, economic, social, and psychological dimensions.

This will require a mental journey into a different world, as different as the other side of Alice's looking glass in Lewis Carroll's famous story. We will have to leave behind many assumptions about how modern economies "must" run, since these assumptions are drawn largely from our own very different system. The assumptions, for example, that government and business are rivals for power in a zero-sum game, that populist politicians beget inflation, that innovation is the monopoly of individuals—all these are unnecessary, even misleading, baggage for the journey. Be prepared to abandon them, since things are not always what they seem in the Eastasian wonderland.

Consider, for example, the role of history. Americans tend to think of history as merely a curiosity that intellectuals fancy but that practical people ignore in favor of the future. In Eastasia, however, history is only yesterday. The Pilgrims founded Massachusetts Bay Colony at the beginning of American historical time, but in Eastasia it was the end of the Ming Dynasty and the beginning of the Tokugawa era—just another period in a cycle of millennia. Japanese remember the Meiji Restoration of the nineteenth century as readily as we recall World War II. This sense of history makes it natural for Eastasians to assume that their own culture, which derives directly or indirectly from that of ancient China, deserves to be the central culture of the world.[15]

One will seldom hear an Eastasian citizen make this claim so boldly, but if we accept it as an assumption on passing through the looking glass, then much of that region's high motivation and sense of direction becomes understandable. It amounts to a commitment to the survival not of individuals but of the larger culture. For this reason, Eastasians highly value education and training, which preserve culture and enhance its ability to meet external threats. This also explains their propensity to sacrifice individual interests to those of the group, and why they so willingly postpone consumption and other gratifications. In an important way, Eastasians have that sense of historical destiny which Westerners seem to have lost at the end of imperialism, if not after the Renaissance.

Consider further the role of the state. In America and the West the nation-state grew out of the need to defend the tribe against outside aggression, and it became part of an international system with relatively open cultural borders. States are expected to be passive toward the economy and active toward the external world and internal order. Since the Reformation at least, nations have left spiritual matters to the church or to private conscience. They primarily deal with business through monetary and fiscal policy—that is, by printing money and taking taxes. States in the West are expected to be militarily strong, religiously neutral, and economically extravagant.

Eastasians begin from a different premise. Nations are the modern extensions not of tribes but of empires, such as the great Chinese states, which claimed universal loyalty and spread civilization to the barbarians. Their emperors, possessing spiritual and economic as well as political power, represented the personification of the culture, the society in its highest ideal. States defended themselves not by military means alone, but through a mix of defenses including the moral power of the emperor and the vitality of the economy. They were, at least until this century, the seats of spiritual power and the source of economic dynamism. States in Eastasia are expected to be militarily creative, spiritually impressive, and economically productive.

This different view of the state helps explain many puzzles about modern Eastasia. For example, why do Eastasians feel themselves weak and vulnerable in the modern world, despite their obvious strengths? The answer may lie in a different view of the source of national power, which in Eastasia depends on the shared values of the citizens. Outsiders who do not belong to the cultural group are less subject to control by such a state, and hence their influence must be kept to a minimum. Xenophobia and its mirror image, low self-esteem, derive directly from Eastasian perceptions of the uniqueness of their culture and the vulnerability of their culture-based state. This explains in part why Japan continues to resist "internationalization" of its economy and why cultural and scholarly exchanges with China seem so one-sided.[16] If Eastasians felt, as we do, that conflicting cultural and ethnic loyalties would not tear society apart and undermine the state, they would be much more open to domestic diversity and outside influences than they are.

Another example is the attitude toward government involvement in the economy, which we will need to explore in considerable detail later. Eastasians expect the state to foster economic growth, not only to benefit the public good but also to build the nation's military potential. Citizens who entrust national resources to the state for defense in ordinary times cannot object when the state demands a role in the economy. Eastasians get from their state more economic support for business and commerce, but they pay for it willingly by losing the privilege of privacy from government interference. If officials are the "foster parents" of the citizenry, then who can be surprised if secrets are shared among the family? The closeness of state and citizen in Eastasia requires cooperation on both sides, just as our Western arms-length relationship requires mutual restraint.

Consider finally the role of society. In keeping with our European origins and frontier traditions, Americans think of society as the occasionally tolerated gathering of individuals or their families for particular purposes—work or worship, entertainment or business. Eastasians view society much more organically, much as we might view a network of extended relatives or the hierarchy of an enormous church. Americans are concerned with what one looks like and how one talks, Eastasians with whom one knows and what group one belongs to. Nothing occurs in an Eastasian neighborhood without all the neighbors finding out, nor is anyone hired without full knowledge of his "background." To Eastasians we appear at times to be insensitive, gregarious, self-centered ingrates. To us they sometimes appear as snoopy, prying, cliquish snobs.

This difference in social outlook explains many fascinating aspects of the Eastasian scene. Why is it that not only the managers (who enjoy a bonus system) but also the shipbuilders, tailors, and ditchdiggers are willing to work sixty hours a week? This high motivation is a function in part of the social system, which holds people responsible to their families, groups, and employers. To shirk one's job, to miss a paycheck, is to fall short of society's expectations, not just one's own. "Face" is an old Chinese expression—to "lose face," or to be shown to be not what society thinks you are, is a fate literally worse than imprisonment. Eastasians who bring these social expectations with them into international life are often shocked to find that the rest of the world has so little concern for their standing, their international face. In many ways, Japan's massive efforts at rapid growth were spurred by the feeling that Japan had to catch up with its industrialized neighbors to "save face," an important element in ensuring national security.

Another corollary of this attitude toward society is the fear of overt conflict. Since society is a carefully knit framework of relationships, great effort must be taken to prevent conflicts from damaging it. This attitude places a great strain on mediation facilities, (which flourish in all Eastasian countries), from marriage matchmakers to international arbitration courts. It also puts limits on political conflict: rivals for political power must work behind the scenes or else be revealed as wreckers of tranquillity. This explains why most political transitions seem so tame by Western standards, but why a few transitions get completely out of hand, as happened in China during the Communist takeover struggle and in Japan during the days before Pearl Harbor. Compromise and tradeoffs rule the day, even through significant changes like that from Mao Zedong to Deng Xiaoping. But when compromise no longer works, then violence and civil war inevitably result.

These looking-glass perceptions suggest how important cultural attitudes are in shaping the Eastasian economic systems. But societies do not succeed on individual striving alone. They need a political environment conducive to economic growth, just as the engine of a car needs the chassis to channel its energy into forward motion. The governments of the region provide a political context that encourages growth.

The essence of a growth-promoting political environment is neither the presence nor the absence of state intervention. It is predictability—predictability of both leadership and commercial policy. There are few analogues in Eastasia to the leftward swing of France in electing François Mitterrand, or to the rightward lurches of Britain under Margaret Thatcher, or America under Ronald Reagan. Ever since the 1949 Communist triumph in China, each of the Eastasian states has been ruled by a conservative, stable coalition of peasants, bureaucrats, and big-business interests. This coalition permits technocrats to formulate long-term policies for business and restrains the desire to tamper capriciously with economic policy. On rare occasions this coalition has been shaken—for example, in the late 1950s in South Korea and the late 1960s in China—with short-term economic losses as a result. But the basic coalition remained intact through these crises. A predictable political environment has been especially crucial to developing capital-intensive basic industries such as steel and petrochemicals, where investments are so massive and long-term that executives will not venture on them if the future seems cloudy and uncertain.

In addition to predictability, ensured by deep underlying political stability, government provides Eastasian economies with strategic direction that is frequently absent in the West. The edge in this area is structural: it comes from the central established role of an elite corps of career bureaucrats in policy positions. Although today their coercive powers are on the wane and the scale of their active intervention in economic affairs has always been overrated in the West, this bureaucratic elite of planners, economists, bankers, and administrators nevertheless continues to help politicans think strategically about the future. Without career bureaucrats, Eastasian development would have been more sporadic and less substantial.[17]

The large-scale structure of "private" business may be the most underestimated element of the Eastasia Edge. General trading companies, industrial groups, and business associations all take pressure off government, allowing it to remain lean and efficient. These groups, in turn, relate to each other through the familiar patterns of social interaction. They can plan for the future with confidence, thanks to the stability of the political foundation. In many ways, "private" business performs public functions and works toward the public interest more comfortably than in our country.

In summary, the Eastasia Edge has cultural, psychological, and, most fundamentally, structural elements. We must reiterate that none of them makes sense in isolation, and that together they partake of synergy. Our job is to comprehend this whole from as many angles as we can. Perceiving the advantages held by an adversary is, in any case, the first step in overcoming them. As the Chinese saying goes, "Know thy adversary, and know thyself; then each battle will be thy victory."

3

The Puzzle of Growth

WHAT are the sources of Eastasia's remarkable economic performance over the last few decades? When did it all begin, and is there a pattern that can be duplicated elsewhere? Economists have begun to grapple with these issues, but their analyses often leave open more questions than they answer. They disagree strongly about the factors that produce rapid economic development in Europe and the United States, so why should they agree about a region so different culturally and politically from our own?

Eastasia: An Economic Profile

Not that information of an economic sort is absent, or that the record is unclear. On the contrary, data abound to confirm the dynamism of the Eastasian region.* As Appendix A (section a) makes clear, the mean rate of growth in the region moved from around 6 percent to nearly 9 percent in real terms (constant prices) from 1956 through 1978. To be sure, there have been some swings on either side of this trend line. China's economic disorders of the late 1950s produced negative growth rates after good performance during the first five-year plan (1953–57). Singapore had some hard times also during the late

*Sources for the data in the following discussion can be found in the source note for Appendix A.

1950s, though the island republic's annual growth rates in the early 1970s were the best of the lot. Hong Kong's economy benefited dramatically from the influx of Chinese refugees in the early 1960s. The recession of 1973–74 took its toll on every one of these economies, including China's. By and large, however, the pattern is one of sustained growth through the region at roughly twice the rate of the Western economies.

Interestingly, there is evidence in Eastasian developmental patterns to support virtually all the standard theories of economic growth. Some theories, for example, stress the importance of investment and savings rates in determining future development. According to this view, no economy can grow unless surpluses are created that can increase the economy's productive capacity. In the long run, it is argued, this surplus can only come from domestic accumulation of capital, or through capital inflows from abroad.

As is indicated in Appendix A (section b), the mean percentage of GNP plowed back into investment in Eastasia rose dramatically during the two decades of growth from roughly 14 percent to over 30 percent. Taiwan was the lead performer on this measure, with the investment share of GNP rising from 13 percent in 1954 to 40 percent two decades later. China's investment spurt took place during the dynamic mid-1950s, but despite the setback of the high-Maoist years in the late 1960s, investment rates have remained consistently above 20 percent ever since. Relatively weaker in investment until the 1970s were Singapore and Hong Kong, whose economic growth long resulted mainly from aggressive export and international service activity. But since the mid-1970s, feverish construction booms in both city-states have dramatically raised investment-to-GNP ratios and the rate of growth itself.

Some economists stress that the main determinant of domestic investment is personal and corporate savings, which generate cash that can be used to invest in productive capacity. Again, Eastasian countries score high on this measure. The most spectacular performer in savings has generally been Japan, which emerged from the postwar reconstruction period with one of the world's highest rates of personal and corporate savings. Japanese gross savings exceeded 30 percent during much of the 1970s. Surprisingly, Taiwan's domestic savings rate has exceeded Japan's since 1973 after a dramatic rise from around 10 percent in the mid-1950s. The domestic savings rates of Hong Kong, Singapore, and South Korea, while more modest by these standards, showed considerable growth from below 6 percent to two, three, or four times that by the late 1970s. In short, as the Eastasian economies have grown, so too have the propensities of their citizens to put aside their wealth for the future. This tendency to save is clearly a hallmark of Eastasian growth.

Still other economists insist that the true explanation of Eastasian growth lies in the ability to export in a competitive international environment. Here again the evidence is unmistakable. The percentage of Hong Kong's GNP accounted for by exports rose dramatically from 26 percent to well over 70 percent within two decades, and Singapore's export growth was even more spectacular. The larger economies of the region, China and Japan, showed relatively more constant export shares, around 10 percent for Japan and from 1–2 percent for the People's Republic. Though Japan is often thought to have achieved its economic growth through aggressive export policies, Appendix A (section d) shows that the Japanese economy since World War II has depended much more heavily on domestic sources than on exports to sustain growth. Needless to say, China, with a passive continental economy, is the least dependent of all Eastasian countries on export markets.

Of course, exports contribute positively to national growth only to the extent they are not offset by imports. Many developing countries today find they are unable to make their export drives pay off because they must endure an ever-increasing import bill. Some have suggested that Eastasian economic growth since the war is a fluke based on U.S. economic aid to our Asian allies against Communism. While this aid may have been a factor shoring up the economies of Taiwan and South Korea in the 1950s, there is little evidence of its significance much beyond 1965. Only Singapore and Hong Kong, which did not receive economic aid from the United States, have shown consistently large trade deficits—the sign of chronic imbalance between imports and exports which must be made up for by "invisible" payments. In their case, the "invisibles" were not economic assistance or military aid but (1) intangible financial services sold to the outside world and (2) long-term capital investment by multinational corporations impressed with their economic prospects. China and North Korea have shown relatively small imbalances on current accounts over the past twenty-five years, while Taiwan's and Japan's accounts moved increasingly toward surplus during the 1960s and early 1970s—an indication that they were beginning to export capital instead of depending on imports of capital for growth. Only the South Korean economy has continued to depend on substantial capital inflows throughout the postwar period. And those inflows have been overwhelmingly commercial-base transactions.

Another characteristic that distinguishes the nations of Eastasia from other developing countries is the importance of manufactured exports in their performance. For Hong Kong and Japan, with few agricultural or mineral resources available for export, manufacturing has continuously been the mainstay of international trade, in each case amounting to more than four-fifths of all exports throughout the post–1955 period. Other countries, however, have undergone major transitions in the composition of their exports, learning increasingly that manufactured goods are a better passport to prosperity than commodities. China increased its manufactured share of exports from 11 percent in 1954 to more than 50 percent in 1978, while Taiwan and South Korea have done even better over the years. Singapore, whose key position at the crossroads of Asia makes it a natural transshipper of agricultural and mineral products, nonetheless increased its manufactured share of exports from 10 percent to nearly 50 percent. The phenomenal performance of Eastasia has depended in large measure on the rapid transformation of the economy from one of primary to secondary production.

Developing economies must arrange to acquire or to produce domestically the capital goods they need for growth. These capital goods include the machine tools needed to build factories, modern transportation equipment, and communications hardware, as well as the other items of technology required by modern competitive economies. Eastasian countries have recognized this need for the tools with which to grow. The two Koreas have been the most spectacular acquirers of capital goods, with roughly one-third of their respective import bills going to this purpose in 1978. Until the Great Proletarian Cultural Revolution, China matched the two Koreas' commitment to capital imports, at one point (1958) devoting 40 percent of its total imports to capital goods. But since then, China has fallen back to the average of the other economies, with about 20 percent of its imports being machinery and other forms of capital equipment. Taiwan and Singapore, with their aggressive government-sponsored industrial development programs, have been the other big performers in capital goods imports after the Koreas; Hong Kong and Japan trail the pack with more modest ratios. Japan, of course, already possessed a well-developed capital goods industry of its own by the 1950s and thus did not need to import nearly so much machinery in order to sustain growth.

Yet another problem besetting developing nations is that of population. Modernization brings improvements in health care and a decline in mortality rates. If extended life expectancy is not matched by an equal or greater decline in birthrates, a population explosion will result, with the attendant problems of crowding in the cities and diminished per-capita production. Eastasia appears to have succeeded in controlling population growth in the last quarter century. Taiwan, Singapore, and South Korea have nearly halved their net annual reproduction rates of the early 1950s, and China's enormous population has been growing at a rate approaching only 2 percent a year, well below China's GNP growth rate during the same period. The unstable political situation around Hong Kong has produced wild fluctuations in the colony's population, but the underlying birthrate, isolated from movements across the boundary, has remained as low as China's or Japan's. For whatever reason, the control of population growth has been an important element in the East-asian success story.

So Eastasian performance continues to confound those who take a narrow economic approach to growth, since virtually any theory can find convincing evidence. Whether we credit the Eastasians with productivity, frugality, resilience, or competitiveness—or all of the above—the striking facts about Eastasia are growth in the face of adversity, and common progress despite diversity.

The Pattern of Benign Growth

Seldom has the world seen such a remarkable pattern of sustained economic improvement. What makes it even more remarkable is that the improvement has occurred without many of the debilitating effects which normally take their toll on growing societies. The "growing pains" of development are remarkably lacking in Eastasia.

Consider, for example, the disease of inflation, which habitually undermines the best-laid plans of economic policymakers. The natural tendency of central planners, and of politicians, is to permit the supply of money to rise—by deficit financing, which makes large-scale government programs possible, and by careless control over interest rates and other monetary policies, which allows the policymakers to favor some interests over others. Inflation is the natural enemy of real growth, since it erodes the value of the currency, diminishes the nation's ability to compete in exports, encourages the flight of capital, and undermines the confidence of people in their government.

What is particularly striking about Eastasia's economic performance in recent decades is that its governments have, with few exceptions, managed to keep inflation under tight control. Figure 3–1, which plots a number of nations on the two dimensions of rate of growth and rate of inflation, shows the results of these firm policies. The developed economies, including the United States, have suffered average annual inflation rates of 4–9 percent over the last two decades—not far from the average inflation rates of the Eastasia countries—but they have not grown nearly so rapidly. They are low-growth, low-inflation countries on the world scale. The other "developing" countries, including Brazil, India, and Indonesia, have all averaged less rapid growth than either Eastasia or the West, but have shown much higher inflation rates. They might

FIGURE 3-1

Growth with Minimal Inflation
(Annual Average Percentages, 1960-77)

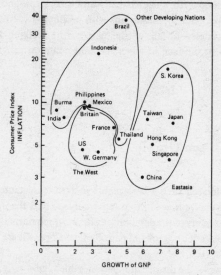

SOURCES: World Bank, *World Development Indicators,* June 1979; U.S. Congress, Joint Economic Committee, *China: An Economic Assessment,* (Washington, D.C.: U.S. Government Printing Office, 1975).

be called low-growth, high-inflation countries. The Eastasian nations, from China (with the lowest inflation rate) to South Korea (with the highest), are grouped together at the lower right, in the zone coupling low inflation with high growth.

How has this remarkable performance in controlling inflation been achieved? First of all, the governments of Eastasia have steadily run balanced budgets or even budgetary surpluses ever since the 1950s. To be sure, there have been periods of disastrous inflation, notably the immediate postwar years in China, Korea, and Japan. Since 1976, Japan has allowed a budget deficit to develop, both to improve the balance of payments and to assuage certain key interest groups in the Liberal Democratic Party through funds for public works projects. But by and large, Eastasian governments pay their bills annually without borrowing, either domestically or internationally.

This self-control, in turn, is a result of the peculiar political makeup of the Eastasian countries, whose politics are dominated by stable coalitions of conservative interest groups without a stake in inflation. "Indexing" is unheard of, treasuries manage the budget like traditional shopkeepers, and individual borrowers—with their built-in interest in currency depreciation—are not numerous or vocal. Eastasian economies tend to run on cash, not credit, as they always have traditionally, and this conservatism continues to inform public policy. We will need to examine later how this fiscal conservatism is built directly into the capital markets of Eastasia, but for now it is enough to observe that government works to control, not to exacerbate, the problem of inflation.

This is not to say that the balance of government budgets is the sole factor behind the control of price movements. In the West, growing demand for consumer goods and for higher wages has driven prices constantly higher. Were it not for Eastasia's increasingly competitive performance in international markets, public policy would have had to weaken and permit the currencies of the region to drift with the greater world tide of inflation. But this has not occurred. Manufacturers have been able to cut costs dramatically, despite modestly increasing costs of labor. Wage levels, though rising, have climbed less rapidly than elsewhere. Moreover, Eastasian workers have remained remarkably less interested than their Western counterparts in increasing marginal consumption rates. For all these reasons, demand-push inflation has been less of a problem than in most other countries.

Another characteristic of Eastasia's growth pattern is that government has been only partly involved in the larger economy. Consider the tax bite that government takes out of the U.S. economy every year, despite our inclination toward deficit financing. As table 3–1 shows, in 1977 nearly a third of our gross domestic product was absorbed by the various levels of government through the fiscal system (of course, a similar proportion of the national "product" comes from government expenditures). The European countries show an even higher degree of government involvement in the economy, with the mean for Western nations above 36 percent in 1977.

Needless to say, not all these government revenues and expenses contribute to rising productivity. In Eastasia, governments are leaner, drawing less heavily on the economies that support them, even though those economies have not been, at least recently, as wealthy as our own. The average Eastasian government absorbs in taxes less than one of every five currency units produced each year. Hong Kong has so lean a government that it is often hard to discern the fine managerial hand which guides the colony's finances.

Not only do these governments absorb less of the economy, they also contribute more to it on the investment side. China and North Korea are almost caricatures of high government investment economies, with more than 30 percent of their budgets going toward "capital construction." Some Eastasian

TABLE 3–1

Lean Government: Tax Revenue as a
Percentage of GNP, 1977

Eastasia:	
Japan	22.2
China	16.9
ROK	17.8
ROC	24.2
Singapore	24.7
Hong Kong	13.7
Average	19.9

The West	
United States	30.3
France	39.6
West Germany	38.2
United Kingdom	36.6
Average	36.2

SOURCES: U.S. Bureau of the Census, *Statistical Abstract of the United States, 1980* (Washington, D.C.: U.S. Government Printing Office, 1980), p. 906; Bank of Japan, *Keizai tōkei nenpō 1980* [Economic Statistics Annual] (Tokyo: 1980); Republic of Korea, Economic Planning Board, *Handbook of Korean Economy 1979* (Seoul: 1980); Republic of China, Executive Yuan, Council for Economic Planning and Development, *Taiwan Statistical Data Book 1980* (Taipei: 1980); Hong Kong, Government Information Services, *Hong Kong 1979* (Hong Kong: Government Press, 1979), p. 262; People's Republic of China, *China Business Review* 1 (November-December 1980): 10–11; Republic of Singapore, Ministry of Trade and Industry, *Economic Survey of Singapore 1979* (Singapore: Singapore National Printers, 1981).

NOTE: The figure for Singapore does not include "public sector" revenues such as those of the various housing boards, the telephone company, the port authorities, and so forth. If these revenues were included, the figure would be 39 percent.

governments, including those of Hong Kong and Taiwan, spend eight times as much on investment in such projects as roads, harbors, and airports as they do on social services.[1] Leanness of government is accompanied by an inclination to put muscle to good use in building what we often disparagingly call "infrastructure," rather than to waste it by redistributing assets or satisfying unproductive desires for consumption.

A final indication of the unusual nature of Eastasian economic growth is that the region has avoided the kind of massive unemployment or underemployment that plagues many developing countries and has been the bane of the "advanced" nations of Europe and America during times of recession. In 1976, at a time when the West had unemployment rates of 6 percent on the average (table 3–2), Eastasia had only 3.4 percent unemployed, and Taiwan left only 0.8 percent of its population unused by industry. There may be certain statistical problems with these indicators—in particular, the bias imparted by the various unemployment compensation schemes of the Western nations, which encourage the reporting of unemployment by offering welfare payments as the reward. Nevertheless, it is certainly true that more Eastasians are gainfully employed than are citizens of the industrialized West.

Table 3–2 also shows that governments in Eastasia not only spend less of the public product but also tend to spend a smaller proportion of it on welfare or other forms of social support. On average, Europe and America spend more than six times as much on welfare (as a percentage of government outlays) as do the Eastasian governments. This is in part because of the lower unemployment rate and the absence of public unemployment compensation

TABLE 3–2

Work, Not Welfare: Unemployment and Welfare Payments, 1976

	Unemployment (%)	Welfare Payments as Share of Government Expenditures, (%)
Eastasia:		
Japan	2.0	8.4
ROK	3.9	4.6
ROC	0.8	12.9
Hong Kong	5.6	5.0
Singapore	4.5	1.5
Average	3.4	6.0
The West:		
United States	7.7	36.1
West Germany	4.6	49.4
United Kingdom	5.7	22.7
Average	6.0	36.0

SOURCES: International Labor Organization, *Yearbook of Labor Statistics, 1979* (Geneva, 1979); International Monetary Fund, *Government Finance Statistics Yearbook, 1979;* Republic of China, Executive Yuan, Council for Economic Planning and Development, *Taiwan Statistical Data Book 1979* (Taipei, 1980); P. Haddon-Cave, *The 1981–82 Budget* (Hong Kong, 1981). Bank of Japan Research and Statistics Department, *Keizai Tokei Nenpō* (Economic Statistics Annual) *1980.*

schemes, but it is also attributable to a belief, pervasive throughout Eastasia, that individual and family welfare are the responsibility not of the state but of private groups. Eastasian government is lean in this way because people expect to take care of their needy in other ways than through the public dole.

In many respects, this description of the leanness of government, the conservatism of fiscal and monetary managers, and the "supply-side" concentration on investment rather than consumption may seem like that of a right-wing utopia. These very characteristics of the region we are describing strongly resemble the recommendations of the "new wave" of economists who are seeking to reverse the pattern of loose fiscal and monetary policies of recent decades in the United States. But other aspects of the Eastasian picture make this parallel unconvincing. For example, it is remarkable that conservative management in Eastasia has not had a regressive effect on income structure. In 1970 the middle 40 percent of the South Korean population (in terms of income) received 37 percent of the national income, despite a decade of high growth and the kind of inflation that normally decimates the middle class.[2] This middle-class share was comparable to patterns in Denmark and the Netherlands, and substantially higher than in West Germany. The share of South Korea's upper 20 percent in total national income was within one percentage point of Sweden's, while that of Taiwan's richest one-fifth was actually four percentage points lower.[3]

Eastasian governments and employers have engineered this apparent anomaly. They are concerned not just with the growth of the national economy in the aggregate but with the welfare of the population as a whole. They take responsibility if their policies harm a segment of the population. Could we visualize the steely-eyed budget-cutters of the Office of Management and Budget resigning because breadlines were increasing in Detroit? Precisely this sort of cross-linked concern is expected of Eastasian political managers, who must be sensitive to both growth and equity.

Even more important is the fact that the population generally supports and trusts government without relying on it or demanding much from it. The wave of "welfare state" measures that swept Europe and America in the last half-century has not yet reached Eastasia, if it ever will. The people expect little from their governments except peacekeeping, national defense, and moral leadership. Governments that undermine the economy in the name of more equitable distribution of wealth (such as the Maoist rulers in China) quickly lose popular support. Governments remain in power in much the same way as did Benjamin Disraeli's in Victorian England or Theodore Roosevelt's in America before World War I: by promising the people a stake in national growth, not by offering them a chicken in every pot, bought with funds out of government coffers. Modern American and European conservatives thus differ from their Eastasian counterparts in having to deal with quite different popular expectations of government. Consequently, Eastasian governments are free to focus on the underlying problems of national growth, rather than on undoing the "mistakes" of earlier politicians.

Finally, there is the fact, most curious from the viewpoint of the Western conservative, that the private pursuit of profit ("pure market orientation") is viewed with considerable distrust in the Eastasian political tradition. Businessmen always stood on the bottom rung of the social ladder in traditional Eastasia because of their tendency to ignore the public interest. In modern times, governments have promoted growth almost in spite of the strong desire for personal gain among private interests, not because of it. Eastasian growth has not occurred because of the absence of controls on freewheeling business activity, but because governments have encouraged certain forms of economically profitable activity while discouraging others. The utopians of laissez-faire will have to look elsewhere for their models than to Eastasia.

Part II

SOCIETY

4

Common Sources of Strength

EASTASIA has an edge on us today because it is organized and thinks differently from the way we do. These modes of thought and action have roots that go deep into the history of the region. They are not easily exported, and not easy for us to copy. But if we are to compete we must begin by understanding their mainsprings.

Many of the patterns we discern might be termed "Confucian," after the great Chinese philosopher of the fifth century B.C.[1] Since the Eastasian philosophical tradition is at least as long and complex as our own, this is clearly a misnomer. We might just as easily term the European tradition "Platonic" or "Aristotelian," after some of our own leading thinkers. In fact, many of the philosophical underpinnings of modern Eastasia lie with non-Confucian doctrines such as Legalism or Taoism. The point is that, to a striking degree, the patterns of behavior and organization which account for the rise of Eastasia are shared commonly across all the countries of the region. Here we can touch only on the highlights.

Westerners who reached the Orient for the first time more than a century ago were tempted to treat it as an undifferentiated whole, since they knew little about the differences between China and Japan, Korea and Vietnam. They called Eastasia the "Far East," following the British, who thought of the region as the farthest extension of their empire reaching eastward through the Suez Canal. To them the Eastasians were "quaint" in their traditions, "inscrutable" in their controlled demeanor, and "mystical" in their occasionally other-worldly religion. Many of these common characteristics were used to build prejudices. Britishers spoke disparagingly of "wogs"—short for "Westernized Oriental Gentlemen." Americans talked of the "Yellow Peril" and designed laws excluding Eastasians as a group from immigration to the United States after exploiting "cheap Oriental labor" for a generation to build our great railroads.

Since the nineteenth century our perceptions of Eastasia have become more sophisticated. We remember Japan as our enemy in the Pacific war, and China as our great ally. We recognize that Japan is presently a democracy and China a Communist dictatorship. We know that geishas are Japanese and Peking duck is Chinese, that Korea is divided, and that China now hopes to be our ally against Russia. In many other ways, specialists have dissected the cultures and histories of the region, so that each country now stands out in sharp relief. It takes an effort to recall the common features which the Eastasian peoples share.

Basic Similarities

The most obvious point is that Eastasians look alike. Though they speak radically different languages, Chinese, Japanese, and Koreans share common physical characteristics. North Chinese may be taller and the Japanese finer featured, but all Eastasians stem from common ancestors who lived together in Central Asia as recently as the last great Ice Age, 15,000 years ago. Eastasians are quite aware of this physical homogeneity, particularly in recent years as foreigners have appeared on the scene. To this day the Eastasian peoples find it easy to exclude those with different physical features from their cultural and social systems.

Written language is another common characteristic of Eastasia. Japanese visitors to China are welcomed with a slogan which means "We share both our written language and our race." All the writing systems are based on borrowings from classical written Chinese, beginning in the case of Japan about the fifth century A.D. and in Korea several hundred years later. The essence of the language is ideographic, which is to say that written symbols represent not sounds but meanings or ideas. An ideograph in Japanese may be pronounced in three or more ways, but the meaning derives from the original Chinese. Koreans and Japanese make use of alphabetlike symbols, *hangul* and *hiragana* respectively, to represent sounds and help with the pronunciation and understanding of ideographs. But both languages, together with Vietnamese, have borrowed extensively from the Chinese vocabulary for concepts and ideas. A nonspeaker of any of the Eastasian languages can often get the gist of a passage simply by knowing the meanings of the ideographs used, and one frequently sees tourists and visiting businesspeople throughout Eastasia vigorously scribbling and exchanging scraps of paper without saying a word. This common storehouse of ideas and written symbols does not ensure perfect communication across Eastasia, but it does make learning much easier. Little wonder that the Chinese have recently turned to Japan to learn about modern technology, just as they did in the early twentieth century.

A third common characteristic is a shared tradition. Although China, Korea, and Japan differed in many ways before the twentieth century, they shared a tradition of agriculturally-based family and lineage organization within centralized state systems. Here we can only touch on some of the key features of that tradition.

Traditional Eastasia was a land of highly specialized farmers. Even today, crop raising in Eastasia more resembles horticulture than it does American mechanized farming. The same care is given to planting, transplanting, irrigating, and harvesting as the most careful gardener would give his prize flowers. In Eastasia, foodgrains such as rice and wheat are the staples and still represent a large portion of the diet. Land is scarce, and rural labor has been cheap until recently. While modernization has driven people from the land into factories and cities, these displaced farmhands are disciplined and tireless. It is no accident, for example, that in Taiwan today some of the most efficient assembly-line workers are country girls who only ten years ago were experienced and careful transplanters of rice seedlings. Agricultural backgrounds have taught Eastasians the importance of thrift, industriousness, independence, and property ownership—all keys to a "modern" attitude.

Eastasian society is rooted in strong families. Respect for ancestry is built into the Confucian religion, which taught that piety towards one's elders is the most important of all virtues. Even the Communist regimes of Eastasia have been unable to shake this basic building block. Family consciousness makes Chinese factories reserve places for sons of retiring workers. Japanese parents treat the education of their children as an investment in the prestige and wealth of their family in the future. Family firms of Chinese origin dominate the economies of many Southeast Asian states. Marriage ties remain important in cementing large groups or cliques: in Japan the man who marries the boss's daughter often assumes her family name. In countless other ways the family system of Eastasia continues to make itself felt.

Long before the European Renaissance, education in Eastasia was the major path to individual success. The class structure, divided into the four classes of scholar, agriculturist, handicraftsman, and peddler, reflected this emphasis on book learning. In premodern China and Korea even a lowly peddler's family could aspire, through education, to achieve the rank of scholar. Unlike the traditional castes of India, these categories were not fixed at birth but could be changed with effort. Educational systems took deep root in Eastasia, offering extensive private education in small academies with individual instruction. In early modern times Eastasia introduced government-sponsored modern education, especially in the military and scientific fields. Japan now graduates more people from high school than any other country and has a higher literacy rate than the United States despite the more difficult written language. In China access to education is considered so important that the issue of how it should be determined provoked the Great Proletarian Cultural Revolution, which disrupted the nation for nearly a decade after 1966. Though there are still serious problems with education in all the Eastasian countries, which tend to teach by rote and not by reason, employers can still pick from eager, well-educated, and highly motivated job applicants. Once on the job, Eastasian workers are quick to learn, loyal, and industrious. The British trained their prime ministers on the playing fields of Eton. Eastasia learned early that education is too important an asset to leave to the aristocracy.

In sharp contrast with the freewheeling Americans, who have distrusted government from the beginning of their historical experience, the Eastasian peoples have embraced government and bureaucracy as a high art. The ancient Chinese conception of public service as a moral responsibility, the traditional stress on ritual as the cement of society, the strict ordering of officialdom by rank and by extensive written rules—all these ancient characteristics lie at the heart of the current Eastasian economic rebirth. Communists are devoted intensely to their organization in Eastasia. Despite China's strong drive toward equality, its officials have a strong sense of protocol and rank. Similarly, civil servants in Japan who start their careers at the same time get equal pay and equivalent rank regardless of performance, except that the natural leaders in the age group gradually take on more substantive responsibilities. Even in relatively individualistic Korea, state officials adopt easily the same elitism found in Japan and Taiwan, where a post in government is considered a mark of superiority.

At the same time, the classic Eastasian demands on government—that it be responsive, capable, and above all concerned for the welfare of the common people—still hold. The ancient notion of the Mandate of Heaven *(tianming),* which may shift to a new political power center if popular needs are not met, keeps Eastasian politicans and officeholders on their toes. The recent purge of thousands of officials in South Korea and perhaps even millions in China for corruption or failure to appreciate the needs of the masses shows the persistence of the Eastasian tradition of a responsive bureaucracy.

Traditional Eastasian government was a government of men, not of laws. In all Japan there are only 12,000 lawyers, whereas in the United States there are over 500,000.[2] The tradition distrusts formal rules and regulations, disdains written contracts, emphasizes ethical rather than legal norms of conduct, and avoids extensive penal sanctions for deviance. The Eastasian tradition relies upon toleration, mutual adjustment, and mediation to solve disputes and accomplish tasks. This is not to say that in dealing with the outside world, Eastasian nations have not learned to negotiate fiercely and to obey the letter of international law—indeed, even the People's Republic of China under Mao was a staunch supporter of written international agreements and the rights of nations. But it does mean that domestically the people of Eastasia waste less time on the niceties of law and spend more time on preserving the human relationships that make rules less important.

If there is a common thread to the Eastasian antilegal tradition, it lies in the word "relationship." Confucius spoke of five relationships—between friend and friend, brother and brother, man and wife, parent and child, emperor and subject—which he insisted should be kept in perfect working order. While a highly modernized Japanese would today find certain Confucian concepts of loyalty and filial piety woefully out-of-date, he or she still lives in a network of intricately ordered social ties which permit individuals to anticipate the actions of others without reference to laws or rules. Protests about rights violations, for example, are rare in Eastasia because the concept of absolute right remains very weak. On the other hand, personal responsibility to a relationship is so strongly felt that it continues to produce suicides under stress. Much of the flexibility, responsiveness, and tenacity of Eastasian nations derives from their commitment to each other as human beings rather than to some abstract principle or written rule.

Political Culture

Eastasia's economic performance rests squarely on a political tradition that facilitates the right decisions while keeping competitors in the dark. Because we know so little about this tradition, we are tempted by incorrect or oversimplified interpretations. One such error, discussed earlier, is the popular notion of "Japan, Inc." Another common misinterpretation is the belief that China is a state ruled solely by a single powerful individual like Mao Zedong, when in fact even the Great Helmsman had to govern by persuasion, politics, and not a little intrigue. Just as American economic performance is often restrained by our political system, success in the Eastasian economic arena is often a result of political and social patterns that are not obvious to the outsider.

Nationalism

Traffic at Independence Plaza in the heart of Seoul is normally among the most chaotic in Asia, with buses, motorcycles, and tiny Hyundai Pony automobiles weaving a mosaic of confusion along access roads to the plaza. But at precisely 6 P.M. daily, traffic traditionally stands still, drivers get out of their cars, pedestrians halt in their tracks, and policemen stand at attention as the national anthem is played. This scene was repeated throughout the country, including such places as the Pohang Steel Mill or the Changwon Machine Building Complex, throughout the 1970s, helping fuel the crucible of Korean industrialization to white heat.

For more than a century, nationalist sentiments—stemming from attitudes of resistance to the West or, as in the case of Korea, to Japan—have been a basic driving force underlying Eastasian economic growth. Such sentiments, of course, have also propelled modernization elsewhere, particularly in Middle Eastern nations such as Turkey and Egypt and among "follower" European states such as Germany and Russia.[3] But love of country has been especially important in Eastasia as a stimulus to growth and effective policy formation. This is partly because of the Eastasians' relatively strong cultural pride and their consequent humiliation at subservience to foreigners, and partly because of the abrupt and threatening circumstances in which Eastasians first encountered the industrial West.

Eastasia attempted in the nineteenth century to resist the European and American imperialist nations by military force, and when that failed began to build up economic forces to compete in other ways. China's response to the West, for example, began as a drive to "expel the barbarians" who were importing opium from India. Japan's modernization was sparked by the arrival in July 1853 of Commodore Matthew Perry's American fleet demanding the opening of Japan to trade. Korea was galvanized in 1878 by the landing of U.S. marines, and then later by an invasion of Japanese imperial troops. In each of these countries, military force from the West was the catalyst that impelled changes in their economic systems, and which etched an indelible relationship between love of country and national economic and military strength in the popular consciousness.

The trauma that fused nationalism and national security so tightly to the processes of economic growth might be termed the "black ship phenomenon," after Japan's abrupt encounter with Commodore Perry's fleet in 1853–54.[4] When Perry's ships arrived at Shimoda over 125 years ago, the Japanese had no oceangoing vessels, no railroads, and no telegraph system. National policy had forbidden for 200 years the creation of an ocean-going fleet. Despite its organizational sophistication, technologically Japan was living in the sixteenth century. Yet within five years of Perry's visit, Japan made decisions committing the country to a modern economy in the Western image. The Japanese reformers used as their motto an ancient Chinese slogan which might be thought of as the theme song of modern Eastasia: "A rich country makes for a strong army." This theme of economic growth in the interest of national security has been struck in more recent times by Taiwan, locked in confrontation with China; by South Korea, facing its North Korean enemy; and by the People's Republic of China, as its Soviet neighbor to the north grew more hostile. In Eastasia, more frequently than in America or Europe, national survival is known to depend on the health of the national economy.

Despite its eagerness to learn modern ways from the West, Eastasia has regarded them as strictly utilitarian and has clung fiercely to indigenous traditions. In China, for example, the popular notion of reformers in the late nineteenth century was "Chinese knowledge is the essence, Western knowledge is utility."[5] The equivalent Japanese expression was "a Nipponese foundation under Western skills." Eastasians have made a fetish of copying Western technology—often going to ridiculous extremes and copying unnecessary details—because of their correct belief, contrasting sharply to that of orthodox Islam, that Western technology can be separated from Western political and religious institutions. This ability to separate technology from what is more basic to Eastasian culture and nationhood gives Eastasians greater flexibility and integrity than less selective peoples. It also has preserved for them the respect for their own nationality that underlies their modern resurgence. Even tiny colonial Hong Kong still identifies strongly with China's national power, as could be seen from its enthusiastic reaction to the announcement of China's first nuclear device in 1964.

Togetherness

Eastasians are known throughout the world for their clannishness, their solidarity, their group consciousness, and their loyalty to their own kind. We are tempted to trace the origins of this togetherness back to Eastasian village life, which depended on cooperation among village members. Villagers were required to help one another in transplanting seedlings, irrigating paddy fields, threshing grain, building bridges and roads, and fighting calamities. This village consciousness still lingers in Eastasia, most strikingly in Japan, where it has been described by the sociologist Chie Nakane.[6] Workers at Toyota or Matsushita eat together, play Mah-Jongg together, drink together, and work together smoothly as a result. Sacrifices for the group—whether it be the company or the nation—are easier to demand in countries with a village consciousness of this sort, whether the sacrifices be acceptance of lower wage increases, acquiescence to automation, or more painstaking quality control. Even in familistic and individualistic China, the Communist Party draws heavily on "village" attitudes: young people universally accept assignment to posts by the state because they believe in national solidarity.

Another result of the persistence of the "village" in modern Eastasia is that political dealings involve primarily groups rather than individuals. Organizations make the claims or state the opinions in Eastasian society, not individuals, who speak only for their groups. In China individuals are even identified by their "unit," or employing organization, on their personal identity cards. This group-oriented tendency is a fundamental factor in the political stability of the region, which regards individual views as divisive and heterodox. Outspokenness in Eastasia is almost always a sign that the speaker is backed by a larger group which has approved his opinions. Decisions do not come easily, but remain firm under outside pressure. Eastasian togetherness means that the entire village, be it a company, a political party, or a nation, acts as a team.

Individuals in Eastasia are always ideally at one with their groups and have no private opinions or thoughts. This pattern is obvious in the way business offices are organized. Foreigners who call on an executive often find that their counterparts have no private offices. An office in Eastasia is a large room with ten to twenty desks in which co-workers make phone calls, write letters, and receive visitors. Everything is done in full view and within earshot of one's peers. Senior managers may be placed farthest from the door to indicate their rank, but unless they are extremely westernized (working in an American company, for example) or rank very high, they have no special form of privacy. This layout symbolizes the deeper attitudes toward relationships which we term togetherness.

Loyalty is the key building block of such a society. Togetherness requires an individual to bare his soul only to members of his "village" and to establish lasting relationships only with them. Hence the disappointment of many Westerners that friendships seem so fleeting in Eastasia. Termination of lifelong ties is often bitter, as was the split between Chinese Communists and Nationalists after a long period of working together in the 1920s. Long-term stability within the tightly knit group requires constant effort, long discussions, concern for minority views, and explicit compensation for disappointments and other contributions to group solidarity. But the payoff is in results, the ultimate reward for good teamwork.

Politically, togetherness expresses itself in the form of factions. Factions are everywhere in Eastasian political life, bridging the communications gap between superiors and inferiors which makes European politics, for example, often seem unreal.[7] They unite people of different ages and experience, bringing together patrons with their clients. In the Japanese parliament, or Diet, factions are formally recognized, even possessing their own office space, administrative staff, and field organization. Factional maneuvering determines the fate of cabinets, having, for example, toppled the governments of Prime Ministers Kishi, Tanaka, Miki, and Fukuda in recent years. Diet factions also contribute to campaigns and negotiate promotions within the cabinet, which makes watching them a favorite pastime of the Japanese press.

In China, factions play a much less public role, belonging instead to a netherworld which lacks formal recognition. Factions there take the form of personal followings of powerful leaders, such as the late Premier Zhou Enlai, who cultivate extensive personal staffs. When promoted to a new job, say, in the capital city of Beijing, a leader will bring several of his subordinates with him in his entourage, as did Deng Xiaoping when he moved from Szechwan. Factions extend downward through the bureaucracy in the form of "systems"—liaison networks which connect officials at various levels who share the same specialty, such as agriculture or heavy industry. Sometimes Chinese factions may engage directly in policy disputes, as did the Gang of Four, who sought to seize power on the death of Chairman Mao. But though the word "faction" is used as a term of discredit in China, it refers to a pervasive way of organizing life which outsiders as well as natives must learn to deal with.

Yet another form of togetherness is provincialism, a kind of regional consciousness often found in the large Eastasian countries. In Japan, for instance, such consciousness was acute during the Meiji era. Many of the founders of modern Japan were Choshu men from a single district in southwestern Honshu; they dominated the army just as men from the Satsuma area of southern Kyushu dominated the navy. In China the Hunan provincial faction within the

Communist Party drew its strength from the fact that Chairman Mao was himself from Hunan, and the Hunanese were the largest provincial group among the party's older generation. In Korea, President Park Chung-hee's followers came heavily from South Kyongsang Province, and those of opposition leader Kim Dae Jung from South Cholla Do. In Eastasia these regional loyalties are often strengthened by dialect differences which may in the case of China be as great as those between the major European languages. China's most modern city, Shanghai, is strongly represented in the circles that deal with foreigners, since Shanghai has had more foreign experience than other parts of China.

The most powerful factions gain followers in the strategic sections of the bureaucracies. Tanaka Kakuei, leader of one of the most powerful Japanese political factions, consolidated his power by recruiting supporters from the ministries of finance and construction, which regulate real estate transactions.[8] In China the faction of economic planner Chen Yun has gained substantial political leverage through its influence on the State Planning Commission since the 1950s. While factions may slow down the decision-making process because of the need to keep members informed, they do ensure that followers cooperate to implement policy once decisions are made.

Often the strongest bonds of togetherness are formed among men (and sometimes women, though Eastasia tends to be "unliberated" in this respect) who share a common formative experience. For example, in Japan a tiny group of technocrats who served together during the late 1940s in a key planning organization, the Economic Stabilization Board, has since risen to considerable power. This group includes the director of the Japan Economic Research Center, Kanamori Hisao, the director of the Nomura Research Institute, Saeki Kiichi, and a former foreign minister, Ōkita Saburō. In Taiwan the men who served on the Council on United States Aid (CUSA) in the 1950s, such as Y. K. Yin and his assistant K. T. Li, have retained multiple posts and moved from one important job to another while retaining strong personal ties.[9] In China the "December 9th" group of anti-Japanese student resistance leaders from 1935 has continued to hold key jobs in the planning apparatus of the Chinese government.[10] Lee Kuan Yew's personal brain trust in Singapore (including Ngiam Tong Dow, the young chairman of the Economic Development Board and permanent secretary at the Ministry for Trade and Industry) and the former key Korean employees of the prewar colonial banks constitute similar long-term "clubs." The virtue of such clublike groups is that they permit their members to get things done rapidly and flexibly by working around bureaucratic roadblocks and by overcoming the information shortages so chronic in secretive Eastasian decision making. The uncanny success of that most British of institutions, the Royal Hong Kong Jockey Club, now packed with prominent Chinese, in no small part is due to this need for informal ties to overcome formal frustrations.

Secrecy

Eastasians have selective vision, enabling them to "see" only that which should be seen. The distinction between the formal world and the real world runs deep. In Japan a popular expression distinguishes between the "facade" and the "root of the matter"; in China it is the "name" versus the "reality." In the drama of both nations, stage crews dressed in black stroll on and off the set in full public view, but they are not "seen" because they represent reality and not the formality being offered to the audience.

The distinction of "name" versus "reality" extends to politics as well. The Japanese Diet, for example, is only the formal representative of the people, just as in China the National People's Congress is merely the "name" of the Chinese government. The reality in both cases is that power lies elsewhere, in the ministries or in the parties that govern.

All Eastasian cultures emphasize ceremony. Ceremony, like a shotgun marriage, often gives legitimacy to events that have already taken place. Confucius termed this process the "rectification of names," since he contended that it was immoral for name and reality to be out of kilter. China held out for two decades until the United States was willing to recognize only one China and not two by excluding Taiwan's claim to be the "Republic of China." Once this ceremonial recognition was performed, the Chinese would not tolerate any further tinkering with the "name," no matter how the underlying reality might change. Giving legitimacy through ceremony helps create consensus and good feeling, while locking in the opinions of majority and minority alike.

In sharp contrast to the world of names, "reality" in Eastasia is unvarnished. Laws and norms do not apply in the pragmatic world, any more than the power of the declining dynasty could reach the rebels on Liangshan in the Chinese novel *Water Margin*.[11] Informal understandings are often hammered out far from the formal settings of government, in teahouses in Japan, in guesthouses in China. There are over 200 high-quality establishments of this sort in Tokyo and more than 60 in Beijing. This version of the "smoke-filled room," where discussions can be conducted privately without the pressure of a formal setting, is more common in Eastasia than in the West. Here we make policy in the full glare of lights, in congressional debate, campaign speeches, and press interviews.

The secrecy of decision making in Eastasia offers the advantage of surprise, since outsiders know little of the all-important behind-the-scenes action. The decisions to bomb Pearl Harbor, to end the Pacific war, to launch the Great Leap Forward, to purge the Gang of Four, and to make General Chon ruler of South Korea and devalue the won in 1980 were made secretly and only later ratified with the proper "names." Eastasia gains great flexibility and initiative by keeping outsiders away from the inner world of reality.

5

Structural Diversity:
A Major Asset

ALTHOUGH the seven Eastasian states share common social and cultural underpinnings, they also differ on important dimensions. Some are tiny, and some great; some are rich, and some relatively poor; some are Communist, and some not; some developed early, and some late. This very diversity is worth noting, since it may become a major asset of the region in the future. Eastasian nations have borrowed shamelessly from one another in the past, and there is no reason to suspect that this process has ceased. Just as variety in genetic background makes for strong and hardy plants, so diversity of structure makes it likely that Eastasian competitiveness will continue.

Since we are interested in explaining the performance of Eastasian nations, we must explore their "political economy"—the way they organize their economies with in their differing political systems. Just as in Europe and America, each country has a unique mix of public and private enterprise, banking systems, government initiatives, and political input from pressure groups. Eastasian nations are similar in the prominent roles of their central bureaucracies in the economy, in the absence of divisive trade unions, and in the lack of detailed public argument over economic policy. These common elements help explain some of the strength of the Eastasian economies, but there are important variations on this major theme.

Japan: A Nation of Organization

Japan's modern manufacturing sector is a half-century older than its counterparts throughout the region. It flourishes within the most organization-minded of the Eastasian political cultures. Japan has, not surprisingly, a well-organized private business sector which speaks out on its own behalf. Three national business federations stand out: Keidanren (for big business), the Japan Chamber of Commerce (primarily for small business), and the Council on Economic Development (for issue-oriented businessmen in both large and small firms). Also active are regional business federations and industry associations for such sectors as steel, electrical power, banking, autos, and electronics. These mouthpieces represent the full range of interests, with greater sophistication and effectiveness than in any other country.[1]

Japanese industrial groups are unique both in regional and international perspective. Centered on major banks and trading companies, which provide funds and marketing services, groups such as Mitsubishi, Mitsui, and Sumitomo organize complex business deals, share the risk of new high-capitalization ventures, and shift resources away from high-cash-flow, low-growth areas toward those with greater future growth potential. Successors to the "financial groups" *(zaibatsu)* of prewar days, although more loosely organized than their predecessors, the Japanese industrial groups function like small governments in allocating resources. If Japan is indeed "incorporated," it is so more because of the strong authority of these groups in relation to member firms than because of governmental authority.

Business in Japan tends to be more highly leveraged with credit than in Chinese-culture-area countries such as Taiwan and Hong Kong, where companies borrow less. There are exceptions to this rule, notably Matsushita Electric, Hitachi, and Toyota Motors, but typical debt-equity ratios in Japanese heavy industry run around 6–1.[2] With this heavy financing burden, industrial firms in Japan rely heavily on banks, and banks in turn depend on the Ministry of Finance and the Bank of Japan. Government thus manipulates the private manufacturing sector only indirectly through banks and industrial associations, not directly through intervention in business activities. Public corporations play a much smaller role than in Western Europe and much of the rest of industrial Eastasia, thus strengthening the impression of Japan as a market economy, with government stepping in only occasionally and selectively to provide a safety net.[3]

As the only parliamentary democracy in Eastasia, the Japanese government finds itself subject to more grassroots interest-group pressure than is common elsewhere in the region. Small businesses, farmers, and other special interests pushed subsidy levels during the 1960s to over twice the average for the advanced industrial nations. Interest groups have distorted public policy in Japan more than in any other Eastasian nation, although their impact on policy formation has not been so striking as it often is in the West.

South Korea: Active Government Interventionism

Like Japan, South Korea is a nation of private firms heavily dependent on banks, as a result of debt-equity ratios even higher than in Japan. It also has relatively strong industrial groups, including Samsung, Hyundai, and Daewoo, as well as emerging industry associations.[4] Most powerful of these private-sector groups is the Korean Traders Association, whose former president, Kim Woun-gie, was prime minister in late 1980. Nevertheless, these groups are not so powerful as Japan's: they are younger, they operate within a more individualistic culture, and Korea's central government is more powerful and has broader regulatory powers than its Japanese counterpart.

Government enterprise controls only the transportation, the electric power, and, in large measure, the steel sectors; the state often achieves national policy goals through intimate ties with private firms, often on the basis of substantial subsidies. Under the regime of President Park Chung-hee, the Hyundai Group spearheaded priority projects to develop a shipbuilding industry and to penetrate the Middle East construction market. It came close to being a private "national policy company," on the pattern of the Industrial Bank of Japan, although its ties to government have weakened somewhat since 1979.

The state bureaucracy in South Korea has more tools for shaping the private sector than was true in Japan even during the Meiji or early pre–World War II periods. As in Taiwan and Singapore, but in contrast to Japan, economic planning is an integral function of government: the head of the Economic Planning Board in Korea serves concurrently as deputy prime minister. The central monetary authority, the Bank of Korea, is also powerful, providing 11 percent of the total funds loaned by commercial banks, versus only 3 percent in Japan.[5] Government financial institutions are also a major force in the economy; the Korean Development Bank, for example, provided three times the level of funding to private industry during the late 1970s that the Japan

Development Bank did during the days of Japanese double-digit growth during the 1950s.[6]

South Korea is split by religious and regional cleavages—more so than Japan or Taiwan. Ever since the wartime independence struggle against the Japanese, Christians in Korea have been highly active politically; their activism has led to evolution of mass media more independent and directly critical of government than anywhere else in Eastasia outside Japan. Regional splits between northeast and southwest, dating back a thousand years and exacerbated under Japanese rule, also plague South Korea and contribute to political polarization and policy rigidity. Interest groups are not well developed, so often the public cannot communicate its wants without disruptive demonstrations such as those at Kwangju in the spring of 1980. As a result, state resources often are given preferentially to insiders, while those outside the ruling coalition (for example, small business, Cholla Do in the southwest, and so forth) find their hands outside the cookie jar. Korea also has a harder time taking politically unpopular measures, such as implementation of a tight monetary policy, than do the other governments of Eastasia. The freedom of financial lords or industrial groups from state control and the wide range of occupational groups and regions to be appeased by government are major reasons for Korea's high-growth, high-inflation policy of recent decades, a pattern very different from that in Taiwan and Singapore.[7]

Taiwan: A Capitalist Land of Powerful Public Enterprise

Nearly one-sixth of Taiwan's population consists of former refugees from the China mainland or their descendants. These "mainlanders" dominate the government, while the business community is mostly native Taiwanese. Government has less direct leverage on business than in Korea or Singapore, since businessmen rely more on multinational corporations or on Japanese trading companies, which handle roughly half of Taiwan's foreign trade.

The state in Taiwan compensates for this weakness by using public corporations to control and manage the economy. China Petroleum, for example, monopolizes both petroleum imports into Taiwan and petrochemical production, and during 1980 ranked among the largest 120 corporations in the world outside the U.S.[8] This company gives the state substantial influence over synthetic fiber and textile producers, such as those of the Formosa Plastics

Group, the island's largest private industrial concern. The Ministry of National Defense similarly influences the policies of the major electronics group, Tatung, by letting defense contracts. State control, through public corporations, of steel, aluminum, fertilizer production, shipbuilding, railways, and electric power, gives the Taiwan government leverage over downstream sectors throughout the economy, as well as some control over the inflation rate through adjustment of raw material prices. In 1979–80, for example, the ROC government kept Taiwan industry competitive (despite rising energy costs and without devaluing the currency) by suppressing the prices charged by public corporations in basic industry.

The government manages the economy also through its central bank, the Central Bank of China, which controls not only monetary policy but fiscal and foreign exchange policy as well. Its governor, K. H. Yu, a former longtime private secretary to the late President Chiang Kai-shek, also heads the Council for Economic Planning and Development, the nation's long-term planning agency, analogous to Korea's Economic Planning Board. Taiwan's top political leadership has invested the Bank of China with considerable power, and appointed men of substantial personal influence to head it, out of a deep concern for economic stability dating from the hyperinflation of 1947–49 on the mainland.

Curiously enough, neither Governor Yu nor most of the top economic policymakers in Taiwan are administrators by training. In sharp contrast to Japan and Korea, where virtually all influential bureaucrats are graduates of the law faculty, in Taiwan the largest number of top administrators, including Prime Minister Y. S. Sun, are engineers. Governor Yu of the Bank of China is an economist, and key economic planner K. T. Li is a chemist by profession.

Interest groups exert less pressure in Taiwan than in Korea and Japan partly because government has relatively less to offer to self-sufficient Taiwanese firms. The repressive purges against Taiwanese of 1949–50 and the lack of a free press also intimidate many who might otherwise make demands on government. A few native Taiwanese well-connected with the ruling Kuomintang political establishment, such as C. F. Koo of Taiwan Cement and T. S. Lin of Tatung Electronics, help bridge the gap between rulers and ruled, despite the lack of strong Japanese-style private business organizations to promote government-business dialogue. Taiwan enjoys perhaps the smoothest, most "apolitical" economic policy management of all Eastasian states, combining moderately high growth with low inflation, equitable income distribution, steadily declining unit labor costs, and an industrial structure steadily expanding its high value-added sectors. Only in the recent failure to conserve energy —because of pressure from public corporations for low-cost energy—has government management been weak. Economic policy made by engineers in Taiwan seems to run more smoothly than that made by lawyers and economists in most parts of the world.

Singapore: Confucian Socialist Capitalism

In many respects, Singapore reflects the outstanding features of the Eastasian model more faithfully than any other state. Singapore's Prime Minister Lee Kuan Yew, although highly westernized, is in many respects a quintessential Confucian leader—austere, remote, authoritarian, and intensely concerned with national welfare. These traits also characterized Emperor Meiji, Park Chung-hee, Chiang Kai-shek, even Mao Zedong—similar figures who galvanized their respective Eastasian states into unity and self-sacrifice for the sake of the nation.

In its pervasive moralism, Singapore public policy is also thoroughly Confucian, perhaps more so than in any other Asian nation aside from the People's Republic of China. Just as wall posters on the Chinese mainland urge higher productivity or resistance to revisionism, public admonitions in Singapore encourage thrift, diligence, and, until recently, short haircuts. The state tells taxis where they may stop, and paints yellow lines on sidewalks indicating where passengers are to queue up. It rewards parents of one or two children and penalizes those with more. It forces citizens to save through mandatory accounts in a moralistically titled "Central Provident Fund," and breaks up ethnic communities by forcing citizens to choose public housing by lot. Singapore executes convicted heroin pushers, and boots out foreign hippies. This tiny city-state may have the most clearly defined and rigidly enforced public morality in the world.

Despite its Confucian heritage, Singapore is, in many ways, the most westernized and Western-oriented of the Eastasian political economies. English, which most Japanese, Koreans, and Chinese in Taiwan and the People's Republic speak poorly, is the common language of Singapore. Legal codes are British in origin, and Western lawyers, doctors, architects, and bankers are welcomed.

More than any other Eastasian state, Lee Kuan Yew's Singapore sees its future in alliance, not competition, with Western multinationals from outside the region. Only 15 percent of foreign investment in Singapore is Japanese, versus nearly 60 percent in Korea and almost 25 percent in Taiwan.[9] Virtually all of the remainder is Anglo-Saxon. In the 1980 budget statement before parliament, Minister of Trade and Industry Goh Chok Tong specifically made this point, noting that in an era of escalating tariffs and quotas, Singapore could succeed in exporting only if it did so through multinational corporations.[10] Singapore aggressively encourages Western investment, through the twenty foreign offices of its Economic Development Board, known informally as the "Godfather of the multinationals." But Singapore tries to maintain leverage against foreign companies, especially the banks, by financing the bulk of domestic investments internally rather than borrowing abroad. About 65 percent of total capital formation in 1980 was domestic—virtually the reverse of the pattern in Korea.[11] Singapore also strives to maintain its autonomy through the active use of public corporations and by encouraging joint ventures between foreign firms and the Singapore government in strategic sectors.

Singapore's leadership sees alliance with foreign business as a strategic necessity in view of possible Soviet intervention in the region and as a means of protecting its access to Western markets. But this alliance has some negative domestic social effects which need to be neutralized politically so as not to disturb domestic stability. The presence of the multinationals, for example, has created a very rich class of managers with incomes far above the national average. At the same time, free-market import policies tend to depress the wages of unskilled workers. Foreign firms' entry as bidders into Singapore's local labor and capital markets also tends to divert resources away from local entrepreneurs who could otherwise use them to grow. Thus, income and wealth are distributed less equally in Singapore than elsewhere in Eastasia. The country's industrial strategists argue that they have little choice. "You have to bake the cake [of growth] before you can eat it," shrugs one.[12]

Alone among the ruling regimes of capitalist Eastasia, Singapore's is of socialist origin. Prime Minister Lee Kuan Yew was once the firebrand attorney of a leftist trade union, and his ruling People's Action Party (PAP) was long a member of the Socialist International. Even today, unions serve as a major source of PAP support. The Singapore government thus has strong ideological as well as political incentives to offset the negative effects of the multinationals on local income distribution with positive social welfare programs of its own. This it accomplishes not by overt intervention but through extensive social programs undertaken by Singapore's semigovernmental union movement, the most active in Eastasia. The National Trades Union Congress operates a chain of twenty-nine supermarkets selling rice, flour, and other commodities at cheap prices to union members. It also maintains an insurance cooperative catering to blue-collar workers, a dental surgery center, and a chain of restaurants where workers can celebrate weddings and hold New Year's banquets at low prices.

In the housing field the government is unusually active for an Eastasian regime, both to fulfill social welfare objectives and to ensure that polyglot Singapore is able to achieve true ethnic integration. By 1979 the state-run Housing and Development Board had placed nearly 70 percent of the population in public housing.[13] Apartment assignments have been by lot so as to break up the old ethnic divisions (Chinese versus Hindu and Malay) which had led to bitter intercommunal riots in 1959.

Singapore, as a well-run authoritarian city-state, experiences few of the mass interest group pressures and counterpressures that render economic management in the West, or even in Japan, so much more turbulent. Government machinery in this country of 2.4 million people—Eastasia's smallest nation—is likewise relatively simple and centralized. (Government securities holdings in the various public corporations and in joint ventures with the private sector are quite literally centralized—in the vaults of the government's holding company Temasek Holding Private Ltd.) Top leaders are close friends: all young personal protégés of Prime Minister Lee Kuan Yew. Bureaucracy is neither old nor institutionalized, and lacks organizational imperatives of its own. For all these reasons and more, it makes better sense to speak of "Singapore, Inc." than to apply the "Inc." to any other Eastasian state.

Because of Singapore's unified, flexible policymaking structure and its mixed Confucian, socialist, and capitalist heritage, the city-state has been able to generate perhaps the most creative range of public policy institutions in Eastasia, encouraging growth and competitiveness while providing for public welfare. Some highlights:

1. *National Wage Council.* Sets nationwide wage standards through bargaining among all major business and labor groups. No strikes since 1977.[14]
2. *Economic Development Board.* Multifunction organization that establishes institutions from industrial estates to tourist promotion centers. Empowered to buy shares in the enterprise being established and to grant tax-free "pioneer status" for 5–10 years in order to bring in attractive venture business.
3. *Activation Committee.* Concentrates on problems of policy implementation, cutting red tape. Places particular emphasis on breaking through infrastructural bottlenecks in areas like road and port construction.
4. *Central Provident Fund.* Compulsory social security savings fund. Proceeds used to finance domestic industrial development.

With these and other policy tools the Singapore government has won popular support at home for the battle to survive against, or with, the West.

Hong Kong: Administering a Chinese Miracle

Hong Kong differs from its neighbors in two important ways: it is the only Eastasian state still ruled by foreigners, and it lives completely in the shadow of its enormous neighbor, the People's Republic of China. A vestige of former colonial administration, the colony exists today solely at the mercy of a country which is the motherland of 98 percent of its population. Despite the People's Republic's loud claims on "unliberated" territories once belonging to China, the Chinese government willingly accepts British administration of Hong Kong, which it nonetheless continues to assert is entirely Chinese territory. When the tiny Portuguese colony of Macao, across the Pearl River estuary, was offered back to China following the 1974 coup in Lisbon, the Chinese politely refused. They would undoubtedly do the same with Hong Kong.

Neither China nor Britain wishes to change the status quo, and with good reason. Hong Kong has been a lucrative investment for British and other multinational corporations. The Hong Kong and Shanghai Banking Corporation, for example, presently holds assets well over twice as large as the colony's annual GNP.[15] Since "The Bank" is a private corporation, many of its assets are held safely outside the colony. China for its part continues to earn more than US $2 million a day through Hong Kong's commercial activities.

In addition, the colony regularly absorbs disaffected elements from China's impoverished economy, people who within a matter of months are usually converted into efficient workers in the capitalist system. Hong Kong employers typically complain of the lack of discipline and skills among these illegal immigrants, but they are eager to take on more hands, given Hong Kong's shortage of labor. Since China's recent improvement of ties with the West, Hong Kong has been a target of Chinese investment, especially the colony's booming real estate market. Hong Kong Chinese, with their knowledge of world trading practice, have been leaders in the new construction projects in south China.

To the leaders of Hong Kong the government of Singapore, with its extensive intervention into the market, appears *dirigiste* by comparison. The British governors of Hong Kong pride themselves on their hands-off approach to the colony's hurly-burly economy.[16] Controls on imports, foreign exchange, foreign investment, and wages and prices are nonexistent. Yet, as in Singapore, the economic affairs of the city remain firmly in the hands of a small elite, highly ordered and predictable in important respects. Interlocking directorates are common among the British-owned firms as well as the Chinese.

But Hong Kong, with its unusual political arrangement, cannot reconcile the political aspirations of the people with their economic desires. Unlike the Chinese of Singapore, who are evenly divided between separate dialect groups, the vast majority of Hong Kong's population speaks Cantonese. Although the Hong Kong business elite includes a number of powerful Shanghai industrialists, the Chinese community tends to speak linguistically and culturally with one voice, that of Canton. Since the PRC will not tolerate even gentle moves in the direction of a Cantonese republic, Hong Kong politics are remarkably tame in comparison with those of Singapore.[17]

The differences between Hong Kong and the Communist province of Guangdong are striking, despite the homogeneity of the population. It is as though the Chinese character were split like Dr. Jekyll and Mr. Hyde: a traveler crossing the border ventures from one world into another. In Hong Kong there is color, diversity, individuation, and the old-fashioned Chinese virtue of apolitical, but not amoral, familism. Business and commerce are at the core of the society. On the other hand, even at the newly developing border town of Shenzhen, China is drab, uniform, and collectivist. It builds on the ancient virtue of loyalty—in this case, not to family but to the state. Hong Kong and Singapore have had the great advantage of the energies of a Chinese population freed temporarily from the demands of the Chinese political system. The PRC and Taiwan have had the advantage of their ability to appeal to the powerful patriotism of Chinese masses. For Hong Kong, however, the knowledge that the colony may become nothing more than a part of Guangdong when China's proper ownership is reasserted "in the fullness of time" is a sober warning. The miracle of Hong Kong, while benefiting Westerners and helping knit together the maritime economic world of Eastasia, is still a miracle performed with Chinese labor and genius.

North Korea: Communist Confucian State

Structurally the Democratic People's Republic of Korea more nearly resembles China than it does the Republic of Korea to the south. Both China and the DPRK are centrally controlled, authoritarian, Communist Party states whose powerful bureaucracies supervise planned economies in the Soviet pattern. Both have diverged from recent Soviet practice in allowing a cult of personality to flourish around two leaders, Mao Zedong and Kim Il-sung. Both have relied heavily on mass organizations to consolidate power, and on carefully planned and executed campaigns to increase self-reliance. North Korea's Juche program has been markedly less successful than China's, since Korea has amassed a larger foreign debt (over $2 billion) than its enormous Chinese neighbor and has recently defaulted on major international loans.[18]

Whereas China, unable to run an enormous country from Beijing, has shifted power down to local enterprises and farms, North Korea still attempts to exercise central control over the economy, paralleling the centralization of South Korea. The personal rule of Kim goes beyond that of the late President Park Chung-hee, who resembled other Confucian leaders of modern Eastasia. (Kim even echoes Chiang Kai-shek in grooming his son as his successor.) North Korea, with less than a third of the Korean population, lacks China's confidence that the Communist portion of the nation will soon dominate. Its political economy therefore is more embattled, less innovative, and less competitive on the world scene. Even so, the North Korean economy has performed better than that of any other Asian state outside Eastasia, except possibly Malaysia, whose dynamic overseas Chinese businessmen are also of "neo-Confucian" origin.

The People's Republic of China: Atypical Archetype of Eastasia

China is the homeland of many of the phenomena we have been describing as Eastasian. Its population constitutes four-fifths of Eastasia's total. Yet China remains atypical of the region today.

China is not, for example, a trading nation. Its vast agricultural population and inaccessible interior still make foreign contacts difficult, despite more than a century of effort by commercial nations. For three decades after "liberation" in 1949, foreign trade was deemphasized in the drive for self-sufficiency. Only since the break with the Soviet Union in 1960 has trade with the West, including Japan, begun to rise. Today China's total foreign trade is less than 5 percent of the GNP and remains at roughly the same absolute level as that of the "province" of Taiwan. The United States today has several times more trade with Taiwan than with the entire People's Republic. China thus stands out as a major exception to the modern Eastasian model of dependence on international trade.

China differs further from the more developed sections of Eastasia in difficulty of transportation, though it has 4,000 miles of coastline and a lively coastal trade. Most of the population lives in the interior, far from railway or steamship communication. China's development will lag behind that of the rest of Eastasia until the infrastructure of a modern transportation system can be built.

Finally, China differs from the rest of Eastasia in the enormity of its population, which hugely magnifies the difficulty of coordinating national policy. This means that attempts to direct the economy from the center or to encourage innovation may be lost in execution, as millions of Chinese fail to get the message. China's decision-making structure, centered on the State Planning Commission and the Communist Party, is the largest in the world and suffers from all the disadvantages of gigantism.

In many ways the Chinese have adopted strategies unique among Eastasian societies. In the late 1950s, for example, Chairman Mao attempted to break through into industrialization by ordering villages and neighborhoods to build steel furnaces in their backyards. This move quickly failed because of lack of both know-how and raw materials. In the mid-1960s an even more ambitious scheme, the Great Proletarian Cultural Revolution, attempted drastically to transform the educational system by admitting large numbers of unqualified workers and peasants; meanwhile, disloyal members of the bureaucracy were removed through a massive purge. These upheavals held back China's growth, even though, surprisingly, China's cellular economy—strikingly similar to those of Taiwan and Hong Kong in this respect—continued to function through years of government inaction.

After the death of Chairman Mao in 1976, China's new leadership under Deng Xiaoping adopted a bold new strategy of learning from the West. This strategy of "four modernizations" (which in many ways resembled the efforts of the Meiji government in Japan and of the Manchu dynasty during 1900–10) involved actively encouraging the study of advanced nations, inviting foreigners to work in China as experts, purchasing technology through joint ventures with foreign firms, and sending thousands of Chinese abroad. Unlike the Meiji oligarchs who founded modern Japan, China's leadership is constrained by the large investment required to move a subcontinent into the modern world. The lack of foreign exchange and the political constraints imposed by a well-entrenched and ill-prepared bureaucracy continue to frustrate China's planners.

China nonetheless has tremendous potential, particularly if aid is forthcoming from outside. The rate of growth of industrial production since 1949 has, despite the ups and downs, averaged nearly 9 percent annually, not far from the level established by Japan in the early twentieth century.[19] The Sixth Five-Year Plan (1981–85) projects 8 percent growth in industry and 4 percent in agriculture. Building on this growth and assuming no major agricultural or political catastrophe, China's performance may become more typically Eastasian. China will never be as committed to the international trading game as its maritime neighbors, but given its massive size and population, China's entry into export markets will have a substantial impact upon them.

Republican China: The Power of Negative Example

In many respects the example of China before the Communists underlines the accomplishments of Eastasian nations since 1950. Despite several decades of intense industrial and financial activity, the Chinese economy never approached its potential in the first half of the twentieth century. Industrial growth remained low. Virtually all modern enterprise was concentrated in a narrow strip of coastal cities known as "Treaty Ports," which were under the economic control of foreign powers. The native government had little grasp of economic matters and less control over the economy. An inept banking system, ineffective monetary policies, and a greedy political and military elite produced rampant inflation—perhaps the world's most spectacular case of economic collapse. In only one year, from September 1948 through August 1949, the value of the Chinese currency fell from 60,000 to the dollar to 20 million to the dollar. Under such circumstances, savings and investment fell to zero and the economy ground to a halt, to be revived only years later by the Communist government that seized power in September 1949.

It was fashionable at the time to blame this disaster on Chinese businessmen or on the meddling of foreigners in Chinese markets. Chinese entrepreneurs, some said, were too shortsighted, too interested in quick profits, too dedicated to the improvement of their own families at the expense of the nation. Foreigners who invested in or lived in China were "exploiters" of the poor Chinese, who in turn developed an excessive dependence on foreign assistance.

History shows, however, that China's problems in the first half of this century were largely political, not economic. Politicians on both sides of the civil conflict were correct when they accused one another of destroying the Chinese economy for selfish reasons. Recent studies show, for example, that Chinese bankers in Shanghai, far from being lackeys of the Nationalist government, attempted to maintain financial independence and to preserve the value of the Chinese currency in the face of overwhelming odds.[20]

The Nationalist government, founded by military conquest in 1928, never controlled enough of China's vast area to bring the economy under its wing. It abandoned the major source of tax revenues, the land tax, to the provinces, and thus was unable to use fiscal policy to influence economic trends. It failed to establish a national currency, since many provinces controlled their own mints and currency presses. Despite the creation of three or four government banks, including the Central Bank of China (which never became a controlling "central bank" in the classic sense), the government failed to carve out a national monetary policy. Most important, the preoccupation of the government with political issues such as unifying the country, fighting the Japanese invaders after 1937, and coping with rampant Communist insurgency after 1945 prevented it from dealing directly with the problems of economic growth, developing an industrial policy, or promoting China's trade position in the world.

The remarkable success of Eastasia outside of Japan and Korea today rests firmly on the foundation of this negative example. Overseas Chinese in Hong Kong and Singapore, still remembering clearly the disasters that befell their families on the mainland, do their utmost to avoid political quagmires. Chinese money is the most "nervous" in the world, easily frightened out of any nation that displays instability—as the flight of Chinese capital from Thailand, Indonesia, or Vietnam during recent turmoils will attest. This nervousness makes Chinese investors prone to save large portions of current income and to stash it away in foreign banks, often in Hong Kong and Singapore. These have become the repository for billions of dollars in Chinese flight capital from other South and Southeast Asian nations. This flight capital, in turn, has become the nest egg for much of the growth in Hong Kong, Singapore, and Taiwan.

Taiwan's rapid economic development since 1949 also rests squarely on the earlier Chinese disaster. The same Nationalist government that failed so miserably when it claimed control over hundreds of millions of Chinese has proved highly competent in managing the economic growth of fewer than 20 million Taiwanese, while using the very same financial institutions and many of the same personnel. Taiwan's economy is lightly managed to prevent, at all costs, the kind of runaway currency inflation that brought the mainland government down three decades ago. Tough, conservative fiscal and monetary policies, as well as aggressive protection and support for export industries, lie behind the confidence of Taiwanese investors in the workers and in the future of their country. It is as if the Nationalist government had said: "Never again will we allow political chaos to undermine our national economy."

But the nation gaining the most from the disaster of 1949 has been China itself. The Communist government rose to power on the Chinese dissatisfaction with political and economic instability. It quickly capitalized on that dissatisfaction to build a tight fiscal and monetary system with a remarkably low rate of inflation and remarkably high rates (even for Eastasia) of taxation and savings. It nationalized all the banks, consolidated all the local currencies, and established clearinghouses, giving control over all monetary policy to the People's Bank of China, a central bank with branches in virtually every village.[21] Thinking that private enterprise was in part responsible for the economic disaster, the government nationalized all industry and collectivized virtually all agriculture by 1956, thus putting the state in total control of the economy. Though these measures seem harsh, they certainly brought China's endemic instability under control, drastically raised the savings and investment rates, and laid the foundation for significant growth in the late 1950s and early 1960s. China's performance since 1950, like those of Taiwan and other ethnically Chinese economies, has shown that the Chinese people, despite their alleged selfishness and shortsightedness, are capable of tremendous frugality and dedication, given the proper political environment.

Thumbnail descriptions of the various Eastasian political economies cannot do full justice to the variety of the region. No country is exactly like any other, and even two parts of the same nation, such as North and South Korea, may be organized very differently. Borrowing across national boundaries has been very important, however. South Korea's structure draws heavily on that of Japan a few years ago. Indeed, the current Korean five-year plan compares Korea's present position explicitly to that of Japan in the 1960s. Singapore followed Hong Kong's lead in a number of social innovations, notably housing. Taiwan's centralized structure evolved in response to the threat from the Communist state across the Formosa Strait, since lack of central control was thought to have been the cause of the downfall of the Nationalist government of China in 1949. North Korea borrowed heavily during the 1950s from the centrally planned Chinese system, itself modified from the Soviet model. In many respects this diversity represents a major asset of the Eastasian countries, which pragmatically look elsewhere in the region for solutions to their problems.

6

The Dual Rule
of Public
and Private Power

IN the modern West we traditionally assume that governments do not promote growth. The European fear of government emerged at a time when private interests confronted monarchists who fed on commerce. In more recent times, democratic and socialist movements have spread distrust of government as the tool of the wealthy classes. Government now is expected to police and regulate the economy, ensure social welfare, and redistribute profits. We distrust private as well as public bigness, and we dismantle the very organizations in the private sector that might successfully compete in the outside world.

Eastasians regard these patterns with amusement. They take a different and much more positive view of organization and of government. Even before the Greeks and Romans, the Chinese invented bureaucracy. They believed that the state was responsible for the well-being of the people, and they established government agencies designed not to dole out welfare but to create it. In modern times Eastasian governments have encouraged production, protected native industry, and rallied the population around economic causes with national significance. In many ways Eastasian societies are geared up for a modern world where economics is the key to the future.

Unlike us, they are not afraid to concentrate and embrace power, whether public or private.

Single-Party Rule: The Common Pattern

Not that conflict and turmoil have been absent from the Eastasian scene. Struggles among dynasties, conflicts between feudal kingdoms, popular disturbances and revolts have recurred with monotonous regularity in the history of the East, even as recently as the Communist-Nationalist conflicts in China, Korea, and Vietnam since World War II. The rise of modern democratic nationalism strained the traditional empires to the breaking point throughout the region. The last of the great emperors to fall was the Vietnamese Bao Dai, a puppet of the French, in 1954. The kindly Japanese emperor has been, except for his decisive role in ending World War II, largely a figurehead, as were his ancestors for centuries. The republic which replaced traditional monarchs in many cases claimed to represent the popular will. But invariably the revolutions of Eastasia have produced effective single-party rule.

China and Taiwan maintain a facade of multiparty representation, including in their respective national congresses several smaller parties, now composed largely of octogenarian former intellectuals with no natural constituency. But there is no doubt in anyone's mind about the dominance of the ruling parties: the Chinese Communists and the Chinese Nationalists. North Korea has long since abandoned the fiction of opposition parties; despite considerable concern among foreigners and among domestic Christian and intellectual elites, the South Korean government periodically declares all political opposition illegal. Singapore has blocked most substantial opposition from the political process, even though its present government originated as a socialist opposition party; Prime Minister Lee Kuan Yew now attends election rallies only because they are "part of his job." Only in Japan, with its complex modern electoral system nearly a century old, is there a substantial opposition party. Even there, the left-wing parties seem bent on self-destruction, with their ideological inflexibility and administrative incompetence. In all Eastasia there has not been a single major legitimate change of party rule since the fall of the leftist Katayama cabinet in Japan in 1948.

This is not to say that governmental politics do not change or that instability is absent from the scene. The Communists defeated the Nationalists in a

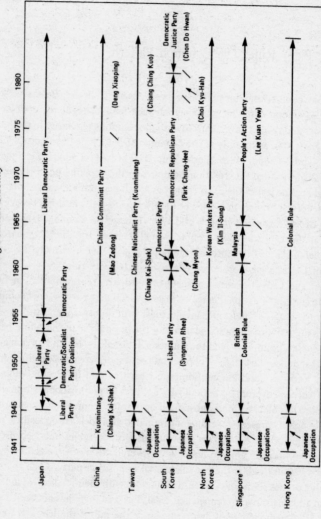

FIGURE 6-1

Eastasia's Striking Political Stability

*The PAP ruled Singapore from 1959 to 1963 while Singapore was a self-governing British colony, and from 1963 to 1965 while Singapore was a part of Malaysia.

massive civil war in China in 1949. Coups d'état by colonels in South Korea changed governments in 1961 and again in 1979. The successions to Mao Zedong and Chiang Kai-shek produced substantial changes of government in China and Taiwan. But the remarkable thing is the continuity of single-party rule, once established. (The details of this continuity are suggested in figure 6–1.) The citizens of Eastasia, especially the businessmen, are more comfortable knowing that their governments do not change. Perhaps this helps explain why Eastasian governments seem more familiar with, and sometimes more competent at, economic policy than those in the West.

Ministerial State

Another striking phenomenon of Eastasian political systems is the dominance of central administration. To Americans who are accustomed to the dispersal of authority among local and state governments, the concentration of power in Eastasia is often striking. Japan's educational and police systems, down to the elementary school and neighborhood district-station levels, are run from Tokyo. China, for all its regional and ethnic diversity, is still run by technocrats in Beijing. Even in Taiwan, local self-government is limited because the "national" administration maintains a pretense of being the government of all of China, not just of the "province" of Taiwan. This concentration of power in metropolitan hands means that the political system exercises more consistent control over society than in the United States. Visitors to Eastasia regularly remark on the homogeneity of policies, whether in the outer islands of Japan or the remoter provinces of China. This homogeneity has its true Western analogue only in France.

In the structure and functions of government ministries, the concentration of power shows through clearly. From Tokyo to Seoul to Beijing, ministries amass resources, manpower, authority, and prestige that no Washington bureaucrat could dream of. The top graduates of the top universities gravitate to them and remain there for a lifetime, partly because ministerial jobs are the most prestigious in society. The word "bureaucrat" (*kanryō* in Japanese, *kwanri* in Korean, *ganbu* in Chinese) has a different ring in Eastasia, striking fear and envy in the hearts of ordinary citizens, whereas it merely fills us with disdain. Ministries form their own specialized networks, establish favored links with certain universities or newspapers, have their own private social lives and entertainment facilities, and provide employees with a strong organizational identity. In China, ministries stand at the apex of large networks (*xitong*).[1] Every ministry—Agriculture, Heavy Industry, or one of the forty-odd other cabinet-level bureaus—makes policy for all of China in its specialized field. It has thousands of employees, including factory workers, accountants, medical personnel, educators, and so on.

Though much less powerful, ministries in Japan exercise their awesome authority often in subtle defiance of the will of the Diet, because only they understand the complex issues of modern government. Unlike Washington, where two thousand or more department heads are fired with each change of administration, in Japan new ministers bring with them only a small handful of political appointees. They are at the mercy of long-term, full-time, loyal ministry bureaucrats who are carefully recruited—again, unlike Washington bureaucrats—through difficult examinations which date back in tradition to the Chinese Tang Dynasty more than a thousand years ago. They advance by consensus among comrades who select out the best and brightest of a "class" of cohorts for promotion to higher responsibility. The selectiveness, solidarity, and professionalism of ministerial bureaucrats in Eastasia help strengthen their influence over the rest of the country.

Of course, ministries do not find economic policies easy to implement. Struggles among ministries are common, particularly on economic issues. In Japan, for example, the Ministry of Agriculture consistently represents the interests of orange and beef-cattle producers, who hope to keep tariff protection high, against the wishes of the powerful Ministry of International Trade and Industry (MITI). In China, the Ministry of Petroleum has different plans for the nation's oil production than does the Ministry of Heavy Industry, which needs fuel for China's furnaces. Much of politics occurs behind the scenes in the cabinets, where issues are resolved without fanfare through ministerial infighting. The political systems are held together by technocrats of varying expertise but of uniformly great influence. In many respects Eastasian officials form a caste of oligarchs vying with one another to exercise authority over a deferential and productive society.

Concentrations of Power

Governments, of course, do not generate economic value. China has 350,000 industrial enterprises,[2] and Japan more than 200,000. These firms range from small, family-run businesses to enormous plants with tens of thousands of employees such as China's Anshan steel mill in Liaoning or Japan's 16-million-ton-capacity Fukuyama Works on the Inland Sea. Such a beehive of activity would produce only chaos were it not for concentrations of power.

Industrial organizations vary, particularly between Communist and capitalist states. In Communist countries direct ministerial control of basic industry is the rule, though provincial authorities may play some leadership role. After 1976, industrial firms in China were organized into larger groups, along the lines of the trusts built briefly in the early 1960s. Despite recent decentralization movements, China's leaders still insist on tight central control over major organizations, particularly those in raw material extraction, transportation, and heavy industry—the 25 or so "key industries." In Japan and South Korea, such large industries as steel and shipbuilding remain in private hands, as does the production of consumer goods. But even here, the levels of concentration are greater than those found in the United States, where antitrust legislation prevents the concentration of power. In the capitalist nations, government also maintains a special relationship with basic industry through the industrial and long-term credit banks. In fact, Japan and South Korea are the only Eastasian nations with laws to break up such industrial concentrations—laws introduced at American insistence and then often ignored.

The traditional Eastasian expression for concentrated economic power is "financial group." This phrase is pronounced *caifa* in Chinese, *chaebol* in Korean, and *zaibatsu* in Japanese, but it is written with the same two ideographs in all three countries. The first such groups, established in Japan during the last two decades of the nineteenth century, were patterned after the European and American "trusts" of the period. Initially these groups concentrated narrowly on specialized product lines; they did not compete extensively with one another except in limited areas such as shipping. Before World War II, for example, Mitsui concentrated on the coal and paper-pulp industries, while other *zaibatsu* had virtually no coal mines or paper mills. Sumitomo focused on nonferrous metal mining and smelting, while Mitsubishi emphasized heavy industry.[3]

After the war, Japan's industrial groups began to assume their present shape. The American occupation order to disband frightened the old-line leadership of the groups, which responded by diversifying rapidly into broad-based financial empires, each possessing a full set of industries. Mitsubishi moved from its heavy industrial base into autos, electronics, and petrochemicals, while Mitsui moved into aluminum and petrochemicals. Within the groups, now known as *keiretsu,* or "affiliations," banks and trading companies assumed the old leadership roles played by the holding companies before the war. Banks and trading companies were growth-oriented, seeking outlets for expanding deposits and commissions from rising trade flows and capital investment. They spurred their member firms on to greater growth and shifted resources within each group's portfolio of industries so as to increase growth. These banks and trading companies have the power to allocate resources on a scale far beyond the dreams of the largest American corporations. At the same time, they are driven forward by the fierce competition among the several groups at the top of the Japanese system.

South Korea has recently evolved a set of industrial groups which resemble the Japanese giants to a remarkable degree. Since the mid-1970s these large companies, led by Samsung, Hyundai, and Daewoo, have come to dominate South Korean external trade and industrial development. These Korean groups grew out of construction and trading companies with international and official ties. Since in South Korea the banks are all state controlled, they have not attained the Japanese level of independence from government, but rather exist with the explicit support of authority. In the early 1980s, government technocrats encouraged the groups to concentrate on specific industries, as had been the rule in Meiji Japan. For example, the Hyundai group was given automobile production and Daewoo received electric power equipment as major spheres of influence. But the groups strongly resisted state efforts to force them to specialize. Whether the natural tendency of these groups to diversify and to compete aggressively in the Japanese pattern can be controlled is still unclear. Samsung's license in December, 1980, to manufacture color television sets for the new national market may set the stage for renewed rivalries and struggles for concentrated power.

In Hong Kong, diversified private-sector groups, which flexibly transfer resources from sector to sector, date from the early days of colonial rule 140 years ago. Jardine Matheson and Butterfield-Swire, for example, are among the world's oldest diversified industrial and commercial groups. In Taiwan, groups have also begun to develop over the past fifteen years. The electronics-based Tatung, for example, got a sharp boost from U.S. offshore procurement contracts during the Vietnam War, and has since been aided not only by consumer sales of television sets and electric fans but also by substantial Taiwanese government military purchases. Tatung President W. S. Lin is a member of the Standing Committee of the Kuomintang and a key figure in business-government relations. The division between mainlander and native Taiwanese can be seen in the concentration of power into government-owned (and mainlander-oriented) enterprises such as Taiwan Power and the massive Retired Servicemen's group, on the one hand, and smaller, privately held, Taiwanese-run groups such as Formosa Plastics and Yuehloong Motors, on the other.

In China and North Korea there is no precise analogue to the private-sector organizations that rule the capitalist economies. But many of the underlying tendencies of capitalist Eastasia may nonetheless be discerned in the Communist countries. The trend toward concentration of economic power can be seen in the decline of the small-scale, nonmodern sector of their economies since the 1950s. Despite the claims for the vitality of native industry made during the Maoist era, large-scale modern industrial organization has been the largest contributor to economic growth. During the first decade of Chinese Communist rule, for example, the contribution to gross value of industrial output by nonmodern enterprises dropped from 43 percent to less than 25 percent.[4] Despite the existence of a central plan for all industry, each enterprise, whether modern or nonmodern, has been from the beginning a separate accounting unit, responsible for its own profits and losses, with each firm accountable for the performance of its subordinates and for its relationships (contractual or otherwise) with other firms.

While the planning system of the 1950s closely resembled the Soviet system of "economic accounting" (*khozrashchet*), by the 1960s planning decisions and control were relaxed by allowing greater profit retention, reducing compulsory targets, and giving authority over many firms to provincial and even lower-level governments. The massive decentralization during the 1960s in China, associated with the Cultural Revolution, produced a system of provincial-level industrial complexes in which each province (with an average of over 20 million inhabitants) controlled its own economy within broad guidelines set by the central government. In many respects the provincial systems are functional equivalents of the industrial groups elsewhere in Eastasia, with their concentration of authority over a number of industries, their need to obey the broad mandates of the central ministries, and their fierce competitiveness vis-à-vis other provincial establishments.

Dual Rule

The system of "dual rule" (*shuangceng lingdao*) that has characterized Chinese industry since the late 1950s is an example of the broader Eastasian pattern of acceptance of organized power. Under this system every enterprise splits its loyalty between obedience to central government—the industrial ministry under the State Council, for example—and private or local authority. In Shanghai, for instance, there are more than 7,100 factories with over a million industrial employees.[5] These factories are directly subordinate to several dozen industrial corporations under Shanghai's industrial bureaus. Each industrial bureau is responsible to the Shanghai municipal government for its economic success or failure, paying dues to local government in the form of profits and turnover taxes—the functional equivalent of dividend streams to shareholders in a capitalist economy. Each bureau, however, must follow the broad rules laid down by the industrial ministry above it in Beijing, which establishes targets for performance, allocates funds for investment, recommends levels for employment and production, and allocates the flow of output. The same kind of tension that links industrial groups and the state in Japan prevails between Shanghai and the government in Beijing, which acts as regulator, benefactor, consumer, and conscience for the local authorities. Ministerial "systems" perform many of the functions of trade associations, linking firms and organizations that are otherwise fiercely competitive with one another. Eastasian countries have all, in one way or another, made use of a form of "dual rule" in managing their growing economies.

General Trading Companies: The Nervous System

Within the economies of Eastasia, a particularly important role is played by general trading companies (GTCs), which act as the central nervous system for economies attuned to the needs of the outside world. In Japan, the first nation to develop the institution, these are known as *sōgō shōsha*. Each industrial group in Japan possesses one of these formidable organizations, and there are several which flourish outside the major *keiretsu*. Each began as a specialized trading firm, somewhat along the lines of the trading companies that presently handle China's exports and imports. But with the inexorable logic of economic advantage, each has become a broad-based trader in commodities and products of all sorts, from metals to machinery, chemicals to fuel, foods to textiles, raw materials to finished products. In some ways the general trading companies of non–Communist Eastasia most resemble the Chinese and North Korean foreign trade ministries in the breadth and depth of their domination of commerce.

These companies differ greatly from Western export-import firms. They tend to be much larger in total turnover, since they handle such a wide range of products. The largest Japanese general trading company bought and sold over $60 billion worth of goods in 1980—a sales volume greater than the entire two-way trade between Japan and the United States in that year ($51.3 billion).[6] GTCs account for half of Japan's total foreign trade, and for an even larger proportion in Korea.[7]

As a consequence of their tremendous size, much larger than non-Eastasian competition in the trading field, GTCs can take advantage of economies of scale not available to competitors. They maintain huge staffs of experts in every subfield of trading, with broad knowledge of languages and foreign markets. GTCs amass and digest an incredible variety of information about foreign economies; because of their tightly knit organization, they can withhold such information quite effectively from outsiders. Because of their close, long-standing ties to major banks, resulting from the industrial-group structure, GTCs can offer financing in the billions of dollars for resource-development and manufacturing projects, as well as pure trade deals.

TABLE 6–1
Japanese General Trading Companies, 1980

Company	Turnover in (billions of (U.S. $)	Japanese employees	International share of turnover (%)	Proportion of Japanese trade handled (%)
Mitsubishi	68.5	9,724	58	14.7
Mitsui	62.6	9,798	56	13.0
C. Itōh	52.7	7,743	54	10.5
Marubeni	50.2	7,657	62	11.5
Sumitomo	47.8	6,064	47	8.3
Nissho-Iwai	32.5	6,276	60	7.23
Tōyō Menka	16.3	3,191	59	3.5
Kanematsu-Gōshō	14.8	2,775	48	2.6
Nichimen	12.8	3,293	68	3.2

SOURCE: Oriental Economist, *Japan Company Handbook: Second Half,* 1981 (Tokyo: Tōyō Keizai Shinpōsha, 1981).

Among the greatest competitive strengths of Eastasia's GTCs is the structure of the business incentives under which they operate. GTCs take a percentage (normally very small) of the value of each transaction, rather than a conventional markup on the products they sell. Since they handle an extremely wide range of products, and many sides of a transaction involving any single product, GTCs can profit just by generating trade flows, even when neither they nor their client firm takes much unit markup on any one portion of a deal. For example, Japan's Mitsui or Korea's Daewoo can cheaply sell coal-mining equipment to China or tire plants to the Sudan because they subsequently plan to market the coal or tires produced. They can also afford to barter or to take inconvertible local currencies in compensation, because they buy as well as sell in the countries with which they deal.

Western manufacturing firms, despite their often enormous scale and financial resources, are not organized to handle complex trade transactions in highly disparate product areas. Western export-import companies are not large enough to afford the information networks of Eastasia's GTCs. Nor do they have the ties with banks necessary to finance massive investment or to match the aggressive support of national governments which Eastasia's GTCs can bring to bear.

In the capitalist economies, trading companies do not always allocate resources in the fashion desired by governments. Often, supporting precisely the sectors not favored by government is the most profitable line of endeavor. For example, trading companies gave major financial support to the textile and paper industries in Japan when those sectors were out of government favor and having trouble with credit. But whatever their relationship to government policy over the short term, these companies often pioneer new lines of industrial development that government later is compelled to follow. They also provide government with large quantities of intelligence information of the sort which the military services or the Central Intelligence Agency presumably provide in the United States. Following the Arab oil crisis of 1973, for example, it was Japanese traders who provided, through their secure information channels, the first status reports on which the Japanese diplomatic response was based.[8] That the Communist trading companies at home and abroad act as the eyes and ears of their governments goes without saying.

Business Associations and Commercial Coordination

Despite the enormous concentration of private power in the Eastasian economies, foreigners are often amazed to find evidence of collusion and self-restraint across entire nations and industries. The temptation is strong to blame the governments for interference or secret masterminding of what appears to be a concerted action directed against the outside world. Japanese pricing of machine tools and steel, Hong Kong textile and electronics marketing practices, and Korean shipbuilding deals often show a single face to the world where we would expect to see many. Often the answer lies in the Eastasian pattern of business association.

There are two basic categories of business associations. First there is the cross-industry federation, of which Japan's Federation of Economic Organizations (Keidanren) is the paradigm. Then there are industry-specific associations, such as the Association of Banks (formerly called the Exchange Banks' Association) of Hong Kong or the Korean Traders' Association, which exist to maximize the interests of a specific sector of the economy. Both types of organization flourish throughout the capitalist part of the region.

The cross-industry federation resembles the Western concept of a chamber of commerce, but with some differences. Interestingly, chambers of commerce were very popular in Eastasia in the late nineteenth and early twentieth centuries, when they were imported from the United States and Europe. Among the Chinese they became ethnically based, representing powerful regional economic interests. To this day, chambers of commerce in Hong Kong and Singapore express the interests of Fukienese or Cantonese traders rather than the entire business community. During the Meiji era the Japan Chamber of Commerce supported big business, fought to retain the land tax, and sought to block corporate taxation. Today this organization primarily represents small business, though large firms are nominally members and though the chairman is the former head of Nippon Steel. By and large, chambers of commerce in Eastasia have limited themselves to a lobbying role on behalf of special interests.

The general business federations we are interested in do far more than that. Keidanren, founded in the early 1950s by war-torn big business, is the principal conduit for political contributions to the ruling Liberal Democratic Party. It has selected prime ministers and helped the party make key policy decisions. When the business world has a consensus position, Keidanran often coordinates industry, makes policy, and conducts diplomacy just like a government. For example, Keidanren was the organizer behind Japan's massive participation in the development of the Amazon Basin in Brazil and the comprehensive aluminum smelting project in central Sumatra in Indonesia during the 1970s. Because it represents firms as diverse as Mitsui Mining and IBM Japan, Keidanren maintains neutrality on controversial domestic issues, such as the clash between Sumitomo Metals and MITI in 1965 over whether Sumitomo should be allowed to expand its steel-making capacity. But in external matters it allows Japanese industry to speak with one voice. Its staff of nearly 200 ranges from experts on energy policy (where it takes an unpopular pro-nuclear stance) to specialists on Latin American economic development.

Because of Taiwan's precarious diplomatic status, that nation's private business federations have also been forced over the past ten years to assume a major role in economic diplomacy, maybe even more extensively than Japan's Keidanren. Spearheading this diplomacy has been C. F. Koo, the urbane, subdued president of the Taiwan Cement Corporation and, simultaneously, of Taiwan's National Association of Industry and Commerce. Koo, who maintains close communications with top local government officials at twice-monthly strategy sessions, reportedly spends one-third of his time overseas on international missions negotiating export and energy supply quotas for Taiwan, as well as promoting his country's economy more generally. The son of a former Taiwan landlord, Koo is fluent in both Japanese and English and has been decorated by eighteen nations.

In Korea, business federations are not as well developed as in Japan. The main such organization, the Federation of Korean Industry (FKI), is patterned after Japan's Keidanren. But it cannot yet match Keidanren's industry-level working committees for generating policy proposals, nor does it have the leverage that grows out of a political funding role. Still, under the leadership since 1977 of Hyundai Chairman J. Y. Chung, a close confidant of the late President Park Chung-hee, the FKI has had a close working relationship with the central government and has assumed some of the "shadow government" characteristics of its counterparts elsewhere in Eastasia.

Unlike the general federations that watch over the interests of the entire business community, specific trade associations protect the interests of particular industries. Throughout Eastasia, merchants banded together traditionally to protect their affairs from the prying of tax collectors, the exactions of military commanders, or the extortions of policemen. Since commerce was considered a lower-class operation, trade associations often resembled underworld "families," with secrecy, mutual protection, and collusive action the rule rather than the exception. The cohesion of business in Eastasia, far from being a government-sponsored unity, originated from the need to protect business from government.

In Japan, modern trade associations sprang up during the 1930s, as the national government discovered their usefulness in getting a handle on the economy and mobilizing for war. The Japan Iron and Steel Federation (JISF), or Tekkō Remmei, which dates from that decade, is one of the strongest in the country and has a staff even larger than Keidanren's. The JISF's functions suggest some of the pervasive influence of such associations in Japan. It monitors the investment, technology, pricing, and export plans of all its members for their mutual benefit—and maintains a computerized file of information about current market shares and inventories of each member. The association works to prevent excess capacity, coordinates production schedules in order to maintain an orderly market, and oversees the steel industry's involvement in national foreign-aid projects, such as those in China and Mexico. Between 1977 and 1980 the Shipbuilding Industry Association supervised plans for scrapping over 40 percent of the nation's shipbuilding capacity, almost entirely without government subsidy or the direct intervention of the Transport Ministry.[9]

The potency of the traditional industry associations can be seen by contrasting them with their younger brothers in automobiles and consumer electronics. Since these industries arose after World War II and never developed the complex intrasectoral control apparatus created to prepare older sectors for war, their members act more independently. Japan's exports of autos and television sets have run out of control in recent years in part because their industry associations lack the power to curb individual manufacturers. A similar weakness may be found in the petrochemical industry, where MITI long found it difficult to regulate capital investment. The relative independence of younger industries may aggravate U.S.-Japan trade relations, since the Japanese government may find it hard to control their aggressive, export-oriented behavior.

In China, the state allocates export quotas by affixing a blue stamp, or "export visa," to trade documents without trade association involvement. But in virtually all the capitalist Eastasian nations, "orderly marketing agreements" have helped create what we might call export cartels coordinated by the trade associations. Taiwan has had such export associations for years.[10] Japan has been forming them as the artificially restricted portion of that nation's export trade gradually expands. In 1970, for example, the Japan Traders' Association, or Nihon Bōeki Kai, was founded to represent the nation's nine large general trading firms, who together handled 47 percent of Japan's exports. In South Korea, trade associations—particularly the powerful Korean Traders' Association—step in often to regulate the flow of exports abroad.

Nowhere are the broad functions of Eastasian trade associations clearer than in Hong Kong. There not only interest rates but even the external value of the local currency is set by such a group, the Association of Banks. Established in 1897 as essentially a social club, this association's objective is, in the words of its 1965 constitution, "to further the interest of member banks in Hong Kong by representing the banking industry in its relationship with its government, other bodies, and organizations and the general public, in all matters touching or concerning banking business." Formally, all the organization does is determine maximum rates on short-term deposits. In practice, however, the group is an interest-rate-setting cartel that performs virtually all the functions, including control of the money supply and in intervention in foreign exchange markets, which would be performed by a national central bank elsewhere.

Hong Kong's Association of Banks illustrates a vital feature common to virtually all the Eastasian trade associations, a feature which both enhances their effectiveness and gives them conservative qualities that might well cause them to be outlawed in Western market economies like those of Britain and the United States. This association is consistently dominated by its two largest members, the Hong Kong and Shanghai Bank and the Chartered Bank. The representatives of these large firms constitutionally alternate as chairman and vice chairman of the association, although the group's executive committee also includes members from six other banks and has the last word on matters of policy. Dominance by the largest members in hierarchical fashion is also a feature of other Eastasian trade associations, ranging from Japan's Iron and Steel Association to the Korean Traders' Association.

Small firms in Eastasia traditionally have also had their organized representatives, however. In Japan virtually every trade group, right down to the taxi drivers and the public bath owners, is organized, although mainly for lobbying purposes rather than to participate in industry regulation. Some of the smaller groups can have considerable political clout. Indeed, in 1968 the traditional innkeepers of Japan were so insistent on government financial aid that they forced Tanaka Kakuei, then secretary general of the ruling Liberal Democratic Party, to agree to set up a special government bank to provide exclusively for their needs and those of a few allied groups, such as the public bath and coffee shop owners.[11]

Public and Private Power: The Keystone Combination

The cliché has it that Eastasia, particularly Japan, has devised a unique government-business relationship. According to this cliché, Eastasians differ from us in their willingness to subordinate business interests to those of the nation. Governments direct and control private enterprise toward the goal of economic growth and output. Japan, Inc., is being followed closely by Taiwan, Inc., Hong Kong, Inc., and eventually even China, Inc.

This cliché is false. Eastasian governments do indeed promote the interests of business in ways that depart dramatically from the adversary relationship we know in America. But businesses in Eastasia pursue their individual interests with a fanaticism and determination that the robber barons of the American West would have envied. At times this "excessive competition," as the Japanese delicately term the phenomenon, leads private enterprise to act directly counter to government dictates, as did Sumitomo Metal in aggressively expanding steel capacity during the 1965 recession in Japan, or Sharp in electronics during the late 1960s. Even where the interests of business and government coincide, initiatives frequently come from the private sector since the bureaucracy is understaffed in relation to the broad range of complex functions it must handle. Indeed, the major role of government in the partnership is increasingly that of providing information and ensuring a predictable business climate rather than twisting corporate arms on behalf of state goals. It is precisely this division of labor between an aggressive, competitive private sector and a forward-thinking, technically oriented bureaucracy that makes the dual rule of public and private power in Eastasia such a strong and formidable partnership.

Part III

POLICY

7

Agriculture:
Root of the Nation

IT may seem odd to suggest that it is
the rual sector that has spurred Eastasian growth. In most countries a backward peasantry has been dragged screaming into the twentieth century, when
its antiquated methods of cultivation, primitive market consciousness, and
atavistic social relationships have made it a burden on the modernizing parts
of the economy. In the rest of the developing world, planners hope at best to
"bracket" the peasantry, isolating it from the externally oriented sectors of
trade and industry, in the hope that peasants will soon disappear—or at least
migrate to the cities to become productive industrial laborers. At worst, leaders
of such countries anticipate the steady deterioration of rural living standards,
increased population densities, and ultimately an endemic rural rebellion that
saps the ebbing strength of modern economic forces.

Problems of Rural Development

There are enough examples of this pattern of rural disability and destabiliza-
tion to have produced a massive literature—often Marxist inspired—of
"peasant unrest." The Communist revolutions in Russia and Cuba are often
alleged to have derived more from rural dissatisfaction than from the suffer-
ing of the urban proletariat. The "peasant" parties of Central Europe in the
1930s and the Latin American land-reform movements based on agricultural
labor in the 1960s are examples of the political potential of a disaffected
peasantry.[1] We may argue that revolutionaries will gain support from disaffected elements no matter where they are found, but the fact remains that in
many developing societies an impoverished agricultural sector has undermined political order and made economic development difficult if not impossible.

Another classic pattern of rural degeneration is called "involution" by the
anthropologist Clifford Geertz.[2] Characterizing this pattern is a vicious cycle
of population growth and intensification of agricultural efforts. Instead of
seeking such technological improvements as mechanization, irrigation, or fer-
tilization, an involuted society simply increases the number of men and women
working each square meter of land. Large families become an economic advantage, providing more labor for further intensification. While involution can
continue for many generations, as it has in Central Java or Bangladesh, the
end product is an equilibrium at a relatively low standard of living. While
involution does not often produce the political instability of less adaptive rural
societies, it prevents nations from making full use of the economic talents of
their village populations, whose energies are absorbed in maintaining a subsistence economy.

A third disaster that often strikes developing countries is that of the plantation economy. In countries where major cash crops such as pineapples,
rubber, coffee, or cocoa are produced for the world market, there is a tendency for large-scale plantations to be more efficient and for peasant proprie-
tors to be gradually transformed into rural laborers. Such latifundia, with
their disaffected proletariat of landless banana pickers or cane cutters, have
often produced extensive political pressures on the national economy (as, for
example, in Venezuela or the Philippines), particularly since the world market for the produce of latifundia is volatile and subject to wild price
changes.[3]

The Eastasian Pattern

It should be clear from this presentation that the Eastasian rural economies have differed sharply from these less happy models. In their own unique way, Eastasian villages have not undermined their political systems but have instead contributed strongly to them. By producing leaders, supporting armies, sustaining elites, and deferring to urban leadership, the "peasants"—if that European word is the correct term for the "cultivating people" *(nungmin, nōmin)* of the region—have provided the underpinning for modern Eastasian societies.

Consider the latifundia issue. Many observers have been puzzled at why Eastasia did not produce large plantation agriculture but instead preferred small peasant proprietorships. The pattern is clear despite the occurrence of latifundia in some peripheral regions such as Malaya (with English-built rubber plantations worked mostly by Indians) and the Southeast Asian hill regions (with tea or opium plantations often worked by hill tribesmen). These cases aside, the dominant mode of ownership in Eastasia is the family farm. Even before land reform decreased the holdings of large landowners, the average farm size in the region was on the order of five acres or less, with the average male agricultural worker tilling less than three acres.[4] With such a scarcity of productive land, it seems odd that Eastasia did not pool it into larger farms with more free-floating agricultural labor.

The secret of this puzzle is rice, a food grain with peculiar requirements for cultivation. Still the staple food for Eastasian peoples, rice is not well suited to large-scale agriculture. It is a finicky crop, demanding steady and individualized attention (in the absence of modern machinery) of a sort that only a highly motivated farmer could give. It rewards the cultivator with high yields, sufficient to support the average family of five from a tiny plot of land— important because only 15 percent of the total land of Eastasia is arable. Since it supplies virtually all the nutritional requirements of a family, there is little reason to convert to cash crops and to expose the rural economy to wider markets, except for a few necessities, such as salt, and the minor luxuries. It demands a stable population, settled on the land for generations, to maximize the potential of each small plot—in the same way that only the home gardener knows the best use for each corner of the garden. The commitment of Eastasian agriculture to grain cultivation, in other words, determined quite early in history the basic patterns of the region's economy.

Of course, other nations have cultivated rice and yet not enjoyed the stability and growth that characterize Eastasia. Particularly in South and Southeast Asia, rice cultivation does not bring with it the larger economic benefits, but rather tends to produce involution. The Eastasian systems evolved a strikingly successful relationship between agriculture and government that made the great Chinese empires strong and enabled Japan to withstand foreign attack for centuries. The political and social systems of traditional Eastasia reflected the mainly agrarian nature of society: taxes were collected largely in grains, not in currency, thus reinforcing the commitment of the population to agriculture. Even in feudal Japan, government protected sedentary landowners from predation by bandits, and in return took more than a third of the rice crop to pay for its armies and officials.[5] Informal economic and political networks— secret societies, chambers of commerce, crop-protecting cooperatives, and irrigation organizations—grew up indigenously in agrarian China. Agriculture was considered to be the "root of the nation," a phrase which in modern times has been used by nationalistic parties on both sides of the Yellow Sea— *nongbenzhui* or *nōhonshugi*. In this delicately balanced system, government itself depended on surplus food-grain production, without which no armies could be raised and no ruling elite had the leisure to pursue education and politics. In this way a unique tradition of pro-agrarian statecraft emerged, a tradition which still survives in the government-rural alliance that dominates most of the region today.

"To Rebel Is Justified"

Many who know of the history of agrarian unrest in the region may take exception to this statement. Indeed, it can be argued that the Eastasian peasantry has been as unruly as any in the world, with dynasty after dynasty falling to rural rebellion, often induced by the collapse of the agrarian economy. Did not the Han, Tang, Ming, and Qing dynasties (not to mention the "dynasty" of Chiang Kai-shek) fall to peasant rebels? Was not rural unrest behind the Meiji reforms, Japanese militarism, the Korean revolt against Japan? Did not the Communists feed on rural dissatisfaction in seizing control of China and Vietnam?

We do not deny that peasant rebellions have shaped Eastasian political history, but we do contend that they have played a somewhat different role here than in other parts of the world. Curiously, the regularity of rural revolt suggests the difference: Eastasian tradition *expected* the peasantry to revolt and to restructure society under certain circumstances. "To rebel is justified," the phrase used by Mao Zedong to encourage his Red Guard radicals in 1966, actually derives from a classical political novel, *Tale of Three Kingdoms,* which describes the massive rebellions after the Latter Han Dynasty in the third century A.D.

What "justified" rebellion in the tradition was the failure of government to meet the standard of performance laid down by traditional statecraft theories: to protect the welfare of the people. The right to rebel was reserved by the peasantry for those times (which came every few generations) when government lost its "heavenly" mandate. Early statecraft assumed, and modern practice confirms, that a vital and flourishing rural sector both supports and is supported by government. Thus, unlike other major peasant rebellions in world history, those in Eastasia have not normally created new forms of government or new ideologies, but rather have reaffirmed the old.

Consider the relationship between Chinese Communism and the Chinese peasantry, one of the world's most striking and powerful alliances. From our point of view, Marxist-Leninist propaganda notwithstanding, this relationship has proved to be profoundly conservative for Chinese society. To be sure, the revolution dramatically altered most aspects of Chinese political, social, and economic life. By expropriating landlords, killing the gentry class, and emasculating the secret societies and the former Kuomintang officialdom, the Communists turned China on its head and brought the peasantry to power. Or so the propaganda goes. In fact, since the Chinese revolution the villages have remained passive recipients of policy, rather than constituencies for further change; the government continues to rule, as the mandarins did, by extracting surplus food grains to feed armies and officials; and state ideology, despite nods to the urban-oriented Lenin, Stalin, and Marx, continues to stress "agriculture as the foundation." The more things change, the more they remain the same.

Uses of Land Reform

Land reform offers another instance of the powerful relationship between government and countryside in Eastasia. The tradition provides many examples of reforms quite similar to those of recent decades. The classical Chinese wrote of a system of communal lands (*jingtian*—literally, "land surrounding the village well") that were periodically redistributed to ensure equal economic opportunity to every villager. Throughout various dynasties, redistribution was used to gain political support for new rulers. In Japan, the Taika Reform of the seventh century was introduced in imitation of the landholding system of the Tang Dynasty in China.

Japan used the rationalization of landholdings as a pretext to gain control of large areas in Korea after the occupation of 1910. The American military government which occupied Japan in 1945 used land reform, in turn, as a device for democratizing the country—and to undercut the Japanese Communists' demands for a more thoroughgoing rural revolution. The Nationalist government, having moved to Taiwan as a last resort against the Communists, confiscated the large holdings of native Taiwanese landowners and thus reduced the likelihood of a rebellion led by rural lords against Kuomintang rule. On the mainland, the ruling Chinese Communist Party likewise carried out an extensive land reform, thus undermining the rural base of their opposition and consolidating their support among the peasantry prior to collectivization in the mid-1950s. In each of these cases the major principle was the sanctity of land ownership and the right to till the land in perpetuity. The major benefactor was, of course, the party in power.

What is striking about the history of Eastasian land reform is the consistency of its political effects. Land reforms have systematically promoted political stability by increasing the security of the vast mass of small freeholders in the countryside. This pattern was as true of the Chinese Communist land revolution, which produced a stable base for the Communist Party, as it was of the Japanese land reform that enabled the Liberal Democratic Party to entrench itself among its rural constitutencies. By displacing landlords to the cities, land reform has had the side effect of creating a class of urban entrepreneurs who are unable to rely on their former base of support in rural rents, and who therefore turn their talents to industry and commerce. Land reform thus has undermined the traditional consumption-oriented landlord elites of Eastasia, while shifting the balance of power toward the growth-oriented cities.

The Reverse Scissors

In 1921, four years after the Bolshevik Revolution, V. I. Lenin instituted a program known as the "scissors" as the foundation of his "New Economic Policy." Prices for agricultural products were set so as to minimize the cost of living of the urban factory workers on whom Lenin depended. On the other hand, the prices of consumer goods which farmers would traditionally have purchased from the city, including fertilizer and agricultural tools, were set so high that few farmers, who by and large were not Bolshevik supporters, could afford to buy even the bare necessities. This squeeze play, which resulted in long-term disruption of rural-urban ties in Russia, ultimately made necessary the draconian measures of collectivization under Stalin after 1930.

Russia could afford the scissors, since there was sufficient grain production to take care of both rural and urban dwellers. Eastasia, with fifteen times the pressure of man on arable land, has not been able to afford this luxury. Not only would large portions of the population starve (in the cities first, of course), but the countryside would quickly reassert its preponderant demographic weight and "seize control of the cities" in one fashion or another. Instead, Eastasian governments have been forced to employ what we call the "reverse scissors": a pricing policy that favors agricultural production and encourages the modernization of agriculture. At the very worst, as in China before 1949, governments have avoided excessive agricultural taxation in the interest of political harmony.

An important side effect of the "reverse scissors" is that industry in Eastasia has not been able to rely on processing of agricultural products as a major first step in modernization. Here Taiwan, with its abundance of marketable subsidiary crops such as onions, pineapples, and mushrooms, may be an exception. Japan's early industrialization depended more on heavy industry for armaments and improvement of transportation than it did on agricultural processing. This characteristic of a northern temperate climate—sufficiency rather than surplus—may be one of the advantages that distinguishes Eastasia from the more abundantly endowed, and hence predominantly extractive, South and Southeast Asian economies.

Whatever their differences from more abundant societies, Eastasian countries, by protecting their agricultural sectors, have reaped broad economic benefits. Shielded from the squeeze of unfavorable pricing and taxation, farmers are free to produce the surplus the society needs from them; sons and daughters are free to pursue the education that will allow them to to get jobs in nearby factories; and families respond to incentives to increase productivity.

Rural Conservatism

Despite decades of propaganda about the "radicalism" of the peasantry, in Eastasia the rural population remains a remarkably conservative force. It resists change because for many years it survived at the bare margin of subsistence in many areas, and because it was in fact the fundamental basis of the agrarian empire's political organization. This reality has colored the Eastasian response to the new international environment. In China, the drive for the "four modernizations" must inevitably include agricultural growth and well-being, since three-quarters of the population still resides in largely self-sufficient villages. No radical economic solutions can be risked that might threaten the delicate fabric of rural China. In Korea there is a widespread sentiment, even among industrialists and city dwellers, that a stable and prosperous countryside is essential for national survival, despite the economic pressure to follow the Japanese path in allowing the agricultural population to dwindle. Hence the ambitious and expensive Saemaul (New Village) Movement, directed by the Ministry of Home Affairs, in which villages are encouraged to preserve their ancient ways, remain loyal to the state, and enjoy American television soap operas. In Japan the Liberal Democratic Party still protects the rural constituency that originally produced it, even though agricultural households have declined to less than 10 percent of the electorate. Many Japanese still remember the dark days at the end of the war, when entire cities were evacuated to live off the land, and the government is inclined to preserve, at least symbolically, this option for the future. Thus, 40 percent of the Japanese Diet still comes from "rural" constituencies.

Agricultural Performance

Agriculture in Eastasia has performed remarkably well considering its modest base in the nineteenth century. Japanese agricultural growth in the late nineteenth century laid the groundwork for rapid industrial growth in the twentieth. Growth in Japan has resulted from the widespread introduction of new seeds (for example, the Penglai variety of rice imported from Taiwan), application of fertilizer, and use of mechanical tilling and harvesting aids (though mechanization has been only marginally helpful in paddy rice production because of the intensive demand for labor at transplantation time). The Japanese farmer today produces roughly four times more food grain annually than his grandfather did.[6] In Taiwan the figure is three times, and in Korea and China about twice.[7] There is no doubt that, given commensurate factor inputs (especially water), Chinese production could begin to approach Japanese levels by the end of the century. China's agricultural development is being held back not by the machinations of the "Gang of Four" or by the inadequacies of the commune political system, but by the lack of phosphate and nitrate fertilizer and of good and timely water sources, themselves a product of industrial development.

China: The Problem of Population

Perhaps the toughest of modern Eastasia's dilemmas is how to turn China's great weakness, its enormous rural population, into a strength. The issue dates back centuries, to dynasties that flourished because they gave free rein to the growth of the agricultural population. As China's numbers swelled from around 100 million to nearly 500 million people, Ming and Qing rulers used this expanding population to consolidate and expand their empires and make China the most powerful nation of its day. Unfortunately, by the early nineteenth century, population growth had become a serious problem. The agrarian economy required to support the humanity concentrated in the Yellow River and Yangtze River valleys was exceedingly fragile. In the Chinese phrase, production depended on "heaven"—sunshine, rainfall, the absence of pests, and an abundance of natural water. When these factors were missing, enormous human losses resulted, as droughts, plagues, and floods decimated the country. As recently as fifty years ago more than 10 million people died of starvation in the great northwestern drought of the early 1930s.

The Chinese Communists came to power in 1949 armed with a number of advantages over their predecessors. They had experience in ruling large parts of rural China before they captured Beijing. The Communist Party had reached its fighting strength by appealing to farmers in remote regions with offers of land, self-respect, and a stake in the takeover of a nation. If any force could grapple with China's enormous rural population, the Chinese Communists could.

During the 1950s the Party rapidly consolidated its control over a country that many claimed was uncontrollable. To do so, it expanded its own numbers to become the largest political organization in the world, with nearly 40 million members, most of them rural, by 1980. It built a governmental structure from the ground up, beginning with village organization and peasant participation. It first offered widespread ownership of land to the farmers, then suddenly, apparently at the whim of Chairman Mao Zedong, chose instead to build an enormous network of agricultural organizations—cooperatives, collectives, and communes. The tightly knit village structure of rural China today was in place by the end of the 1950s.

In this rural transformation, Chinese leaders have drawn heavily on yet another Western model, that of the Soviet Union during its collectivization drive. The present-day Chinese government, the dominant role of the Communist Party elite, the rigid central planning structure centered on the capital city —all this seems very Russian, despite the two-decade-long estrangement between Beijing and Moscow. But even during their years of copying Russia, the Chinese seemed to recognize the uniquely Eastasian character of their rural problem. They deftly avoided "scissoring" the population with exploitative price differentials; they allowed villages to select Communist Party leaders from their own ranks; they delayed intensifying collectivization until the Party was firmly rooted; and despite zealous claims to the "communization" of rural life in 1958, they quite carefully avoided tampering with the family unit. After the disastrous failure of the highly innovative but poorly conceived forced-draft industrialization program of the Great Leap Forward, they reaffirmed their fundamental notion that a healthy agricultural population was the basis for China's future development.

This policy of "agriculture as the root, industry as the leading factor," laid down in a series of directives between 1960 and 1962, still holds way and remains the basis for China's ambitious attempt to control the size of the rural population. Here the experience of other Eastasian countries was of little help. Japan, South Korea, Taiwan, and Hong Kong have essentially relied on market forces to bring population growth rates under control. Migration to cities simply made large families an economic burden. China could not adopt this laissez-faire strategy because it can hardly expect to feed a half-billion urban citizens without a drastic improvement in agricultural production. Instead, the Communist government actively discouraged migration to the cities, and in the late 1950s became the only major developing country to show a net decrease in urbanization, a phenomenon which has been only slightly reversed since. China's policy is very strictly to limit movement from villages. Except for a small handful of select young people recruited into the People's Liberation Army or higher education (less than a total of 3 percent for both), rural Chinese are restricted to their native villages for life. A massive program to resettle educated youth, many with paramedical and other skills, began in the mid-1960s, sending at least 20 million young people down into the villages for the first time.

The policy of isolating the countryside in this way might have been impossible had it not been for pill-sweetening policies. Increased rural participation in Party membership and deliberations assured the villagers of favorable pricing of agricultural products and liberal profit incentives to units with high productivity. The promise that the fortunes of the villages would at least not be allowed to worsen has been met for nearly two decades.

Birth control became a stated policy in the mid-1960s, despite robust pronouncements from Chairman Mao that China's great and growing population was an asset. Quietly, through the expansion of clinics, the work of paramedics ("barefoot doctors"), the thorough distribution of contraceptives, and the provision of facilities for abortion and sterilization, the government has actively sought to reduce the birthrate. Taking advantage of the fact that China produces a large portion of the world's diosgenin, the natural vegetable product from which estrogens and other reproductive hormones can be synthesized, Chinese scientists have developed inexpensive and potent oral contraceptives administered in the form of postage-stamp-sized pieces of impregnated rice paper.

In the final analysis, however, all these policies will be ineffectual unless they are backed up by economic forces. So long as additional family members are believed to bring economic benefit, families will grow. Even in today's tightly controlled China, observers suspect a substantial underreporting of the rural population. While the official claim is that the birthrate has declined to less than 2 percent, there is reason to suppose that in rural areas the rate is substantially higher. Rural families are told that beyond the second child they cannot expect additional work points allocated for their children, nor is there a guarantee of other community and government services for the additional offspring. This strategy resembles that of Singapore, where third and later children may be denied access to free public education—and schools of their choice—a devastating penalty for the ethnic Chinese, among whom it has worked remarkably well. In the cities a major constraint on large families is the serious housing shortage, along with the long-term economic liability that children impose. There is little wonder that some cities in China are reporting essentially zero population growth, and that Singapore is steadily approaching it.

The population problem in China is far from completely resolved. Seven out of eight Chinese still live in villages, where birth control is harder to achieve. China's population will probably not stabilize until well into the twenty-first century, at a level approaching 1.3 billion persons. But in contrast with many other developing societies, including India, Indonesia, Bangladesh, and Mexico, the Chinese record to date has been striking.

It is worth speculating on what a China, fully modernized, might look like. Industrialization of the countryside itself, rather than the movement of population to the cities, seems the only logical answer, and this tendency has already begun with the development of widespread small-scale industries in the 1960s. For all the quarter of a million villages of China to enjoy the living standards of the farmers of Korea or Taiwan seems only a dream today, and the possibility that every village family may someday own its own China-made automobile seems very unlikely—the drain on the steel industry alone would be incredible. But the likelihood of substantial growth in China's industrial power, including the power to produce consumer items such as electronic goods and home appliances, is very great. When the time comes, the people of China will be able to thank the innovative leaders of the 1950s, including Chairman Mao Zedong, for their foresight.

Case Study: China's Agricultural Miracle

Three decades ago, China was an economic disaster area. Not only was its industry in shambles after the devastation of war and revolution, but its agriculture had deteriorated to the point where widespread famine and malnutrition were endemic. Relief efforts by the United Nations in the late 1940s concentrated on China, the world's most serious starvation problem. The problems of turning China's agriculture around seemed as great as in Bangladesh or parts of India today.

Yet thirty years later the Chinese are not only fully capable of feeding themselves, they have also become exporters of certain agricultural products to the outside world. From 1949 to 1978, food-grain production increased 175 percent, from 111 million to 305 million metric tons—an annual rate of 3.5 percent, considerably greater than the population growth rate of 2.2 percent during the same period.[8] A rice-importing nation in the late 1940s, China in recent years (1977–79) has annually averaged over a million tons in exports of the high-priced grain, which the People's Republic uses to purchase relatively low-cost wheat and other food grains on the world market. While some will still quibble that China remains a net grain importer, that the gains of the last three decades have been hard won and unlikely to continue, and that China's agriculture still seems backward when compared to, say, Japan's or Taiwan's, the record is nevertheless impressive. Compared with other "developing" countries, which increased food production only 2.7 percent a year between 1954 and 1973, China has done rather well, and is starting on the path toward rapid agricultural modernization.[9]

In many ways the Chinese performance follows the path pioneered by Japan earlier in this century, and duplicated by Korea and Taiwan in more recent decades. In the West, agricultural growth has resulted from expansion of the acreage under cultivation or from the intensive use of mechanical power to extend the capabilities of farmers. In the process of growth, the traditional family farm has virtually disappeared, to be replaced by large spreads managed by a small number of professional agribusinessmen. In Eastasia, by contrast, growth has been the product of increased irrigation, double cropping and other intensifications of the agricultural cycle, and the application of chemical and biological technologies. This pattern has been dictated by the fact that the leading Eastasian crop is paddy rice, while in the United States soybeans, wheat, and corn predominate. China produces nearly three times as much food grain per cultivated hectare as the United States, but it requires 100 times as many Chinese as Americans to produce a ton of foodgrain. Scarcity of land, and the high concentration of labor on the land, have forced the Chinese to turn to other inputs in order to increase agricultural production.

The factor that produced the greatest growth in the 1960s appears to have been chemical fertilizer. As table 7–1 shows, total chemical nutrients added to the soil increased sixfold from 1960 to 1970; less than one-third of the increase was due to increased fertilizer imports. Added to this chemical fertilizer was a considerable amount of natural organic fertilizer from increased hog and other livestock production during the period. To absorb this stepped-up application of nutrients, Chinese farmers have made use of fertilizer-sensitive seeds developed quite independently from those used to feed the Japanese and Taiwanese growth spurts.

As was the case in other Eastasian countries, China's growing fertilizer output derived essentially from expanding production of small-scale nitrate and phosphate plants; in the mid-1970s, for example, more than half the domestic production came from such plants. Increasingly, however, China has had to build large-scale chemical fertilizer plants, often with foreign help (the dozen urea plants exported to China by M. W. Kellogg in the mid-1970s are an example). It may be that returns from increased fertilizer application will diminish in the future, but there is no denying the positive results to date.

Water is the other major growth-producing input. As table 7–1 shows, the acreage committed to irrigation in China has grown from 20 percent to nearly 50 percent today, as a result of enormous human efforts to harness rivers, build canals, and dig wells. Remarkable strides in "water conservancy," including a massive program of upstream dams in the Yellow River watershed and large projects to divert and control the Hwai Ho, have decreased the risk of floods and dramatically raised the level of production in the arid north China plain. The limits of rice cultivation have been pushed northward through this effort, so that the region around the city of Beijing now produces a crop of rice to feed the many southerners who have migrated to that city as Communist officials.

Mechanization of agriculture has been somewhat less important, though it receives strong support at the policy level from the government. Though the number of tractors available to agriculture has grown enormously since the 1950s, there are still too few of them, and except in the newly developed

TABLE 7–1

Inputs to the Chinese Agricultural Sector

Year	Chemical Fertilizer (thousand metric tons)		Tractors (thousand 15-hp units)	Rural hydro-power (million kwh)	Irrigated Acreage (percentage of arable land)
	Total	Imported			
1949	5	0	0.4	0	20
1960	710	215	79.0	0.5	31
1970	4,266	1,485	320.1	0.9	39
1977	9,088	1,523	634.5	4.0	45

SOURCES: National Foreign Assessment Center, *China: Economic Indicators,* December, 1978; Dwight Perkins, "Constraints Influencing China's Agricultural Performance," in U.S. Congress, Joint Economic Comittee, *China: A Reassessment of the Economy* (Washington, D. C.: U.S. Government Printing Office, 1975); and authors' extrapolations.

wheat-growing regions, Chinese agriculture remains heavily dependent on human labor. Mechanization is still in its infancy in China's enormous rice-producing zones south of the Yangtze. South Korea, for example, has more than 5 million small rice-paddy tractors, compared to less than a million for all of China in 1980.[10] The key to mechanization in China lies in expanding local, small-scale production of tractors and tools, since the country lacks the nationwide distribution network and large-scale manufacturing capability of more advanced nations. In this field, too, the Chinese can look toward earlier parallel development of Japan and Taiwan.

Ultimately, the source of China's agricultural improvement has been the farm family. The declines in production of 1959 and 1967 can be attributed directly to disruptions of the system and to negative production incentives. In the same way that the collectivization drive in the Soviet Union encouraged millions of peasants to slaughter their livestock, the aftermaths of the Great Leap Forward and the Cultural Revolution gave Chinese farmers license to produce less for the state and more for themselves. Since then, incentives to produce have been improved, gradually for the most part but dramatically since 1978. As table 7–2 shows, agricultural taxes now constitute less than half what they were at the end of the land reform period of the early 1950s. The land tax was established as a fixed amount per hectare, and as output has increased, the tax rate has remained constant, thus reducing its burden on producers. Furthermore, the pricing policy of the planned economy has shifted in favor of the farmers. By 1973 a Chinese dollar's worth of agricultural goods would buy 37 percent more industrial goods than it would have in 1952. The Deng Xiaoping regime's new enthusiasm toward agriculture since the Communist Party's Fourth Plenum of September 1979 entails further incentives to increase agricultural production and tap this source of growth.

TABLE 7–2

The Reverse Scissors:
Incentives in Chinese Agriculture

Year	Rural/Urban terms of trade*	Agricultural taxes (percentage of crop output)
1950	0.90	-
1952	1.00	13.2
1957	1.20	11.5
1963	1.23	-
1973	1.37	6.0

SOURCE: Dwight Perkins, "Constraints," pp. 362–63; and authors' extrapolations.

*Farm product prices divided by prices of industrial goods sold in rural areas.

To Western eyes, perhaps the most surprising fact about China's agricultural pattern is that the "peasants" have continued to produce and to turn over a portion of the fruits of their labor despite a lower standard of living than their urban compatriots, and despite the loss of their personal right to land ownership. Collectivization in the mid-1950s did not substantially decrease production, to the surprise of many foreign observers. Chinese farmers have adapted readily, at least in the short run, to the notion that their "family" is really their village. Communes, brigades, and teams have taken on many of the ownership rights formerly held by families, including the right to invest or consume the aftertax surplus. Individuals and families have clung to their modest "private reserve plots"—up to 5 or 10 percent of the cultivated land—to satisfy their personal needs. They have also engaged in such subsidiary occupations as handicraft making, and they trade eagerly, when allowed, in the "free markets" for agricultural produce that open from time to time.

The Chinese leadership is currently committed to increasing these incentives even further. If they succeed, it seems likely that China's miracle of agricultural growth will continue. The point is not that China will become a major source of food for the rest of the world: the three great English-speaking agricultural nations of Canada, America, and Australia will continue to play that role. Nor is China likely to transform itself overnight into a nation of wealthy, well-fed meat-eaters. That outcome, which would require rates of growth greater than any Eastasian nation has shown, is unlikely both because of China's enormous size (demanding enormous inputs to agriculture) and because of the relative poverty of China's rainfall and soil chemistry compared to nations with great arable plains.

But at least for the foreseeable future, China has turned agriculture from a liability into an asset. Its effect on industrial growth has been changed from negative to neutral or even positive. And China's great population has been kept intact, ready to supply abundant manpower, talent, and energy to the process of growth. In these ways agriculture continues to be the root of the Chinese nation.

8

Cities of Industry and Commerce

THE CITIES Of Eastasia are the jewels in the crown of success. Seventy-six of them have populations exceeding 500,000, including nine in Japan, six in South Korea, and fifty-six in China.[1] Among them is Tokyo, the largest metropolis in the world for three centuries until Shanghai passed it in the 1960s, as well as the most populous city-states in the world, Singapore and Hong Kong.[2] Eastasian cities are massive and teeming with humanity, but at the same time they are orderly microcosms of the dynamic countries they represent.

Eastasia's urban problems of the past have long been a journalist's paradise. Shanghai in the 1930s was a nightmare of chaos, full of beggars, prostitutes, gangsters, and millions of displaced peasants eking out an existence as refugees from Chinese domestic turmoil. Present-day Tokyo is still a mass of confusion to the visitor, without even a coherent system of street names. It is a nightmare for the commuter, who often must travel two or three hours to reach his employment. Europeans and Japanese alike took umbrage at the statement by a hapless European Economic Community official in 1978 that the Japanese were "economic animals" who despite their newfound prosperity still lived in "rabbit hutches." Nevertheless, there is no denying the difficulty of Japan's current housing situation. Intensely urbanized Hong Kong has always struck travelers arriving from quiet and dignified China as a neon-illuminated den of iniquity where capitalism ruthlessly exploits a proletariat of newly-arrived "freedom swimmers."

However truthful these characterizations once may have been, today there is a world of difference between Eastasian cities and the other 300 or more large cities in the world. Beggars are virtually nonexistent, prostitution and gambling have gone underground, mass transit systems are improving the "commuters' hell," and urban crime, so familiar in Europe and North America, is significantly less frequent than in the West. There is little sign of "urban decay" in any Eastasian city today, as developments only a decade old are regularly torn down for more modern construction. In many ways Eastasia appears to have survived the urban crisis of the twentieth century unscathed. Problems of crowding, poverty, inadequate housing, and inconvenient transportation have not been entirely eliminated, but these cities give every appearance of being vital and productive.

How have Eastasian countries managed this miracle of urban transformation—or at least of urban survival? The answer does not lie in their having prevented the growth of cities. In fact, population density in Eastasia is the highest in the world—as much as 150,000 people per square kilometer in the Mongkok section of Hong Kong.[3] Between the end of World War II and 1970, Japan added 55 million new city dwellers—over half the present population —and the proportion of Japanese living in cities nearly trebled, increasing from 28 to 72 percent.[4] In South Korea the proportion living in cities of more than 50,000 rose from 25 percent in 1955 to 59 percent in 1981.[5] Hong Kong, flooded with refugees from China and Southeast Asia, has more than tripled its population since 1946.[6]

With this growth has come an imbalance in urbanization typical of many developing countries: the tendency is for population to grow faster in the larger cities than in the smaller. The population of Seoul, for example, has increased fivefold since 1955, and one in five South Koreans now lives there.[7]

There have, however, been some cases of successful restraint on urban growth. Hong Kong has forcibly evicted unwanted migrants from the People's Republic who come seeking jobs in a housing-short city—and who often wind up living in squalid shantytowns on the hillsides. China during the late 1950s actually succeeded in decreasing the proportion of people in cities, in part through a youth rustication program that sent tens of millions of students to live in villages after graduation. China still has the strictest controls on migration in the world. To travel anywhere, a Chinese citizen must have the permission of his employer, carry an identity card, and have a valid domestic travel passport. Tokyo's population, while not subject to administrative controls, declined somewhat in the 1970s as urban housing gave way to commercial development. But by and large, urban growth, often explosive, has been a part of the Eastasian pattern.

One attractive but somewhat misleading explanation of Eastasia's success at urbanization is that the automobile has been kept under control. American critics of the private car contend that it has caused the decay of the cities by drawing citizens away to the suburbs. Certainly this has not happened yet in China, where autos are luxuries available only to higher bureaucrats and where most people travel on foot or by bicycle. Cars there are so rare that citizens on an outing pay to have their pictures taken behind the wheel of the photographer's auto. Bicycle traffic jams may produce headaches for Beijing commuters, but bicycles do not emit fumes, nor do they remove their riders far from the urban center every weekday afternoon. The late Chinese Premier Zhou Enlai is said to have assured visitors that China would never make the mistake of putting a car in every garage, since that would only waste energy and create confusion.

Elsewhere in urban Eastasia, the layout of the streets and the disinterest of Eastasians in suburban country living discourage widespread use of the auto for commuting. Only 15 percent of Japanese commute by car to work, as opposed to 80 percent of Americans.[8] Eastasians flock to mass transit in droves not because they enjoy packing like sardines in commuter trains and buses, but because there is as yet no alternative. What is striking is not the rational avoidance of automobiles but the toleration for high levels of discomfort in transportation—traffic jams, crowding, complex regulations, and high prices for vehicles, fuels, and maintenance. Eastasians renovate their inner cities and they remain there. They do so not because they hate the auto, or are wise enough to avoid using it, but because they prefer to live cheek-by-jowl in the neighborhoods where they feel comfortable, despite what to Americans would be intolerable inconvenience.

Housing Policy and Urban Planning

Nor does the answer to the question of urban viability lie in "urban planning" of the sort demanded by Western reformers. Except for the central portions of the old imperial capitals like Beijing, Kyoto, and Seoul, where streets were laid out by the ancients on a neat rectangular grid and where directions can be given reliably by the compass, there is little order in the planning of Eastasian cities. Much as the streets of old Boston were originally cowpaths, the streets of Eastasia were traced out by farmers walking to market or by schoolchildren taking shortcuts to class.

Zoning is virtually unheard of, and buildings of all shapes and sizes abut one another. Wealthy homes are interspersed among smaller dwellings, and factories adjoin residential areas. Though basic services like garbage collection, street cleaning, and power connections function well, public facilities such as theaters, zoos, and sports arenas are often overcrowded and poorly kept. Parks are few and relatively small. Tokyo, for example, has only 3 square meters of parkland per person (about the size of a double bed), compared with 13 in New York, 23 in London, and over 40 in Washington, D.C.[9] Eastasian cities have all the orderliness and public luxury of a bowl of spaghetti without the meatballs.

Public housing has played little role in Eastasian urban growth. The major exception to this rule is Singapore, where government dominates the public housing market. More than 80 percent of Singaporeans live in some form of government housing. In Japan, by contrast, only 6 percent of the housing stock is publicly owned; the state provides mortgage loans only for the purchase of new homes, and there is no functioning mortgage market for home loans. There is no analogue anywhere in Eastasia to U.S. Veterans Administration loan guarantees for private home buyers or to such government mortgage-market schemes as "Ginnie Mae" and "Fannie Mae." In China and North Korea, where all real estate has been owned by the state since the nationalizations of the mid-1950s, investment in new housing still is very low by world standards, and maintenance levels would embarrass the worst New York slumlords. Urban housing was largely a matter of squatters' rights at the time of the Communist takeovers, and families have not moved because there is no place to move.

Throughout the region, urban real estate is in great demand, and the family remains at the mercy of larger forces. Rising land prices in the free market nations reflect this unmitigated pressure on the land. Japanese urban land values went up 3,400 percent between 1955 and 1974, and by 1980 land in the Shinjuku commercial district of Tokyo was selling for nearly $17,000 a square meter—more than $65 million an acre.[10] Annual leasing prices in commercial Hong Kong exceeded $5 per square foot in 1981—twice the level of the downtown financial area of New York City.[11] With these prices in the commercial sector, one can understand why private housing is cramped, undersupplied, and poorly financed.

It is also easy to understand why "urban renewal" in Eastasia so often resembles the reconstruction of war-torn Europe. Ten-year-old housing becomes obsolete and subject to destruction by bulldozers preparing the site for pile drivers: for example, 32 percent of all new housing units built in South Korea in 1978 were replacements for existing housing, virtually all of it less than two decades old.[12] Rapid returns on urban investment in commercial and apartment buildings have pushed out lower-income inhabitants, who are driven to seek shelter in more distant suburbs. Private investment in housing in capitalist Eastasia naturally concentrates on high-income, high-cost sectors at the expense of low-income housing. What is remarkable about this pattern is not that government intervenes to protect urban dwellers, but that lower-income citizens whose living environment is disrupted so massively tolerate this constant displacement without serious protest against their government.

Not that city "fathers" are benevolent and protective leaders of their flocks. Wherever free market forces develop, there is a class of powerful leaders whose business is the escalation of urban land values—speculators, developers, land-lords, and power brokers. These special interests control valuable land, favor public works such as highway building, and oppose welfare programs, zoning, and urban planning. Not surprisingly, they are politically well connected. Indeed, some of the most influential movers in Eastasian politics, men such as former Prime Minister Tanaka in Japan, or Executive Council member Y. K. Pao in Hong Kong, have extensive real estate interests. Though such "urban landed elites" (to use the sociologists' jargon) exist in other countries, what is surprising is that in Eastasia their power is generally accepted and not countervailed by populist or regulatory forces. This pattern also holds for the Communist countries, where municipal governments maintain the authority to make or destroy neighborhoods, create new towns, or lay out new transportation grids without benefit of popular input.

Industrial Pollution

Another Western ideal of city dwellers is conspicuously lacking in Eastasia: the concept of good citizenship. Whereas American reformers on both left and right deplore the failure of citizens to heed the public interest, in Eastasia the principle is seldom raised. Private-mindedness, the minimal concern for public welfare, seems to be the rule even in the Communist states which preach against "selfishness."

A good example is the problem of industrial pollution. The rapid industrialization of the region has occurred virtually without concern for the environmental impact of adding new industry. In the United States, the growth of industry in urban centers drove residents into the countryside to escape pollution; in crowded Eastasia, on the other hand, urban dwellers found escape much more difficult. Between 1968 and 1978, industrial air pollution reduced by half the hours of sunshine in South Korea's largest city—surprisingly, without protest from the people of Seoul.[13] Japan's rapid industrial growth in the 1960s ruined fishing beds, contaminated drinking water, poured toxic chemicals into the air, and created worse photochemical smog in Tokyo than ever was experienced in Los Angeles. The beautiful blue waters of Hong Kong's deep harbor turned green with sewage and the flotsam of industrial society. Even in "socialist" China, factories pursued their private interests without regard to emissions standards or public interest tests of environmental damage.

To be sure, Eastasian governments in the 1970s, stimulated partly by the flurry of concern expressed by Western travelers, began to issue regulations on industrial pollution, and they have gradually begun to enforce them—in many cases more stringently than in the West. Japan, for example, now has in place the world's strictest emissions standards for industry, equaling in the air pollution field the unenforced Muskie Act regulations in the United States. The government now entices new industry to build in the countryside, as in the case of integrated circuits. South Korea's Environmental Preservation Law operates along similar lines, and the Korean government now concentrates on building greenbelts around major metropolitan centers. Japan's bureaucrats at the Ministry of International Trade and Industry have turned concern for environmental quality to Japan's economic advantage by making pollution control devices a major foreign sales item. Furthermore, the constraints on pollution have been imposed only *after* industry has developed and become profitable, not before.

Crime Control

Crime control, another conspicuous Eastasian success, has not been the result of tough courts, capital punishment laws, or highly mechanized SWAT teams. Despite the absence of these pet recommendations of those who would "reform" American justice, Tokyo in 1978 had 10 times fewer murders, 14 times fewer rapes, and 225 times fewer burglaries than New York.[14] Japanese arrest and conviction rates were strikingly higher: 78 percent of all robberies ended in arrests in Tokyo, as opposed to 28 percent in New York.[15] Police concentrate on crimes where there are obvious victims, especially crimes of violence, and waste little effort on such evils as white-collar crime, which does not occur with great frequency. Police are largely unarmed, in part because the population is unarmed: private possession of firearms is outlawed in all Eastasian countries. The criminal justice system—the courts and judges—carries a remarkably light workload. Even in the mobilized, martial countries of China, Taiwan, and the Koreas, where political crimes are firmly prosecuted, there is no critical shortage of prison space, and the courts operate with remarkably free dockets.

How does this apparent miracle come to pass? The answer lies in the Eastasian perception, remote from our idea of justice, that the enforcement of behavioral norms in society is not a matter of law but of social ethics. Violations of property and person are violations of the social fabric, not of individual rights. People have an obligation to their social units—their place of employment, their neighborhood, their nation—to report transgressions. If there are fewer criminals, it is because Eastasians detect them earlier and tolerate them less. Eastasia is a society of industrious stool pigeons.

Consider the peculiar role of the police in Eastasia. Policemen do not cruise in squad cars responding to telephone or radio alarms. Instead, they stand on duty in their boxes—the *koban* in Japan, the *paichuso* in China and Taiwan —observing each neighborhood in minute detail. Neighborhoods are organized around these boxes, which are the authority centers of the residential block or "street committee" (as the residential unit is called in China). Residents in turn rely on the police to handle disputes, convey information to other residents, and communicate with higher authorities to a degree unheard of in America. Policemen are part of the microcosm of Eastasian society, and not above it. This helps explain why, even in emergencies such as the 1960 student riots in Japan, the 1967 "cultural revolution" in Hong Kong, or the 1980 riots in Seoul and Kwangju, the police have adopted passive and humane crowd-control techniques.

Of course, this method of crime control has its drawbacks. The individual's rights against society are scarcely recognized. Eccentrics, recluses, and open malcontents are not well tolerated. Political deviance is too easily categorized as a social evil, as in the two Koreas and two Chinas today, with dissent seen by government as a threat to national security. Alternative lifestyles enter slowly from abroad, and foreigners (even those who have lived in Eastasia for years or even generations) are seldom assimilated. But for all these faults, the system works, and the streets of Eastasia are safe to walk, day or night.

Private Aid or Public Responsibility?

Visitors are constantly surprised to find that Eastasian cities lack public mechanisms for handling unemployment, poverty, or child welfare. There are, even in the darkest times, no breadlines, no orphanages (except those run by compassionate foreigners), no welfare checks, no "aid for dependent children," no state-run employment agencies. The absence of many of these hallmarks of the liberal conscience might lead one to conclude that Eastasians are cruelly unconcerned for their fellow man.

This conclusion might be true in the abstract. Many have noticed the tendency of Eastasians to avoid involvement in cases where an American would intervene: to protect a stranger from attack, to aid an injured pedestrian, to break up a fight. These are all cases in which Americans feel a public responsibility but Eastasians feel only confusion, because they do not know the parties or the issues involved and fear becoming implicated or responsible. But the other side of this coin of public unconcern is a powerful tradition of private mutual aid far stronger than anything known in the West. One must go back to the myths of Robin Hood to find European parallels to the camaraderie of Eastasian neighborhoods, families, or companies today.

Mutual aid is the message of the Confucian ethic of filial responsibility—children must take care of their parents—and it also informs the cooperative attitude that Japanese villagers have toward their village. Philanthropy exists, often quite generous philanthropy, but it is used to serve or reflect credit on one's clan or one's neighborhood, not society in general. Private subunits of society are strong and emotionally cohesive, and provide for one another from cradle to grave. Hospitals run by companies for their employees, midwives who serve their neighbors only, and graveyards that belong solely to families —these are the rule, not the exception.

This may seem a surprising statement to make about the Communist countries of Eastasia, where the state has apparently usurped so many private functions that there seems to be virtually no privacy left. But to focus solely on the formal "ownership" of assets or institutions is to miss the reality that even state-owned functions are turned to essentially private ends. In China's countryside, for example, villages still employ the old time worn mutual-aid schemes for improving irrigation and bridges, harvesting ripe crops, and watching for theft. Even in Chinese cities, ownership by the state really only means ownership by the enterprise or by the neigborhood, since these entities are the practical extensions of government. Because these "units" seldom change, individuals in China and North Korea receive the same implicit guarantee of "lifetime employment" that Japanese corporations offer their workers. Despite decades of expropriation and "socialist transformation," the fundamental welfare system of China remains the family unit: old folks take care of children, the healthy care for the sick, distant relatives take the place of lost close relatives. The welfare system of China is virtually identical to that of Taiwan or Hong Kong—the cohesion of the private family. In Europe this sense of mutual aid among relatives went out in the Middle Ages, if it ever existed.

To be sure, the private mutual aid system will be sorely tested. In Japan the elderly population is rising three times faster than in the United States, so that within thirty-five years one out of five Japanese will be over sixty-five.[16] Housing shortages in China make the large extended family under one roof a thing of the past in many cities. In such cases the state may have to take on some responsibility, at least to encourage the development of homes for the elderly or children's day-care centers. But it appears likely that even these interventions will be implemented by some form of private mutual aid, rather than through public agencies of the American type.

Industrial Peace and "Confucian Benevolence"

Another puzzling characteristic of Eastasian cities is the tendency of labor unions to be quiescent and captive. Japan, one of the world's most industrial nations, with a strong socialist movement, has remarkably fewer strikes than other developed countries. Singapore had only forty-four strikes during the entire decade of the 1970s.[17] Outside Singapore, organized labor plays virtually no role in the political process of any Eastasian nation—and even there, despite the origins of the present government as a trade union party, the National Trade Union Congress is increasingly dominated by the government. Despite enormous gains in productivity in all Eastasian countries, workers have seldom demanded the full yield as wages. China, Taiwan, and the two Koreas have union "movements" that are nothing more than extensions of the government bureaucracies. How do we explain that labor in Eastasia is seemingly so docile?

TABLE 8–1

Labor Discipline: Eastasia vs. the West, 1978

Country	Days lost to strikes per 1,000 workers	Index (Japan = 100)
Italy	720	2,000
United States	428	1,189
Great Britain	414	1,150
West Germany	203	564
France	125	347
Japan	**36**	**100**
Singapore	**0**	-

SOURCE: International Labor Organization, *Year Book of Labor Statistics, 1979* (Geneva: International Labor Statistics, 1979).

NOTE: Strikes are illegal in South Korea, North Korea, China, and Taiwan.

The answer hardly lies in the poverty and "immiseration" (to use Karl Marx's often-quoted word) of the Eastasian working class. As noted earlier, Eastasian workers are not "cheap labor." Wage levels in Japan are substantially higher than in Britain, France, and Italy, and are approaching the levels of the United States and West Germany.[18] (The Japanese Self-Defense Forces, swollen with officers, have a higher average income than American forces stationed in Japan.) Though the incomes of workers elsewhere in Eastasia are much lower than in Japan, their wages are still higher than in most developing countries, and are rising rapidly enough to force the reorganization of export industries throughout the region. Yet all these gains have taken place without a strong tradition of collective bargaining.

Nor is the answer that Eastasian industry is too small and parcelized to support a vital labor movement. It is true that a number of low-paying jobs in electronics and textiles have been filled by young women seeking only enough income to prepare for marriage, and that some manufacturing tasks, such as the production of toys and Christmas lights, are done as cottage industries in the homes of families. By and large however, the labor force of Eastasia works in medium to large factories with long-term employment by identifiable management—precisely the situation which has made organized labor such a force in Britain and the United States.

Admittedly, governments have put some constraints on the independence of unions. A 1971 law in South Korea, for example, limits the collective bargaining rights of unions on grounds of "national security." Taiwan's government, understandably paranoid about possible infiltrators after its disastrous experiences in the 1920s on the mainland, observes all organizations for signs of political opposition and requires government arbitration of all labor disputes. The Singapore government requires a two-week cooling-off period before any work stoppage is permitted. But even in Hong Kong and Japan, where government plays no such limiting role, powerful industry-wide unions have not formed, and work proceeds with little interruption.

This is not to say that labor unions are never the source of controversy or policy debate. Indeed, in Japan the unions are divided cleanly between those in private industry, which by and large support the Democratic Socialist Party with their votes and contributions, and those of public employees, which tend to support, ironically, the antigovernment Socialists and Communists. In Hong Kong, unions can be identified as Communist or non-Communist by observing whether they display the flag of the People's Republic's on "National Day," October 1. The more vociferous union leaders in these politically free parts of Eastasia often take stands on national political issues, such as relations with the United States or the "liberation" of Taiwan. But their belligerence is unleashed only on foreign policy issues, not on the bread-and-butter questions of working conditions or take-home pay.

The answer to the puzzle of industrial peace lies once again in social attitudes. Eastasians tend to prefer compromise rather than confrontation, and the workplace is an arena for cooperation in the process of growth, not for conflict over the spoils. Unions tend to coalesce around their enterprises, like the now passé "company unions" of the West. There is only one industry-wide union in Japan, the Seamen's Union. The rest all belong to their companies. Their presidents are company employees (who often go on to become company presidents), and they work for the interest of the company. In Singapore, national wage settlements for all major industries are determined annually by panels composed of businessmen, labor leaders, and government bureaucrats. Collective bargaining in this context more resembles a board of directors' meeting than the strong-arm confrontation of pickets and goons.

Perhaps the key element in harmonious labor relations is what we might call "Confucian benevolence," a quality akin to the U.S. corporate paternalism of the 1920s—now, considered decidedly out-of-fashion in America. In the case of Singapore this benevolence is practiced by the government-affiliated labor union, the National Trade Union Congress. The NTUC operates a supermarket chain to provide workers with staples at bargain prices; it also runs an insurance cooperative, a dental surgery center, and a chain of restaurants where members can entertain guests and hold functions such as wedding receptions. In addition, the union offers cheap loans to help taxi drivers buy their taxis and it sells schoolbooks to children at cost. In both Singapore and Hong Kong the government helps cushion workers from soaring land prices by subsidizing public housing. In these cases, labor organizations, supported by government and management, act benevolently to avoid the crises that produce labor unrest elsewhere in the world.

In Japan, Confucian benevolence is the monopoly of the private firm. Mitsubishi, Matsushita, and other companies provide dormitories for young single workers and mortgage money for married employees buying homes. Company guesthouses provide a place to vacation, and company dining halls and study programs offer a chance for diversion on workdays after work is done. Wrapped in a cocoon of corporate paternalism, within a web of human ties centering on the workplace, the Japanese worker cooperates closely with management.

In China and North Korea, labor paternalism is the province of the state, which owns the enterprises in which workers spend their lives. The myth that the workers own their government informs the reality that factories provide permanent employment. Chinese laborers, for all their lack of independent unions, may be the most spoiled in all Eastasia—as foreign investors in joint ventures with Chinese factories are learning to their dismay. They have come to accept as natural a system in which no one is ever fired, workers are paid as much as their foremen, and the three-hour lunch is a sacred right. With this kind of benevolence, who needs a union?

To many this description of the Eastasian city may seem unreal. What has happened to the aggressive, self-seeking, individualistic side of human nature which we assume even Eastasians possess? The answer lies partly in striving for education and personal advancement within the system.

Education

Cities in Eastasia for centuries have been centers of education and careerism. In traditional China, cities grew up as administrative, and not as commercial or industrial, centers. They attracted the sons of scholarly bureaucratic families who hoped to pass the official examinations and thus qualify for a government post. The quarter around the Imperial Examination Hall in old Beijing was a student hangout for centuries. Tokyo today is home to over a million university students from all over Japan, who make up more than 10 percent of the city's population. Higher education is a main function of Eastasia's largest cities.

This is entirely fitting for a part of the world where education—regarded almost as a sacred right—is a major responsibility of government. Japan introduced compulsory primary education for both boys and girls in the early 1870s, nearly two decades earlier than the leading Western power of the period, Great Britain.[19] Currently, Japan has the highest proportion of enrolled school-age population in the world, outside North America.[20] Seoul, Taipei, Hong Kong, and Singapore are not far behind. Even the urban masses of China are approaching 100 percent literacy after three decades of educational effort.

Urban schools throughout the region share a general bias toward rote learning and away from individual creativity. But they effectively teach the "three Rs" and provide a solid technical education to enable workers to handle complex tasks on the job. National policy throughout Eastasia encourages technical competence and offers incentives for training engineers and scientists, while conspicuously ignoring the liberal arts and the training of lawyers. Hong Kong government supports vocational and technical training explicitly to supply much-needed labor for industry. In Japan the number of engineers doubled between 1970 and 1980, while the number of lawyers remained constant at around 12,000; the United States, with over a quarter million in 1970, doubled its legal population during the same period, while failing to increase the number of engineers.[21] Despite nearly a decade of antieducational Maoist policies, China is flooding the world with eager scientists and technicians who have been told to learn the best from the West.

City and Nation

One reason why Eastasian cities seem so manageable is that they are extensions of their nations, not enclaves within them. There is no federalism to separate them from national administration, no state-within-a-state tradition to justify selfish behavior, no "Big Apple" chauvinism to isolate them from their environment. Eastasian cities are tightly controlled "municipalities" within nations that dominate them absolutely.

The city-states of Singapore and Hong Kong are the obvious exceptions to this rule. These two great cities were born of British colonial expansion at roughly the same time. They are overwhelmingly Chinese and singlemindedly commercial. All these characteristics are inconsistent with their being part of any Eastasian national system. Were they politically to merge with the Asian mainland, they would chafe miserably under the control of Kuala Lumpur or

Beijing. Their independence has made possible a rapid economic growth that might otherwise have been restrained by the larger political needs of Malaysia or China. Nevertheless, the basic principle that Eastasian cities respond to national priorities still holds. The difference is that Singapore and Hong Kong have been at least temporarily able to redefine the nation to include only the city.

Eastasian tradition requires that urban affairs—including police, education, taxation, and social services—be controlled by the national, not the local, government. Especially in Taiwan, Korea, and China this continues to be the pattern, as there is little room for local initiative. Postwar Japan saw a flurry of independence on the part of Socialist mayors such as Asukata Ichio of Yokohama, but their initiatives were quickly co-opted by the conservative national leadership. City administrators outside Japan tend to be drawn from other regions; despite considerable local pride, municipal administrations thus take on a national rather than a local color.

This nationalization of urban affairs has not prevented a certain anticentral bias among the urban masses, not unlike the distrust that New Yorkers hold for Washington. In the last South Korean national election before the assassination of President Park Chung-hee in 1979, opposition parties got 42 percent of the city vote, as opposed to only 27 percent for Park's party.[22] In Taiwan, "nonparty, nonclique" votes against the ruling Kuomintang are heavily concentrated in the southern cities of Kaohsiung and Tainan, which traditionally support anti-KMT candidates for mayor and council. The city of Taipei consistently reelected anti-KMT candidate Henry Kao until the Nationalist government declared the city a nonvoting muncipality in 1964. In Japan during the 1960s and 1970s, socialist candidates opposed to the conservative Liberal-Democratic coalition did far better in the cities than in the countryside.

Case Study: Land Policy in Hong Kong

The British crown colony of Hong Kong was founded in 1842 by opium traders on "a barren island with hardly a house upon it," to use Lord Palmerston's phrase. The British fought three wars with Imperial China to expand their foothold on the Pearl River estuary: in 1842, 1860, and 1898 they sought to gain breathing space for their small colony of traders and for the

Chinese who chose to work with them. The island of Victoria and the peninsula of Kowloon were ceded outright (in perpetuity, according to treaty), but the so-called New Territories, some 600 square miles of land forming a defensive buffer, remain under a ninety-nine-year lease that expires in 1997.

After the Japanese occupation and the Communist conquest of neighboring Guangdong Province, Hong Kong's commerce and industry, growing rapidly with the population, expanded to make use of a large part of the available territory. Today Hong Kong once again seeks to push back its borders, as it watches China open up industrial and recreational estates in neighboring Guangdong. Since 1945, when Hong Kong was a tiny town of a quarter million, the population has grown nearly tenfold.[23] More than 83 percent of the population lives on 7 percent of the land, yielding a density of 3,500 persons per acre.[24] Downtown Mongkok in Kowloon is the most densely populated district in the world, with more than 150,000 people per square kilometer.

The meager land area of the colony has not only absorbed into the labor force an average of 40,000 illegal immigrants a year for two decades, but it has doubled the amount of territory devoted to export industry. Much of Hong Kong's expansion has taken place without planning or zoning. The Hong Kong government believes strongly in free enterprise, and beyond exercising its rights as owner of all the land in the colony, permits the purchase and sale of land-use rights to the highest bidder. The result is an unsightly mess imposed on the world's most spectacular natural harbor. Thousands of squatters' huts scattered along the hillsides abut the most luxurious modern apartment buildings. An impractical international runway juts into a bay heavily moored with junks. Modern office buildings, renting at astronomical prices, rise out of the ancient "city" of Kowloon, to this day a hotbed of gangsters and secret societies. That Hong Kong works at all is a miracle, but that its land-use system works is even harder to believe.

The government of the colony, managed largely by lifetime expatriates from Britain, performs mainly custodial duties over a population which is more than 98 percent Cantonese. With the strong support of the Chinese business community, the government keeps taxes low, encourages exports and foreign investment, and leaves social and urban policy where it belongs—in the hands of the informal Chinese elite. A small number of elected councils, for which only one in 400 Hong Kong residents may vote, deals with minor matters such as museums and the dates of public holidays, leaving the important decisions (such as monetary policy) to powerful private institutions like the Hongkong and Shanghai Banking Corporation ("The Bank"). Since the government chooses not to use deficit financing, it relies heavily on the sale of land to raise public funds. There being no government bonds to redeem or sell, the government sells land to absorb excess liquidity in the economy.

Technically speaking, land in Hong Kong is not sold but leased for periods of from 25 to 999 years. Leases may be reacquired at expiration for their original value, or with an exchange for new land further away from the central city. Despite the technical limit imposed by the 1997 deadline in the treaty on the New Territories, land there continues to trade at a brisk rate. Land speculation, fiercer than elsewhere in Eastasia, runs free.

The Hong Kong government is also interested in the colony's economic growth. Despite its apparent laissez-faire attitude, it has intervened massively since 1954 (six years before Singapore began a similar program) to make available inexpensive housing on government estates for the working population; now roughly half the population lives in rent-controlled public dwellings. A rent-control statute applies to part of the private housing market, but much of the remainder is subject to the ruinous inflation that has affected land values in general, thus putting especially great pressure on the small expatriate community. A square foot of land in North Point, for example, sold for HK$7–10 in 1948. Twenty-five years later the same tract went for HK$4,000.[25]

Land policy in Hong Kong is the cornerstone of the colony's economy. The recent profitability of major Hong Kong firms such as Jardine, Matheson has depended heavily on earnings from real estate, which in turn reflect the earning power of their tenants. The ability of the colony to absorb a further influx of refugees depends on timely resettlement work by the government. The cost of labor in a manufacturing economy is directly related to rents, which the government has chosen to control directly as well as indirectly, through subsidized public housing. Finally, land in the colony is a major source of revenue, permitting the government to maintain the fiction that it is a merely a figleaf on the body of Hong Kong's economy.

In many ways the Hong Kong pattern is unique in Eastasia. Hong Kong, like Macao, is still nominally under foreign rule, but its Chinese residents continue in their traditional way to regard real estate as a vital asset, much as their compatriots in the Chinese hinterland still cling to the land of their villages or to their ancestral urban dwelling quarters. Perhaps it is natural that an ancient civilization which first adopted settled agricultural life over 4,000 years ago should be preoccupied with land. Other Eastasian governments also have difficulty putting land policy in a neat European-style cubbyhole. The tendency is strong to treat land use as a public good and a moral responsibility. It is not in Hong Kong alone that the struggle for scarce resources is hidden behind the facade of national unity and public policy, while being conducted in private in the boardrooms, restaurants, and guesthouses of the elite.

Environmental, housing, and transportation problems continue to plague Eastasia's rapidly growing cities. But in many ways the region has survived the urban crisis of the twentieth century. The crime rate remains low; labor unrest is rare; education spreads. The Eastasian urban village may not be a creative, free, or liberal community. But it is a cohesive, productive, and motivated city of industry and commerce—the physical and spiritual locus of the Eastasian challenge.

9

Capital for Growth

LIKE the sluggish cobra before a mongoose, we are transfixed by the blur of rapid movement. Growth, imports, deficits, dumping, shocks—all these pop before our eyes and are gone before the next move can be anticipated. We lose sight of the underlying pattern that is the key to Eastasian mastery of the current economic world: the ability to amass and apply capital.

We are accustomed to thinking of Eastasian peoples as peasants, as cheap labor, as cannon fodder in "human sea" warfare. We still think of their economies as labor driven but undercapitalized. We have not yet learned that throughout the region, even in dirt-poor China, the efficient use of scarce resources has been raised to a consummate science.

In economics this translates into quiet yet systematic savings and the channeling of accumulated capital toward the investment with the greatest impact. Eastasian societies, despite a history of poverty in comparison with the Western peoples of plenty, have for generations had among the highest savings ratios in the world, together with the world's most efficient institutions for turning savings to useful purposes. Like the heart of the warm-blooded mongoose, which beats faster and pumps more nourishment than the snake's, the engine of capital formation drives the Eastasian economies faster than we can follow.

The Eastasian Urge to Save

The most obvious method of capital accumulation, with the clearest link to the economics of the family and the individual, is savings from current income. As indicated in table 9–1, Eastasian nations by that criterion are extraordinarily frugal almost without exception. Japan has a savings rate over four times that of America and double those of most European countries;[1] Japanese savings deposits, which since 1977 have exceeded a total of $1 trillion, are the largest in the world and serve as a vast reservoir for funding industrial development.[2] Savings ratios in Taiwan and Singapore are even higher than in Japan.[3] On the Chinese mainland the rate is so high, despite meager income levels, that the government has stepped up consumer goods production since 1979 to absorb excess savings. Those who have heard stories of vast hoards of gold bullion found in Eastasian backyards and mattresses can readily suppose that the people of this region are compulsive misers holding out for a rainy day.

Does psychology explain why Eastasians save? Take, for example, the case of modern Japan, a nation whose per capita GNP briefly passed that of the

TABLE 9–1

The Eastasian Urge to Save

Eastasia	Savings Share of National Income (1980)
Japan	18.1%
ROC	33.4
ROK (1979)	16.5
Hong Kong (1978)	13.0
Singapore	28.4

The West	Savings Share (1980)
Italy	12.7%
France (1979)	11.8
Germany	11.7
Britain (1979)	7.2
United States	4.3

SOURCES: For the West, Bank of Japan, *Kokusai hikaku tōkei* [International comparative statistics] (Tokyo: Nihon Ginkō Chōsa Tōkei Kyoku, 1981), pp. 27–28, 39–42; for Eastasia, national statistical yearbooks.

NOTE: Figures are for domestic savings as a proportion of national income. All data are for 1980 unless otherwise indicated. Savings rates for China and North Korea are in the 25–35 percent range.

United States in the third quarter of 1978. Many Japanese still find it hard to believe that their country is as rich as it is thought to be in the outside world. Families there have become accustomed only slowly to the high incomes they began to receive as the economy took off in the 1960s. Unlike Americans, who tend to assume that growth in individual welfare is virtually a constitutional right, Japanese have been taught by years of warfare, patriotic drives, and austere budgets to believe that prosperity is not a permanent feature of their lives. In many ways this psychological uncertainty about growth characterizes all the economies of the region, not just Japan's. Vulnerability, or the belief that calamity is around the corner, drives Eastasians to save. Government welfare benefits are meager, so personal savings must sustain Eastasians in illness and old age. Moreover, they tend, unlike Westerners, to increase their savings as economic circumstances become more turbulent and uncertain. Following the oil crisis of 1973, for example, personal savings ratios in Japan rose substantially, providing additional funds for government and private-sponsored investment, while those in the United States and Europe fell.[4]

Reinforcing the Eastasian's constant striving for security are imperatives to save which appear to have their roots in ethical commitment. One famous theory, developed by Max Weber and Ernst Troeltsch, has it that Europe required a religious revolution before it could modernize. During the sixteenth century, according to this view, mysticism and devotion to the afterlife gave way to a commitment to practical "works," thus leading the way to the rise of capitalism. This change in attitude made Europeans work harder, since work became a measure of one's piety.

Eastasian history offers no direct analogy to this religious transformation, since except for a little Buddhist mysticism from time to time, its peoples have remained profoundly pragmatic and this-worldly. But Confucian philosophy, with its stress on proper behavior and respect for one's position in life, hailed prudence and frugality, demanded sacrifice for future enjoyment, and condemned parents who failed to provide for their offspring. Though Japan avoided ancestor worship, its people too were concerned for the future of the group, be it family or village. In this sense, Eastasia has always been "otherworldly," if the "other world" is taken to mean the world of the future for one's associates and descendants. For Eastasia, the roots of modern capitalist attitudes toward accumulation lay in the past. They have been recently nourished by the powerful psychology of contemporary nationalism—the belief that it is patriotic to save in order to support national economic development.

Psychological motivations are important, but there are other institutional reasons for the high personal savings rate. Eastasia is crowded, with little room for expansion of personal "living space." Room for more appliances in the house, for example, is limited by the small size of living quarters. Room for a family automobile is limited by the lack of highways and parking space, both linked to the scarcity of land. Eastasians do not have the expansionist, acquisitive outlets for spending that absorb so many Americans.

Furthermore, Eastasians have not yet developed many of the facilities of the consumer-oriented society. Installment buying and credit-card purchases have been very slow to develop and are mainly confined to the employees of large corporations. Most people finance the purchase of a house out of savings rather than by taking out a mortgage. In Japan, the most financially sophisticated nation in the region, consumer credit relative to GNP is still only about one-seventh the U.S. level, despite a tenfold increase during the 1970s.[5]

As noted earlier, Eastasians have always conceived of social security as being a family rather than a government responsibility. Government social security benefits are accordingly meager, so Eastasians feel they must save for their old age. The system of bonuses, widely practiced in Eastasia, encourages employees to think of their monthly take-home pay as their disposable income, while seeing their semiannual rewards, often equal to one-third of their total salary, as windfalls to be stored away for a rainy day. Relatively low inflation rates assure savers, especially in Japan, Taiwan, and Singapore, that the funds they invest in the banking system will be worth something when withdrawn. All these institutional practices work against the spendthrift and give families incentives to save money.

Governments encourage savings in Eastasia, though the mechanisms of this encouragement vary from country to country. In Japan, for example, savings are spurred by the tax system, which exempts interest on savings accounts from taxation, along with interest on newly issued bonds up to $40,000.[6] Capital gains from sales of stock are entirely tax exempt. In addition, the Japanese government implicitly tolerates extensive tax evasion through the postal savings system: there are twice as many tax-free personal accounts as there are people in Japan, despite regulations limiting Japanese to only one account apiece.

The Singapore government promotes savings through large mandatory contributions to the Central Provident Fund, whose operations are described in greater detail at the end of this chapter. In the People's Republic of China and in North Korea, personal savings receive only very low interest—typically, less than 5 percent a year. But the People's Republic, much like the Japanese government during World War II and the Koreans during the 1970s, often appeals to patriotism to encourage personal savings. The result is a nationwide average of about $50 in bank deposits per person, representing one-tenth of annual per capita income. Only in Hong Kong have citizens been immune from government pressures to save. And there the insecurities of life in a highly volatile laissez-faire economy make saving mandatory for the prudent in any case.

Of course, thriftiness is not universal, even in Eastasia. In many periods of history, savings rates have been low or even negative. In Meiji Japan, gross saving was little more than half the rate of the high-growth post–World War II period, and considerably closer to Western levels: 19 percent during 1905–17 versus 16.6 percent in the United States and 15.2 percent in Germany (1905–13).[7] In postwar South Korea, household savings fell to nearly zero before the interest-rate reform of 1965; savings again fell sharply in the late 1970s, as real rates of return became negative in the face of rampant inflation. Savings were also low during the period of disaster and national crisis in China from 1931 through the 1940s, an era when many had to live off meager previous savings. But under the proper institutional and social conditions, Eastasians have proved able to exercise remarkable frugality and to channel their savings toward public institutions where they can be harnessed for the greater good of society.

The Foreign Component—How Crucial?

Some analysts claim that Eastasian economic performance has depended heavily on foreign investment and aid. There has, of course, been substantial foreign involvement in the economies of the region throughout the postwar period, and international movement of capital has been substantial. During the 1950s, foreign aid predominated, with Soviet assistance to China and North Korea paralleled by American assistance to South Korea and Taiwan. Over the past generation, aid has largely been supplanted by overseas private investment.

United States economic aid to Taiwan, typical of much early foreign assistance, began with the outbreak of the Korean War in 1950 and ceased in 1964. The total amount of nonmilitary aid granted to Taiwan over the 1950–1964 period was $1.5 billion, or about $10 per year for every man, woman, and child on the island.[8] Most of this money was given as grants or as soft-money loans repayable in Taiwan dollars, which were then used to underwrite the functioning of U.S. official operations on the island, as well as to support American scholars there. In addition, the United States provided the ROC with more than $2.5 billion in military equipment which Taiwan would otherwise have had to procure on the open market at a much higher price.[9] American aid to Taiwan in the 1950s and 1960s clearly helped the island to become essentially self-supporting in the 1970s, especially by financing infrastructure such as the major port complex at Kaohsiung, the largest export-processing facility on the island.

But this does not mean that American aid was indispensable, or that Taiwan was incapable of developing on its own. American assistance was used largely to offset the enormous military expenditures required to defend the island against the Communist Chinese. Certainly after the termination of aid in 1964 the picture suggests a vital native economy, able to repay international loans and build up current account surpluses. The share of domestic savings in gross capital formation rose from 65 percent in 1961 to 96 percent in 1969, with foreign capital accounting for only 5 percent.[10] Indeed, Taiwan was the first U.S. aid recipient in the non-Western world to become self-sufficient enough to "graduate." Within ten years it was dispensing aid of its own to friendly nations in Africa and Latin America.

The Taiwanese pattern was repeated in South Korea, which stopped receiving U.S. aid in 1980; but that aid had ceased being crucial to the nation's development many years earlier. In both Korea and Taiwan, substantial foreign investment has helped to fuel growth since the mid-1960s. But this investment has been small in relation to the regions' rapidly expanding economies. Moreover, the bulk of it—over half of Taiwan's $1.9 billion and roughly two-thirds of Korea's $820 million from 1962 through 1978—has come from sources within Eastasia, chiefly the Japanese and overseas Chinese.[11] Since 1960 most Eastasian countries have shown dramatic decreases in their dependence on outside financing; several have become net exporters of aid, trade, and investment while maintaining their own internal capital formation.

In this respect, many Eastasian countries have benefitted from what Lenin called "the advantages of backwardness." Having come into the modern world late, Eastasian countries could study the models of advanced Western nations and could turn to outsiders for help in the capital-formation process. Even though Japan resisted foreign investment during the early stages of growth, there were occasional windfalls, such as the massive indemnities paid by the Chinese in gold to atone for their defeat in the Boxer Rebellion of 1900. This indemnity, which amounted to more than a third of Japan's annual GNP, enabled the Japanese for many years to run a favorable balance of payments while importing parts and materials from Europe and America. The massive influx of American foreign aid into Taiwan and the Republic of Korea in the 1950s also came at a crucial time when those nations were struggling to generate capital for growth. More recently, the bursts of growth in Singapore and Hong Kong have been fed by extensive investment from multinational corporations, including some from Japan. But even in Singapore, long seen as one of the Eastasian states most dependent on foreign investment, the domestic share of total capital formation rose from 56 percent during 1970–73 to 65 percent during 1980.[12]

Communist Eastasia has shown a similar degree of recent independence from foreign savings. The Chinese government did receive large amounts of Russian military and technical aid in the 1950s. From 1950 to 1955, China consistently imported more from the Soviet Union than it exported to that country; the cumulative deficit amounted to nearly $1 billion, all of it financed by Soviet loans to China.[13] But after 1956, the People's Republic reversed the trade balance, running a surplus with Russia well into the 1960s. In addition, China began to repay its Soviet loans immediately after the end of the Korean War and had liquidated them completely by 1964.[14] Much of China's reluctance to draw down a line of credit of over $10 billion offered by Japanese, American, and European banks since 1978 lies in the leadership's determination not to repeat its unhappy experience as an international debtor to the Soviet Union in the 1950s. Many Chinese also remember with regret how foreign governments and banks came to pick their own political winners in China before the Communist victory by using their economic leverage to support their favorite warlords. This may explain why the Chinese have placed such strong restrictions on the acceptance of foreign equity investment under the new Joint Venture Law announced in 1979.

Putting Savings to Work: The Key Institutions

No amount of saving, whether generated domestically or infused from abroad, can produce growth unless it is channeled effectively into productive investments. Effective investment depends on the knowledge, foresight, and persistence of the experts who offer credit, as well as on the productivity of the debtor or entrepreneur. In the West, especially in the traditionally market-oriented Anglo-Saxon states, capital markets have been the crucial mechanism for channeling savings into investment; since the mid-1970s their importance has been rapidly rising in Eastasia as well. But traditionally Eastasia has relied on rather different and more indirect means of deciding who gets what funds for investment and commerce, as well as when, where, and how.

The Indigenous Economy and Native Banking

Even before the twentieth century a lively commercial economy existed throughout Eastasia. Though the region was largely closed to Western contact, intranational trade flourished in traditional commodities such as tea, handicrafts, vegetable oils, lumber, and food grains. Despite the low status of peddlers and merchants on the social ladder, commercial activity in key centers such as Edo, Seoul, and the lower Yangtze River delta grew steadily in the immediate premodern era as the population of the region increased. In these centers, tradesmen developed traditions that would prove useful in the burst of growth in the twentieth century. Closely held ownership of firms, usually small or middle-sized, ensured that profits would not easily be funneled away from the families who ran the businesses. An informal but highly efficient credit structure, often in the form of collective credit associations, provided startup and emergency capital, albeit at rather high interest rates. Indigenous banks *(qianzhuang* or *yinhao)* verified and circulated the coin of the realm, usually in the form of copper coins and silver ingots. Pawnshops, extensive in number, offered liquidity in exchange for the family clothing or jewels. Until very recently, a large portion of the businesses and credit organizations in Hong Kong were structured in this traditional way. Only with the advent of prosperity, as wealth in the form of real estate and paper securities surpassed the traditional forms of wealth in portable objects, have modern institutions such as finance companies come to dominate the Hong Kong scene.

In the mid-1970s, Hong Kong had some 182,000 business establishments, about one for every twenty-two persons (the U.S. ratio is 1 : 36).[15] Each year, one in seven of these businesses fails; new entrepreneurs replace them. The vast majority of the establishments are single proprietorships, the classic form of Eastasian business. While much of the flashy side of Hong Kong business is in the hands of foreigners or large Chinese organizations, the traditional shops and restaurants supply the infrastructure for Hong Kong's growth. In the small family assembly plant where the children help out after school, in the store where the grandfather makes a small profit selling sweetmeats or popular books, in the trucking company where the father supplies industry with transportation—in all these enterprises, Chinese learn how to keep business records, how to maintain equipment, how to calculate depreciation and manage loans, and how to minimize taxation. These tiny shops are found throughout Eastasia in one form or another, even in the darkest corners of the Communist-run states. As far south as Indonesia the main streets of virtually every town are lined with such shops—managed not by *pribumi,* or native Indonesians, but by second-, third-, and fourth-generation immigrants from southeast China.

The native banks of Hong Kong exemplify the vestiges of the older financial system that provided the underpinnings for modernity. Most of them, including Hang Seng, Kwong On, Wing Lung, and Dao Heng, began as money-changers, exactly like the ones presently found at the approaches to the Star Ferry or in Kaitak Airport. Virtually all belong to the Kam Ngan gold exchange, another traditional institution where spot and forward metal is traded frenetically in machine-gun Cantonese. While these traditional banks are quickly fading from the scene, usually bought up by foreign banks eager to find a way around the government's recent restrictions on new banking establishments, they still perform some important functions. The native Chinese banks of Hong Kong and Singapore have long played a critical role in communications with the overseas Chinese and in the black market for gold and other valuables in Southeast Asia. In many Asian countries, Chinese ethnics are moving into key roles in the creation of modern banking systems, as in the case of the Bank of Central Asia in Indonesia.

Students of Japanese economic history need not look far to discover the Japanese analogue. Many of the financial houses that supported the Meiji Restoration began as traditional bankers and traders in the Kansai district of southwestern Japan. The houses of Mitsui and Sumitomo, big names in contemporary Japanese trading and banking, began as tiny traditional banks at least three centuries ago. Even today, small family-operated shops, whose demise Western economists have been forecasting for decades, continue to underlie the Japanese economy, supplying parts for industry and services for consumers as they have done over the centuries. Those involved in industry, such as the small business subcontractors of Toyota and Nissan Motors, play a critical role in buttressing the international competitiveness of Japan's economic colossus.

Modern Private-Sector Banks

Building on the sophisticated traditional framework of native banking—and in some cases, such as Mitsui and Sumitomo, arising from it—are the modern commercial, long-term-credit, and trust banks of Eastasia. In Japan, particularly, these modern banks are the heart of the financial system and were so powerful before the first oil shock in 1973 that Japan was known as the "Bankers' Kingdom." During 1971–75, 50.4 percent of the total supply of all new funds for plant and equipment in Japan were provided by banks, with a further 23.7 percent provided by the insurance companies and other financial institutions closely affiliated with them.[16] By 1979 the share of private financial institutions in total capital investment financing had fallen to 69.3 percent, but that was still extremely high by international standards.[17] Only 12 percent of

Japanese capital investment funds in 1979 were raised in the equity or bond markets.[18]

The major commercial banks in Japan have, since the late nineteenth century, served as the linchpin for the massive industrial groups—Mitsubishi, Mitsui, Sumitomo, and others—which dominate the nation's basic industry and trade. They provide the bulk of the short-term finance in Japan, together with a major share of long-term credits in such sectors as shipbuilding and petrochemicals. But their most important financial role is in funding the nine general trading companies, which together handle over half of Japan's foreign trade and also serve, in turn, as the primary source of capital for a myriad of smaller firms. Indeed, even Kentucky Fried Chicken in Japan gets the bulk of its financing, together with the fryers for its restaurants, from the Mitsubishi Corporation.

The industrial groups, led by their main banks and trading companies, pool risk and allocate credit from mature sectors into rapidly growing sectors largely without government intervention. Sometime in the late 1960s, for example, the Mitsui group, after months of behind-the-scenes discussion, proposed at one of its regular Thursday meetings that the company enter the field of aluminum refining. Mitsui Aluminum shares were subscribed to by all the major firms in the group. Mitsui Bank joined the trust bank and the insurance affiliates of the group to supply the financing, and the trading company, Mitsui Bussan, proceeded to buy bauxite and take contracts to sell the product. In this way a multimillion-dollar company was conceived, financed, and launched entirely in-house.[19]

The key industrial finance institutions in Japan, aside from the main banks of the major groups, are the long-term credit banks, established early in the century and patterned after the French Crédit Foncier. They have no direct analogue in the United States, but they play a vital role in "socializing risk" and in giving basic industry confidence to invest aggressively in large projects. They raise funds primarily through the issue of bank debentures, which in 1980 amounted to 20 percent of total bonds outstanding in Japan, and as much as 2.6 times the value of all corporate bonds.[20] Largest and oldest is the Industrial Bank of Japan (IBJ), the source of nearly 12 percent of all long-term financing by Japanese banks over the eighty years since its foundation. IBJ now has more than $7 billion outstanding to the Japanese steel industry alone, and is lead banker to Hitachi and much of the explosively growing Japanese electronics industry, toward which it is currently directing considerable resources.[21] Because IBJ and the other long-term credit banks are neither government-owned nor members of a major industrial group, they can allocate credit with neutrality and flexibility.

In the smaller Eastasian nations, private banks are generally smaller and less influential than in Japan. The exception is Hong Kong, where the massive Hong Kong and Shanghai Bank, with assets amounting to 243 percent of Hong Kong's gross national product, actually serves as the major currency-issuing bank as well as the major source of investment and commercial funds. In Taiwan the trust banks have become increasingly important since the mid-1970s, but the government has been restraining their development to prevent the emergence of industrial groups largely independent of state control. In South Korea all the major financial institutions in the country except the Commercial Bank of Korea, one of the five large city banks, are under government control: no other non-Communist Eastasian nation has such a substantial public presence in its financial system.

Development Banks

The two dominant realities of Eastasian economic life as the region began its striking economic transformation a generation ago were insatiable demand for capital and inadequate supply. There was, inevitably, a need to concentrate resources on strategic sectors whose growth would, in turn, have favorable effects throughout the economy. Investment in such sectors as steel and petrochemicals involved huge infusions of capital, undertaken at considerable risk. The private sector, with the exception of Japan's long-term credit banks, either could not concentrate its resources in these risky but strategically vital sectors or did not want to. Government-sponsored development banks were created to accomplish the task.

Every non-Communist Eastasian nation except Hong Kong has a vigorously functioning development bank or its equivalent. In Japan and South Korea, devleopment banks were set up in 1951 and 1954, respectively, to aid reconstruction from war; subsequently they helped fuel the growth that continued long after prewar levels of affluence had been regained. In both nations, development banks have been important in funding basic industries such as electric power, coal mining, shipping, and steel in their early stages, and then in financing new industries (such as electronics) and urban development as the economy grew progressively more advanced. Because of the generally greater sophistication of Japan's private financial system, other organizations, especially the long-term credit banks, have gradually assumed many of the Japan Development Bank's original functions. In 1979 it provided only 4.4 percent of all new funds to Japanese industry for plants and equipment.[22]

The Korean Development Bank (KDB), in contrast, supplied 52 percent of all new capital equipment loans in 1978 and 17 percent of all loans outstanding to South Korea's deposit-money banks.[23] Indeed, it was and is the single largest and most important financial institution in Korea, and perhaps the most powerful and versatile development bank in Eastasia. It draws its funds largely from the government budget and from international development organizations such as the World Bank. Nearly 90 percent of KDB loans go to provide long-term equipment capital for South Korea's growing industry, with a preference for sectors that will increase exports.[24] The chairman and the board of directors are appointed by the president of the Republic of Korea at the nomination of the Ministry of Finance. The government-run Korean Development Institute does economic research into industrial and market conditions, much of it under contract to the KDB.

Singapore, like Hong Kong, has grown without foreign grants in aid. The Development Bank of Singapore (DBS) was established in 1968 to assume the development financing functions of the Singapore Economic Development Board.[25] But it was given a license at the same time to act as a commercial bank, a role it now enjoys to the fullest. Like the Hongkong and Shanghai Bank, the DBS leads the local money market, helps determine interest rates, and has spearheaded Singapore's role as the capital of Asiadollar lending. Over the past few years, DBS has also attracted fresh foreign investment to Singapore. The government owns 47 percent of the bank's shares, grants the bank lines of government credit, and supplies more than 80 percent of its funds.[26] In turn, the bank makes loans for terms usually up to ten years to companies interested in bringing new industries or services to Singapore; there were seventy-five of these firms through the end of 1977.[27] Just as the Japanese ministries coordinate policy with the long-term banks in Japan, Singapore's bureaus maintain close liaison with the DBS in screening loan and investment applications.

Central Banks

The conventional wisdom in much of the Western world is that central banks have played a key role in organizing and coordinating the explosive Eastasian growth of the past generation. Many of the same people who espouse this view concede that the so-called "gnomes of Zurich" are in other settings often thought to be highly conservative and uncomfortable with dynamic change. But they fail to note the contradiction.

Central banks, especially the one in Taiwan, have often been important in damping overheated booms and in ensuring the stability of the financial order. But they have rarely played the active, growth-oriented coordinating role often ascribed to them. In the crucial early days of postwar Japanese growth, Ichimada Naoto, the governor of the Bank of Japan, actively opposed the development of a Japanese auto industry and the precipitate expansion of the steel industry because he felt Japan did not have a comparative advantage in those areas and could more safely ensure a balanced foreign exchange position by producing textiles. In subsequent years, Bank of Japan officials rarely exhibited much more entrepreneurial spirit than had Ichimada. The bank's so-called "window guidance" after the mid-1950s rarely involved qualitative judgments on where domestic Japanese banks should lend.[28] And by the late 1960s the Bank of Japan had little leverage on the private financial sector in any case, because of growing liquidity in the economy and the proliferation of financial institutions not subject to central bank control.

The role of central banks has been somewhat greater in Taiwan and South Korea, the only other two Eastasian capitalist states to have full-fledged central banks. Ever since the disastrous inflation of the late 1940s, to which many Nationalist Chinese leaders still ascribe their defeat on the mainland, considerable political power has been concentrated in the Bank of China, Taiwan's central bank, which its leaders have used to help decisively direct the economy. The chairman of the Bank of China, Governor K. H. Yu, is also chairman of the Council for Economic Planning and Development and a confidant of top leaders in the ruling Kuomintang. His strong political position thus augments the role of the central bank in directing the economy.

The source of the Bank of Korea's influence over economic policy formation lies, ironically, in the relatively underdeveloped character of Korea's commercial banking system. The deposit bases of the commercial banks are relatively weak, which forces banks (and, indirectly, industrial corporations) to borrow from the central bank. But since the Bank of Korea, unlike the Bank of China, lacks an independent political base, it is severely constrained by pressure from large firms, especially exporters, for credit. At the end of 1980 the Bank of Korea had over $4 billion in loans out to commercial banks on behalf of industrial firms, about 54 percent of which was to finance exports.[29] The Bank of Korea has over the past ten years become a major tool of Korea's export policy, although it has lost some autonomy in the process.

Government Ministries

Economists generally concur that the market makes the most efficient allocation mechanism. But when the issues are (as they seem to be in periods of capital shortage and escalating capital costs) how to allocate funds to the highest-priority sectors and how to insulate corporations from destructive uncertainty as they make major investment decisions, then government does have a role to play, in the view of many economists. Such a coordinating and pacifying role is particularly important in Eastasia, where the subterranean character of most decision making and the shortage of horizontal communication mechanisms make a governmental organization oriented toward coordination and communication most helpful for the private sector.

Japan's Ministry of International Trade and Industry is such an organization. MITI began in 1949 as a transformation of the prewar Ministry of Commerce and Industry and of its wartime successor, the Ministry of Munitions. Its early responsibility was to restore Japan's war-torn economy and to integrate the nation with the world economy through international trade. In the early postwar years MITI was quite control-oriented: it was able strongly to influence private-sector business decisions by allocating foreign exchange and thereby access to raw materials and technology from abroad. But these strong allocative powers were largely dismantled by the end of the 1960s, except in the energy field.

MITI has never had the power directly to influence the flow of credit into specific investment projects, because it does not regulate the banks and other financial institutions that dispense it. But it can and does act to make the cost, market share, and profitability parameters in terms of which businessmen make investment decisions sufficiently predictable to allow them confidently to invest massive sums of their own accord. One element in this approach is *yamagoya*—literally, "the creation of climbers' shelters." On the basis of long-term growth projections for various sectors of the economy, and after making a detailed assessment of optimal production scales for plant facilities in these sectors, MITI calculates the appropriate number and scale of new investment projects. Then it assures those firms which invest in accordance with its guidelines that while they are responsible for any failures which result from mismanagement, they will be sheltered from major unavoidable "storms" as they are "scaling the rock face" of new investment.

One "storm" that illustrates this policy was the world recession of 1973–74. As energy prices tripled in late 1973, many of Japan's energy-intensive industries, including fertilizer, aluminum refining, and petrochemicals, were suddenly rendered noncompetitive through no fault of their own. MITI responded to the plight of affected firms first with recession cartels and then with a systematic program for scrapping surplus capacity and moving the affected firms into new, more competitive sectors.

MITI's policy for making the consequences of investment decisions more predictable has other dimensions. It changes incentive schedules only rarely, and virtually never downward without substantial notice. Together with the Economic Planning Agency and virtually all ministries in Japan to some degree, MITI disseminates, to both business and the general public, long-term "visions" of where it believes the Japanese economy is heading; these "visions" are supplemented by frequent informal private briefings. MITI also employs a practice colorfully known as *mugifumi,* or "thinning the barley sprouts." This practice, the obverse of *yamagoya,* involves jawboning firms which propose investments in excess of MITI guidelines not to do so, in order to ensure profitability for those ventures that do receive permission to invest.

Elsewhere in capitalist Eastasia, governments play a somewhat different role in the investment process. Those countries that have received extensive foreign aid, such as South Korea and Taiwan, have used this aid to expand government's hand in the investment process. In Taiwan the Council on United States Aid (CUSA), established in 1948, for many years selected aid projects, allocated commodity imports, and invested local currency without any responsibility to the government budget. In 1963 this council was reorganized into the Council on Economic Cooperation and Development, which, like MITI, worked on long-range economic planning and technical cooperation. CUSA's agricultural counterpart as recipient of aid money was the Joint Commission for Rural Reconstruction, which for many years functioned as the Taiwan government's agriculture ministry and which masterminded an extensive land reform program in the early 1950s. Many of these agencies' Chinese members, who learned how to conduct government-sponsored investment by handling foreign funds during the brief time they were available, retain key leadership positions on Taiwan today.

The Postal Savings Program

The conversion of hoarding into usable savings has been an important issue of public policy for all the Eastasian countries. A revealing example is Japan's postal savings system, which today is the largest financial institution in the world, with three times the assets of the world's largest commercial bank, New York's Citibank.[30] Created in the Meiji period, the postal savings fund, together with its postal insurance affiliate, receives around 8 percent of Japan's disposable income in deposits. It pays low and stable interest rates to its customers, who have access to more than 22,000 branches at post offices all over the country. Income from postal savings accounts is tax-free to depositors. Although there is a legal limit of ¥3 million (about $15,000) per person on postal savings deposits, the system informally condones multiple accounts and thus has become a major tax shelter for Japanese depositors. The bulk of the fund's resources, like those of many corporate pension funds and life insurance funds, is available to the government for investment purposes.[31]

This immense fund has in recent years even helped cover rather large government budget deficits, permitting the ruling party to enjoy the fruits of deficit spending without paying the penalty of inflation. Fifteen percent of the fund's resources went to buy national government bonds in 1978.[32] Over the last century the postal savings system has helped Japan maintain the highest savings rate in the industrialized world, because of the grassroots savings network it creates and because of its competition with commercial banks for deposits. Similar schemes have been or are being tried in other countries of industrialized Eastasia with considerable success.

Capital Markets

In absolute scale and functional significance in the international monetary system, Eastasia has some of the most important capital markets in the world. The Tokyo Stock Exchange, capitalized at $356 billion in early 1981, is the largest in the world after New York's.[33] The Singapore Asiadollar market, whose gross size increased from $30 million to $65 billion in the thirteen years up to 1981, ranks second only to London's as a short-term hard-currency money market.[34] Hong Kong is also a major world financial center.

Ironically, the international prominence of Eastasian capital markets has had surprisingly little direct impact on Eastasian corporate finance. Eastasian companies as a rule operate with debt rather than equity financing, and they borrow their funds largely from banks rather than directly via the capital markets. In many ways it is precisely because shares of ownership, equity, and bond markets are *not* well developed that Eastasia has been able to direct resources so narrowly toward priority purposes. Yet governments throughout non-Communist Eastasia are encouraging the growth of stock markets by sponsoring stock exchanges, granting tax breaks on capital gains, and conducting propaganda campaigns to encourage private investment in what we in the United States call public companies. So far, this has been to little avail: these markets are still extremely thin, highly volatile, and filled with speculators rather than investors. Despite the fact that capital gains to investors in the Hong Kong, Tokyo, and Singapore markets far outperform those in Europe and the United States (see figure 9–1), there have not historically been many takers other than large financial institutions. The securities markets in Taiwan and South Korea are, of course, still closed to outside investors—at least those who wish to be able to repatriate their money.

There are many reasons for the chronic weakness of equities in contemporary Eastasian investment. Historically the Japanese empire, including Korea and Taiwan, showed a much higher preponderance of equity financing than

FIGURE 9-1

Bull Market in Eastasian Stocks: What $100 Invested in 1967 Would Have Earned

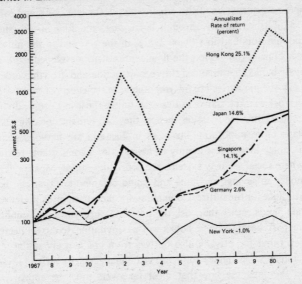

SOURCE: 1967–78 Far Eastern Economic Review, *1980 Asia Handbook;* 1979–81, year-end indexes and currency exchange rates. America—Dow Jones Industrial Index; Germany—Frankfurter Commerzbank; Japan—Nikkei Index; Hong Kong—Hong Kong Index; Singapore—Fraser's Industrial Index.

FIGURE 9-2

Eastasian Reliance on Debt:
Equity to Bank Debt Ratios in Capitalist
Eastasian Manufacturing, 1980

Republic of Korea	**1:2.7**
Japan	**1:2.3**
Singapore	**1:0.9**
Taiwan	**1:0.7**
U.S.	**1:0.68**
Hong Kong	**1:0.6**

SOURCES: *Kigyō Keiei no bunseki* [An analysis of enterprise management] (Tokyo: 1979); Bank of Japan, *Kokusai hikaku tōkei* [International Comparative Statistics] (Tokyo: Nihon Ginkō Chōsa Tōkei Kyoku, 1981); Bank of Korea, *The Korean Financial System,* December 1978, p. 80.

has been the case since 1945, though much of this came through private placements with holding companies rather than through public sale of stock. The rapid reconstruction of these economies in the late 1940s and early 1950s was accomplished largely through borrowing, and foreign aid, since most potential investors had lost their savings in the war and in the inflation that followed. During this period the finance ministries developed close ties with the private banks that financed the reconstruction and growth; consequently, to this day the ministries are unsympathetic to the efforts of other agencies to create a stock market. Banks in Eastasia, unlike those in Europe, do not profit from underwriting stock issues; hence, they too remain unenthusiastic.

Perhaps more important, investors in Eastasia are nervous about stock markets, since they invest mainly to help secure a comfortable retirement in lands where social security systems are poorly developed. Most prefer to keep their money in savings accounts and liquid commodities that can be cashed in as insurance for the future. Companies, for their part, often prefer to remain in private hands rather than risk the potential uncertainties of public ownership—in part because open books are an invitation to tax collectors. The Eastasian thirst for privacy also derives from concern about the impact of takeover bids or struggles for control of management on employees. This explains the Japanese law that most takeovers must be approved by the government.

With Eastasia's dramatic economic success, interest in Eastasian equities has risen sharply outside the region. Over $3.5 billion in petrodollars from the Persian Gulf region poured into the Tokyo stock market alone during 1980, powering it to spectacular new highs.[35] The shares of Hitachi, flag carrier of the Japanese electronics industry and a focal point of Arab interest, tripled in value within a year before the Japanese government suspended sales in the interest of national security.[36] Responding to developments in Tokyo and to the prospect of massive capital inflows from abroad, share prices in Hong Kong and Singapore also surged. In April 1981 the Saudi Arabian Monetary Authority (SAMA) directed two British merchant banks to invest $1 billion for it in Japanese equities, SAMA's first move into equities markets anywhere in the world.[37] This major development spurred the Tokyo Dow-Jones average up 5 percent in ten days and paved the way for what many felt would be a major further advance.

With foreign interest in Eastasian capital markets intensifying, the terms on which Eastasian firms can raise funds through equity issues are growing ever stronger. In sectors where these firms are not heavily reliant on banks, such as the consumer electronics and leisure-goods industries, equity issues are steadily increasing. But in the capital-intensive industries at the heart of Eastasia's political economy—steel, shipbuilding, and petrochemicals—capital needs are so massive and volatile, and the likelihood of short-term profitability so uncertain, that industrial firms, investors (mainly banks), and government do not see reliance on equity as a viable or strategically desirable proposition.

The preference of Eastasian government and industrial leaders for debt financing is more than just a local peculiarity that will pass as countries of the region "modernize." This preference actually helps explain the tremendous growth and resilience of the region's economies. Banks, especially the long-term and quasi-governmental ones, adopt a longer time horizon than do shareholders anxious for high returns. Governments use the credit structure to spread the risks of high-gain projects across society. Competition among banks (in the capitalist countries) and among state credit-allocating bodies (in the Communist world) ensures that projects will be judged on their likely long-term return, not on short-term profit or loss.

Consider the case of the Japanese financial system, the largest in the region and the model for many of the other nations. More than Europe or the United States, Japan emphasizes large bank loans, "indirect" financing by borrowing, and control of credit availability rather than money supply in monetary policy. There are some important exceptions to the general pattern of corporate reliance on banks, Toyota, Hitachi, and Matsushita among them.[38] Indeed, many such firms are so liquid from massive profits on export sales that they exercise many banking functions, lending out substantial sums to smaller affiliates and even to banks. But large firms with small debts are unusual in the basic industries at the heart of Japan's economy.

Japanese government financial institutions such as the People's Financial Corporation, the Housing Finance Corporation, and the Japan Development Bank own far more of the nation's outstanding loans than is the case with their American counterparts. In 1978, for example, government financial institutions owned 30 percent of all loans in Japan's financial sector, as contrasted with less than 10 percent in the United States.[39] By deciding who has access to the credit of public financial institutions, the Japanese government serves as a major intermediary in the financial sector, although the role of its central bank in credit allocation is often overstated.

The point is not that government in Japan controls the financial markets in highly direct ways that unknowing critics might call "interventionist." The Japanese government probably exercises fewer direct controls over the banking system than does the government of the United States. There are no restrictions on branch banking, no requirement to distinguish between commercial and thrift functions, no prohibitions on equity investments by banks. In many ways, Japanese banks are more freewheeling, more market-oriented, more toughly competitive, and less profitable than American or European banks, which are excluded from many normal markets for capital. Indeed, the most profitable Japanese bank, the Long Term Credit Bank, has a return on assets of only 0.25 percent.[40] But because of the relatively centralized character of the banking system and the general reliance on indirect finance, the state is able to exercise more guiding influence than in most Western nations.

Policies for Spurring Investment

The fact that the enormous flow of savings generated in Eastasia moves through efficient institutions is an important contributor to the Eastasia edge. But in the final analysis, these institutions are not responsible for Eastasia's aggressive and unusually farsighted pattern of investment. For this the honor goes to the individual businessmen who actually decide to invest. Their decisions turn ultimately on what the mixture of market and policy signals tell them are the likely consequences of their investment decisions. Policy shapes the investment decisions of businessmen in two crucial ways: (1) it makes business calculations concerning the future more predictable, and (2) it directs investment toward strategic sectors. We must explore these two levels in more detail.

Government Planning

Plans are endemic in the region. China is into its Sixth Five-Year Plan, managed like its predecessors by the all-powerful State Planning Commission. North Korea has been more erratic; it is entering the ninth in a series of one-, two-, three-, six-, and seven-year plans. Taiwan has preferred a series of four-year plans, although the latest is a six-year Plan ending in 1981. In Japan, the Economic Planning Agency's programs have been more hortatory than indicative, but they have come with some regularity. After a series of small postwar plans issued by the Allied headquarters, the agency began with the Five-Year Plan for Economic Self-Support (1956–60). The New Long-Range Economic Plan (1958–62), the National Income Doubling Plan (1961–70), and the Medium-Term Economic Plan (1971–76) followed.

Perhaps most ambitious and provocative of all is Singapore's ten-year development plan for the 1980s, unveiled in March 1981. It sets forth Singapore's aim to become a regional center for such "brain" industries as computer programming, consultancy, financial services, and medicine during the present decade. Among the financial services Singapore's plan targets are insurance— including such nontraditional areas as specialized risk and offshore business —and regional-fund management capability. The plan also suggests additional incentives to attract more regional and international companies to the Singapore Stock Exchange and to promote other markets, including a currency-futures exchange.

In much of Eastasia, the plans of the government are treated mainly as forecasts, as reliable or unreliable as the government's efforts at meteorology. They tend to be forecasts for the economy as a whole, but are often supplemented by forecasts for specific sectors. Often they can have a powerful positive effect on investment by giving evidence of the sorts of sectors—and the scale of production capacity in those various sectors—that the government is willing to support. In Japan, for example, capital investment jumped massively in 1961–62 after Prime Minister Ikeda Hayatō revealed his plan for doubling national income by 1970. Firms in steel, petrochemicals, shipbuilding, and a host of other capital-intensive industries began investing feverishly to increase their share of what promised to be massive new markets, or at least to preempt others from doing so.

In China, on the other hand, plans exist to control the physical flow of commodities and include stipulations about manpower levels, delivery schedules, and raw material allocations. The weaker the free-market economy for trading goods and services, the more important the plan appears to be. Since the First Five-Year Plan, China has moved away from the rigid Russian style of planning, but the lack of an efficient distribution network based on a free market gives each plan continuing importance in China. In any case, a Communist government's dominance of budgetary investment decisions virtually ensures that people will pay attention to its plan and that individual production units can invest confidently in accordance with it.

The government's role in the credit system is most pronounced in the Communist states, where all banks are nationalized and where most investment funds come not from the banks but from the government budget. China has recently issued regulations urging firms to rely more on the People's Bank of China, a huge institution with deposit branches in every village, for their commercial credit. But the annual economic plan, which apportions investment to enterprises based on their proposals, will continue to allocate the lion's share of long-term loans.

Channeling Investment

Eastasian governments have long been plagued by a shortage of capital and bombarded with a constant stream of proposals as to how to employ it. Except in the case of Hong Kong, where the market has normally mediated among investment priorities in good Anglo-Saxon fashion, Eastasian governments have not hesitated to set credit allocation priorities to encourage the "patriotic use of money."

The heart of Eastasian credit allocation has normally been the apportionment of development bank loans in accordance with intersectoral objectives of the national plan. Basic industries such as steel, energy, shipping, and more recently electronics have generally received the strongest support. In Japan and, increasingly, in the other nations as well, specialized government financial institutions have also channeled funds into fields like housing and urban development, as the fundamental requirements of industry were satisfied.

Especially in Korea and Taiwan, as noted earlier, central banks also have helped channel the flow of credit toward priority uses. The Bank of Korea, for example, channels extensive loans to industry through the commercial banks, as in France. At the end of June, 1981 the Bank of Korea offered six different loan and rediscount rates ranging from 5 percent to 22 percent.[41] High priority was placed on export finance, which received a preferential 10 percent rate and more than $2.2 billion in credit directly from the Bank of Korea during 1980.[42] Rather than directly coercing individual businessmen, Eastasian policy shapes the parameters around them in a fashion that makes them want to invest in a manner consistent with national policy. In keeping with their minimalist orientation, Eastasian states rely heavily on tax policy as a tool for promoting investment.

Eastasian tax policies tend to be shaped not by ideological concerns for social welfare or equity, but rather by a pragmatic desire to maximize economic growth. The basic principle, insofar as this pragmatism leaves room for principles, is that taxes on businessmen in favored industries should be as low as possible, to give them strong incentives to invest and thus to promote growth. This is the aim of the two principal strategies now in vogue within the region.

The Japanese "carrot and stick" approach is to establish relatively high nominal rates of taxation—nearly as high as in the United States, although substantially lower than in Europe—and then to create exceptions to them. Special tax-free reserves and accelerated depreciation are targeted specifically to spur investment in sectors the bureaucracy considers strategic. Exports in the 1960s, pollution control in the 1970s, and energy conservation in the 1980s have received this sort of special tax priority, with the flow of investment responding accordingly.

Hong Kong has adopted a somewhat different approach. It encourages private investment by keeping taxes low not just for favored industries but across-the-board. The personal income taxes rate is a flat 15 percent, and corporate taxes are equally lenient. Singapore, which imposes somewhat higher tax rates on individuals and domestic corporations, is extremely good to multinationals, often offering long tax holidays in order to spur foreign investment. Among the most important Eastasian devices for luring investment into priority sectors is subsidizing infrastructure, training, and research costs that a firm would otherwise have to meet independently. Japan pioneered such practices in the 1950s, when more than 20 percent of the national budget went to the construction of ports, roads, and other infrastructures, mainly for new industrial complexes.[43]

All the developing Eastasian states except Hong Kong, which is itself a free port, have export-processing zones; even Hong Kong made a major departure from its laissez-faire tradition by constructing a major container shipping port with government funds in the early 1970s. Since 1975, Japan, Taiwan, Singapore, and most other Eastasian states have developed new high-technology research and development parks, where land is cheap, science-oriented universities are close, and public utilities are already provided. Both Japan's Tsukuba and Taiwan's Hsinchu science parks, among others, are encouraging not only domestic but also foreign computer, telecommunications, and precision-machinery firms to invest in research and production facilities on or near their premises.

In the final analysis, Eastasian capital formation and investment policies merge into broader approaches to development that involve intense concern for the evolution of industrial structure. While not denying the ultimate dictates of the market, as has such a prestigious European high-technology project as the Concorde, Eastasians strive continually to upgrade the national portfolio of industries through a policy of dynamic, rather than static, comparative advantage. Such a strategy takes them out of competition with poorer, less sophisticated economies. But it also helps give Eastasia an edge over the industrial West.

Case Study: Singapore's Central Provident Fund—
The Integrated Approach to Financing Social Security and
Industrial Growth

Over the half century since the Great Depression, the unconditional responsibility of the state for the indigent and unemployed, as well as for the social
welfare of citizens more generally, has seemed increasingly axiomatic in the
industrialized West. Not so in Eastasia. There the family and the private
philanthropic society shoulder the major burden of caring for those who
cannot care for themselves. In Singapore, only 22,000 of 1,800,000 citizens
were on welfare in 1966, and this figure had declined to only 6,300 of 2,200,000
by 1978.[44]

In view of the People's Action Party's claims to socialist origins, the Singapore government has found it ideologically difficult to downplay social
security issues in the manner characteristic of several high-growth Eastasian
states. The nation's technocrats have succeeded in fashioning a social security
system which both respects traditional norms of self-help and strives to promote national economic security. Thus Singapore, to put it in recently fashionable parlance, has found a way to have both guns and butter.

In essence, Singapore's Central Provident Fund (CPF), initiated in 1955, is
a compulsory savings scheme whose formal objective is to ensure that workers
are provided for in their old age or in the event of permanent disablement. All
700,000 workers in the city-state of Singapore participate in the fund, even if
covered by government pension schemes or other "provident" funds. Universal and compulsory, the CPF is in these respects functionally similar to conventional social security systems in the West. As in the West, a portion of each
employee's salary (18 percent as of July 1, 1980) is withheld from his or her
monthly paycheck and matched by a corresponding employer contribution (22
percent in 1980).[45] Minimum contributions do not become proportionately
larger as income rises; they represent flat proportions of income. The only
progressive feature is that an employee receiving under about US $85 per
month need not contribute, while the employer's obligation remains. All contributions credited to an individual's account accrue quarterly interest, 6.5
percent annually as of mid-1980.[46]

The sharp contrast between operation of the Central Provident Fund and
Western practices comes in how the funds deposited into the social security
system are ultimately used. In the West, there is typically only a limited
correspondence between contributions and ultimate benefits; in the United
States, for example, secondary employees in a household unit, such as work-

ing wives, typically forfeit contributions made. Redistributive provisions of Western social security systems often tend to reward less affluent or more unfortunate workers and their families at the expense of the more well-to-do and those who do not experience misfortune. Singapore's CPF, on the other hand, has no such welfare-oriented provisions. What a person saves and what his employer saves for him, plus interest, determine what he gets back —period.

In the West, social security funds are disbursed only in the form of retirement or disablement income, usually after the contributor has reached roughly sixty years of age or has become unable to work. In Singapore, however, the employee has a substantially wider range of options. He can receive the funds upon retirement or disablement, as in the West. But he can also use his deposit to purchase a home, thus acquiring a "stake in society," as John Locke would put it. Or he may use the bulk of continuing contributions to the CPF to pay his mortgage, with only a minimal share set aside for retirement purposes. Since 1978, Singaporeans have been able to use their CPF deposits to buy shares in the local bus company, Singapore Bus Service Limited, again on the theory that, as commuters, they would gain a more definite stake in the broader community by so doing. Social security policy, in short, has been used to promote social consciousness.

The Central Provident Fund has also been used to promote industrial development and to undertake macroeconomic policy management, functions that institutions concerned with social welfare almost never perform in the West. These CPF functions have become progressively more important since the late 1960s, as the fund has expanded relative to the Singapore economy as a whole. In 1969 contributions to the CPF were only one hundred million dollars; by 1980 they had spiraled to $2.3 billion, or over 10 percent of the GNP and 36 percent of gross domestic savings.[47]

This rapid growth is attributable both to rising wage rates and to increases in the percentage of wages that workers have been forced to save. From 1955 through 1967 only 5 percent of a worker's salary was withheld. The rate rose to 10 percent by January 1971, to 15 percent by July 1974, and to 18 percent by July 1980.[48] As the size and relative strength of the CPF increases, so does the importance of CPF mandatory deposit rates as a tool of aggregate demand management. By manipulating the percentage withheld, the government can influence the savings rate of the economy as a whole, a feat that is virtually impossible anywhere else in the world. It thus became possible in 1979 for Singapore's wages to increase 20 percent (at government initiative, no less) while consumer-price inflation was actually declining from 4.8 to 4.3 percent.[49]

The Central Provident Fund offers numerous advantages for the conduct of public policy in Singapore. As we have seen, it reduces the pressure on prices that increases in wages create, by giving government an additional means of restraining aggregate demand, aside from politically unpopular tax increases. Moreover, the CPF provides government with a noninflationary source of funds for development finance, much as postal savings systems do in Japan, Taiwan, and Singapore itself. The state need not run deficits or crowd out private borrowers in domestic capital markets in order to secure the necessary funds for priority government projects; it can simply sell government securities to the CPF and then lend the funds raised to Singapore Airlines, to public housing authorities, or to whomever else it chooses. In 1979, seventy-two percent of the Singapore government securities issued were purchased by the CPF, thus providing funds for various public purposes.[50]

The Central Provident Fund system also has provided Singapore with a means of financing most of its industrial growth domestically, much as Japan did, and of avoiding heavy reliance on foreign banks for development financing of the sort to which South Korea and the Philippines have been forced to resort. (Because of this low reliance on foreign banks, Singapore has been able to secure favorable terms on the development funds it has borrowed from abroad.) As a result of steep increases in the rate of mandatory contributions to the CPF (in effect, a steep increase in the rate of forced savings), Singapore has been able to raise the contribution of domestic funding sources to total capital formation from 56 percent during 1970–73 to 65 percent in 1980.[51]

The Central Provident Fund system strongly reflects a number of basic traits of Singaporean public policy. Most strikingly typical of broader policy patterns is the strong moralism of the CPF scheme, which is evident even in the name of the program. The Singaporean leadership has no philosophical reservations about forcing people to save or about limiting the support due an individual from the public sector to what has already been saved, just as it has had no qualms in the past about fining men wearing long hair or forcing them to cut it. The legitimacy of the simple, unambiguous, conservative morality espoused by the government leadership is assumed. The CPF case also shows the sensitivity of government technocrats to the interrelationships among various policy areas. Social security policy, industrial policy, and macroeconomic policy management are not compartmentalized, either in the operation of the CPF or elsewhere in Singaporean public policy. Indeed, it is this holistic approach to policy which is one of Singapore's—and Eastasia's—greatest strengths.

10

Technology for Competition

FOR CENTURIES, EASTASIANS brought up on the Chinese classics resisted the Western scientific attitude toward nature. A nineteenth-century Confucian refused to view nature as something to be studied as if it were a dead thing: to him, Western science was not only impious, it was a waste of time. The superior man strove for a harmony with nature that was beyond the grasp of sordid experiment.

A century later, Eastasia has discovered science and technology. China has produced its own indigenous weapons, synthesized insulin, and predicted earthquakes. Japan has pushed laser and chip technology to new limits, and now dominates the foreign filings of patents in the United States.[1]

In many Eastasian nations, engineers enjoy positions of prominence once monopolized by literati, including, in strongly Confucian Taiwan, the prime ministership. Eastasian states uniformly agree that new technology and knowledge-intensive industries are crucial to their growth. Naturally, since these countries are at different levels of economic development, the science and technology policies designed to meet their distinctive strategic requirements will also differ. Yet there are some common elements worth noting.

From the early days of history through the seventeenth century, Eastasia easily exceeded Europe in technological sophistication. Gunpowder, writing paper, and movable type were all invented in Eastasia; the first two diffused westward from China to Europe. Beginning with the Industrial Revolution of the eighteenth century, however, all the nations of Eastasia (with the partial exception of Japan since the early 1970s) have been essentially follower states in the progress of modern science. The strategic imperative for them has not been invention; it has been the assimilation and adaptation of technical ideas originating in the West.

To a greater degree than in any other part of the developing world, Eastasia has developed institutions for systematically assimilating foreign technology. The first of these institutions was the foreign enclave, where the ways of foreigners could be observed at close range without contaminating the broader society of which the enclave was a part. Japan's Dejima and China's Canton both performed this function in the early days of Western involvement in Asia, and Hong Kong has played a similar role for the People's Republic during the past three decades.

Two other institutions for assimilating foreign technology are the centralized technology staff offices, established to coordinate the inflow of information, and the national productivity centers, jointly financed by business and government. During 1955–61 alone the Japan Productivity Center sent 2,500 businessmen, engineers, and other researchers to the United States to investigate advanced technology and how it might be applied in Japan.[2] Singapore and South Korea have each established productivity centers in more recent years as a means for introducing technology into their own nations. China, North Korea, and Taiwan perform the same function through active academies of science, with their own laboratories and educational branches. The People's Republic has sent tens of thousands of Chinese abroad since 1976 in search of Western skills.

Another key to the Eastasian edge in technology is what might be called "reverse brain drain." Whereas developing countries like India and Nigeria regularly lose talented people who prefer to settle in the countries where they were educated (this often means Europe or America), Eastasia has a peculiar hold on its loyal citizens. Many of China's key nuclear and aerospace engineers were educated in the United States; indeed, the "father of the Chinese H-bomb," Qian Xuesen, was a long-time professor at Caltech whose return to postrevolutionary China was delayed five years by the FBI for national security reasons. Similarly, several members of the Taiwanese engineering team working on ballistic-missile guidance systems capable of striking at China's industrial heartland were educated at MIT, although the United States has banned the direct transfer of strategic aerospace technology to Taiwan.

How Does Eastasia Reverse the Brain Drain?

All the Eastasian states, aside from Japan, have offered strong financial and psychological incentives to their Western-educated nationals to return home, or at least to harness their technical skills to the cause of national development. Taiwan does this through periodic reunification seminars, to which prominent ROC-oriented Chinese living abroad are invited as key participants. South Korea systematically searches for top Korean-born scientists overseas through the Korean Institute for Science and Technology (KIST), a multidisciplinary industrial institution founded in 1966. KIST offers such scientists jobs as senior investigators with plenty of foreign travel opportunities and long sabbaticals. In its first two years, KIST enticed home twenty-seven prominent Korean scientists living in Europe and North America.[3] Very few Chinese scientists abroad have defected—in part because they invariably travel without their families, but also because they remain loyal to the ideal of national progress.

Perhaps the most important institutions for absorbing technology are the trading organizations of Eastasia. The general trading companies act as clearinghouses for Western technology, repackaging it to suit Eastasian needs. Japanese companies were the source of 487 out of 737 know-how agreements signed with foreign licensors between 1962 and 1976 in South Korea.[4] Western corporations, too, are the vehicles for much "technology transfer"—and Eastasians have learned how to extract the most from our own corporate systems. For example, the Japanese computer industry, which today is the worldwide rival of America's great IBM, started from a group of patents granted by IBM in 1961–62 in return for permission to manufacture the company's equipment in Japan. Similarly, patents granted in 1968 by Texas Instruments in return for market access became the technical base for the current strength of Nippon Electric, Fujitsu, and Hitachi in the strategic, high-growth integrated circuit field. South Korean and Taiwanese electronics and telecommunications industries have also recently been vitalized by technological diffusion through U.S. multinationals. Singapore's precision-machinery and optics industry has received similar impetus from infusions of new West German technology. And China is currently extracting major know-how concessions from Western firms eager to cash in on an illusory market.

It is difficult to calculate the precise scale of Eastasian technological borrowing from the West, especially when diffusion via the multinationals is taken into consideration. But the results have been staggering. In fiscal 1979, for example, Japan sold technology worth $342 million in exports, 30 percent more than in 1978, and purchased patents and other technology worth $1.26

billion.[5] Japan's technology export-import ratio has been rising rapidly since
the late 1970s and leaped 5 points (to 27.1 percent on a flow-of-royalties basis)
in 1979 alone.[6] It will not be long before South Korea shows a similar growth
rate, and we are currently building China's know-how at a pace comparable
to Japan's in the 1950s. Virtually all these imports have come from the West,
while less than half the exports have been directed toward Europe and North
America. Japan, which still pays net royalties to the West of nearly $1 billion
per year, has been rapidly gaining on its teachers. In fact, Japan has enjoyed
a surplus on *new* technology contracts since 1973, and now sends more technology to the United States than it receives in certain sectors, such as construction, textiles, and iron and steel.[7]

The Eastasian Policy Response

All this technology has not been fueled by large research and development
efforts. In 1978, Japan spent only 2.15 percent of national income on research
and development, versus 2.48 percent for the United States, 2.64 percent for
West Germany, and 4.57 percent for the Soviet Union.[8] The other non-Communist Eastasian countries spent less than 1 percent of GNP for this purpose.
Only China, under the pressure of maintaining a technically sophisticated
defense establishment in an economically backward nation with little outside
assistance, devotes what is by world standards a really substantial proportion
of national income to domestic science and technology development.

Support for science, though generally modest, is heavily concentrated in
areas yielding rapid dividends for industrial growth. Most research and development spending goes into product development and modification, activities
with quick payoffs; such spending represented 83.4 percent of total Japanese
research and development expenditures in 1978. Little support goes for high-
risk, long-term projects. And, except for China and, increasingly, Taiwan, little
is spent on defense research and development, which bears an uncertain relationship to industrial competitiveness in most sectors. Relatively low salary
levels for scientists add further to the cost-efficiency of the funds spent by
Eastasians on science and technology.

At the outset of the 1980s, Japan is at rough parity with the United States
in proportion of national income spent on nondefense-related research and
development. But Japan, unlike the United States, tends to use research funds

for commercial applications. And the trends in support for science are moving in precisely opposite directions. In 1969, for example, the United States graduated about 40 percent more electrical engineers annually than Japan. But by 1979 the ratio had been nearly reversed.[9] Since a significantly larger proportion of research and development expenditures go for defense in the United States than in Eastasia, Eastasian states will significantly outstrip the United States in civilian-oriented research and development over the next decade.

Although Eastasians have eagerly combed the globe for state-of-the-art technology, their governments have tended to be selective about which technology is actually imported, who the licensees are, and what terms the recipients negotiate with their foreign licensors. Technology imports have been concentrated in areas of greatest strategic importance in industrial development. Japan's Ministry of International Trade and Industry, for example, has since 1950 kept a detailed list of desired technologies for use in evaluating licensing agreements between Japanese and foreign firms. MITI has used its powers under the Foreign Investment Act to prevent or delay undesirable transactions, or to improve the terms favoring the Japanese party. Taiwan and South Korea have used similar mechanisms, although their leverage vis-à-vis foreign licensors has generally been much weaker than Japan's. China demands that any major purchases from abroad include full drawings and engineering specifications.

Eastasian governments, especially those of Japan and China, have kept close watch on know-how. Government organizations help collect and disseminate information: China operates a large-scale copying operation that distributes over 600 foreign technical journals around the country. Japan has intervened, to ensure that all major firms in a given industry have adequate access to improved technology. In the early 1970s, for example, when Hitachi indicated that it was making an agreement with RCA for computer technology, the Japanese government held up the agreement until one of Hitachi's competitors, Nippon Electric, found a similar foreign licensor. MITI also insisted that IBM and Texas Instruments license their technology broadly to Japanese firms when those two American multinationals first began manufacturing in Japan during the 1960s. China encourages competition among firms importing know-how, but it urges them to share their information. This tactic seems more successful than the European practice of designating "national champions" like ICL in Britain or CIE in France, which are more privileged than others.

To a greater degree than Western nations, Eastasian states tend to see technology as part of a larger, integrated economic and social whole. To create and adapt technology, a nation needs scientific researchers; to apply it, a nation needs engineers. Eastasian educational policy is therefore closely coordinated with technological objectives to ensure a strong mix of specialists and lay people educated in general science. The science and especially the mathematics curricula in Eastasian high schools tend to be extremely rigorous by international standards. Japanese students sixteen and seventeen years of age regularly place at the top of their peer group on standardized international mathematics tests.

Rigorous secondary school training creates a high general level of scientific knowledge among the work forces of Japan and the newly industrializing countries (NICs) of Eastasia. Eastasian educational policies at the university level vary in their emphasis on the basic sciences, but they all target engineering, a discipline vital for follower nations seeking to apply technology developed elsewhere. During the 1970s the number of accredited engineers in Japan, South Korea, and Taiwan more than doubled; by 1980, Japan was annually graduating as many engineers of all types as the United States, although its population was only half as large. China, after losing a generation of students during the Cultural Revolution, has begun breeding engineers as rapidly as it did in the 1950s, when 100 percent annual growth in engineering manpower was typical.

To a much greater degree than in the West, Eastasian invention and innovation take place in the workplace and in the research institute rather than in the university. In Japan, concern for orderly human relationships and a pervasive lack of empirical orientation cripple the ability of universities to serve as scientific innovators; Japan's ultra-elite Tokyo University, for example, has never graduated a Nobel Prize winner in the sciences, and it plays a major scientific role only in Japan's space exploration program. In China and, to some extent, in both Koreas, involvement in the political process has crippled the universities' ability to serve as forums for systematic scientific research. In Hong Kong and Singapore, the local industrial community has not been large enough to serve as the catalyst for major university-based programs of technical innovation. And nowhere in the region is the concept of the polytechnic institute well established.

Research institutes and "think tanks" play a key role in scientific activities throughout Eastasia. Typical in many respects is the Korean Institute for Science and Technology, operating on an annual income of more than US $10 million from a government endowment, but without direct government subsidy. KIST employs a staff of more than 50 Korean scientists and engineers, many of them educated in the United States and Europe.[10] They work on a contract basis for private firms (60 percent of total revenues) and for the Korean government (the remaining 40 percent), formulating detailed plans for steel mills, devising production processes for automobile engine bearings, developing electronic switching boards with foreign high-technology firms, and so on. KIST's companion institution, the Korean Advanced Institute of Science, serves as a more purely theoretical think tank, providing answers to practical questions rooted in basic science.

Japan and Taiwan also have sophisticated networks of research institutes, which, like Korea's, harness the expertise of government and business in the service of common technological goals. In Japan the central element in this network is MITI's Agency for Industrial Science and Technology, which sponsors the national research and development program. This program has, over the past fifteen years, done extensive work on seawater desalinization, direct-reduction steelmaking, development of the electric automobile, pattern-recognition information-processing systems, and so on. Research work is done by sixteen MITI-operated industrial laboratories in cooperation with private groups, such as the Nomura and Mitsubishi research institutes, as well as the universities. In Taiwan, key scientific research institutes have traditionally been affiliated with the military, although business circles and industrial planners inspired creation of the Industrial Technology Research Institute in 1973–74 and the Institute for the Information Industries in 1979.

Throughout Eastasia the links between technology and production are close; technology is useful primarily insofar as it leads to new, competitive products, be they consumer goods or military hardware. Not surprisingily, the research-industrial park, which includes both high-technology laboratories and sophisticated industrial facilities, is becoming a prominent part of the Eastasian landscape of the 1980s, as the region moves increasingly toward a knowledge-intensive industrial structure. As has often been the case, Japan was the pacesetter with its $15 billion Tsukuba Science and Industrial Park in Ibaraki Prefecture, near Tokyo, initiated in the early 1970s. Among the major high-technology firms moving into the Tsukuba area is Intel (of California's Silicon Valley), which will be opening an integrated-circuit design center there. South Korea consolidated its various science-related institutes in a Science Park on the outskirts of Seoul during the mid-1970s, while Taiwan on August 15, 1980, opened its Hsinchu Science-based Industrial Park outside Taipei. Singapore also is joining the research-park competition with a major new facility at Kentridge, near the National University.

Differing National Strategies

With mounting energy prices, rising labor costs, and the threat of low-wage competition from developing nations like China, Japan and its non-Communist Eastasian neighbors must quickly shift their industrial emphases away from such sectors as textiles, shoes, and even shipbuilding toward low-energy, knowledge-intensive enterprises. (Strategic imperatives force China in the same direction.) But strategies for moving into high-technology industry and for defining and attaining the proper "market niche" vary significantly from nation to nation. So, too, as a result, do technology policies.

For China, sophisticated, state-of-the-art technology is necessary chiefly in the military sphere. The People's Republic aims to acquire military technology through independent nuclear, electronics, and aerospace programs, supplemented by military purchase and technology-transfer arrangements with Western, particularly European, nations. Otherwise, China's need is primarily for relatively unsophisticated technology that can be adapted to China's underdeveloped economic situation. Scientific research in all but a few areas (earthquake prediction, for example) is a matter of adapting foreign technology to suit domestic conditions.

South Korea and, in some fields, Taiwan are aspiring to reach world-class levels in certain areas of electronics and communications technology by the early 1990s. But they, like Hong Kong and Singapore, are still followers, less sophisticated than Japan, Western Europe, or the United States. Their strategies must thus inevitably focus on adaptation of Western technology to Asian conditions, both for domestic use and, increasingly, for possible reexport to China.

Japan has come to dominate the flow of technology from the West to the Eastasian "Gang of Four"—as Singapore, South Korea, Taiwan, and Hong Kong are sometimes called, in mock reference to the Chinese radical opposition group. Singapore, which has the most diversified contacts of the four and which sees itself in a basically symbiotic relationship with Japan as a producer of medium-technology precision machinery, is receptive to an expanded technology-exchange relationship. Exemplifying such cooperation, Japan and Singapore during 1981 opened a major training center for data processors from throughout Southeast Asia.

In contrast to Singapore, Korea and Taiwan see themselves more directly in conflict with Japan in high-technology fields, partly because of their pronounced current dependence on Japanese technology. Officials of both Taiwan and Korea stress the compatibility of their respective national interests with those of Western multinationals competing with Japan in high-technology fields. Korea's KIST is cooperating with the U.S. firm GTE in developing and producing electronic switching boards in Korea, and Motorola is likewise active there. In Taiwan, Wang Laboratories, Western Electric, and other American high-technology firms are already establishing research and production facilities for possible competition with Japanese firms in Eastasia.

From the Western point of view, newly industrializing nations like China present little direct technological challenge to the West. But in their adaptation of Western technology to the conditions of developing nations, they do create products that are often highly competitive with Western goods in the Third World. Aggressive Korean marketing of the Hyundai Pony in Africa and Latin America, for example, has constricted markets for the automotive output of Western Europe. The chief Eastasia Edge in high technology, of course, lies with Japan, which already has a formidable capital equipment base, efficient production processes, and a growing ability to innovate technology. In 1980, Japan ranked second in the world in nondefense research and development spending (behind only West Germany), with a growth rate that is the fastest among advanced nations.[11]

Through the 1950s and 1960s, Japan's strategic problem with respect to technology was that of Korea and Taiwan today—how to efficiently adapt and implement inventions made elsewhere. During the 1970s, however, it became something more. As the technology gap with the West began to close, and as foreign firms became more reluctant to license technology to Japanese competitors, Japan came under increasing pressure to develop its own technology as well as adapt the innovations of others. There have been two basic types of innovation in Japan. One type, epitomized by very large scale integration (VLSI) circuitry, has involved fundamental scientific and engineering breakthroughs. The other, exemplified by the video tape recorder, has involved bridging a gap in existing product lines with relatively standard technology put together in new ways.

MITI's strategy for getting technology introduced has been to encourage rivalry (as long as it is not "excessive") in putting production facilities on line. But its emphasis in creative research and development projects has been to make them cooperative, involving almost all interested parties technically and financially competent to exploit likely breakthroughs. In addition to MITI's national laboratories, which in cooperation with private research institutes and universities handle such research projects as direct-reduction steelmaking,[12] research cartels involving both the private and the public sector also help to create technology. One such cartel recently completed path-breaking work on VLSI circuitry in a program described at the end of this chapter. Another research cartel has begun a sequel project on computer software, with the results to be ultimately distributed to the cartel's member firms.

The Eastasia Edge in Japanese high technology is multifaceted. In electronics, steel, textiles, and construction technology, Japan is approaching world standards and has favorable trade balances even vis-à-vis the United States. In other sectors, such as autos, superior process technology (including the use of robots) gives Japan the upper hand. Clearly Eastasia's understanding of the potential of technology and the region's willingness to seek optimal means of integrating it into ongoing processes are key elements in the overall challenge facing the West from Eastasia today.

Case Study: VLSI—Government-Business Cooperation in Creating Technology

Ever since the advent of IBM's System 360 and the acquisition of France's independent computer maker Machines Bull by Honeywell in 1964, the Japanese government has seen computers as a strategic industry.[13] It has marked domestic computer firms for special assistance in its struggle with the giants of the U.S. electronics world. In 1971, despite substantial private-sector resistance, the MITI organized two specialized research and production cartels to prepare the Japanese computer industry for the liberation of restrictions on foreign investment in the industry, scheduled to occur four years later. Subsequently, in an effort to lay the technical foundation in logic and memory devices for the development of advanced computer systems independent of foreign technology, and to seize world leadership in semiconductors for Japan, the Japanese government in 1976 organized the VLSI program for the development of sophisticated new computer circuitry.

The goals of this project were ambitious. One was to develop state-of-the-art electronic devices fitting hundreds of thousands of transistors onto a single 4-inch silicon chip—a chip that would be capable of sweeping applications in pocket-sized computers, portable translation machines, voice-recognition devices, and electronic-mail transmission systems. In addition to creating a basic VLSI memory chip, the project proposed to develop sophisticated equipment for manufacturing VLSIs, including an electron-beam-based mask testing machine, an electron beam transcriber, and high-speed electron-beam lithography equipment. The aim, in short, was nothing less than to bring Japan abreast or ahead of the United States in commercially strategic areas of advanced electronic technology.

Given its ambitious reseach goals, the VLSI project operated on a remarkably lean budget of roughly $240 million over four years (1976–80).[14] About $120 million of this came from the Japanese government, strengthening MITI in its efforts to induce the five private Japanese computer companies involved in the project to coordinate their activities with those of the ministry.[15] The program as a whole was administered by the VLSI Technology Research Association, a special agency of MITI. Under the auspices of the association, three laboratory groups were established: one group had the responsibility of developing the basic component and manufacturing technologies, while the other two laboratories were responsible for applying the new technologies to two independent lines of computers.

The first group, known as the Cooperative Research Laboratory (CRL), was specifically established in connection with the VLSI project and included personnel from the five major private-sector participant firms and from MITI's Electrotechnical Laboratory. The CRL, established in Kawasaki, a suburb of Tokyo, provided a forum for private- and public-sector researchers to exchange ideas flexibly, without fear of revelation to domestic or foreign competitors not participating in the research cartel. It typified broader patterns of Japanese public policy in the favoritism shown by government to established firms in an industry.

The other laboratories were operated independently of government by two groups of private companies—one by Fujitsu, Hitachi, and Mitsubishi, which were developing IBM-compatible computers, and one by Nippon Electric and Tōshiba, which were concentrating on systems incompatible with IBM's. The VLSI Technology Research Association coordinated the activities of all these research groups through control of their access to government funding.

Because of the VLSI project's high national priority and the important role of government funds and research personnel in supporting it, the private sector cooperated more smoothly with government than has often been the case in Japan. But intragovernmental rivalries still had some effect on the VLSI development effort. In 1976, Nippon Telephone and Telegraph (NTT), the government telecommunications monopoly, launched a parallel VLSI program, under the auspices of its Electronic Communications Laboratory. Fujitsu, Hitachi, and Nippon Electric, all participants in the MITI project, also took part in NTT's research effort, gaining strategic advantages from their dual involvement that were less available to the governmental participants.

The Japanese government contribution of $120 million to the VLSI project pales by comparison with the billions the French and British governments spent on Concorde, or the even larger sums the U.S. Department of Defense routinely devotes to high-technology research and development projects of its own. Some ask whether the VLSI project was really necessary. Clearly the joint government-business research project generated some important technical breakthroughs, especially in developing circuit technology and primary equipment for the production of one-megabit large-scale integrated circuit (LSI) chips. The project did generate 600 patents, virtually all of which were ultimately opened to the public and to domestic or foreign firms paying royalties to use them. But the persistent question seemingly remains: was the dynamic Japanese private sector, with a demonstrated ability to foresee long-term market demand and to develop a diversity of products to meet it, really incapable of achieving the same results on its own?

If the employment and decision-making structures of the Japanese electronics industry and of the Japanese business world as a whole resembled those of the United States, the need for government-business endeavors like the VLSI project might indeed be less pressing. California's "Silicon Valley," where scientists move rapidly from firm to firm, and scientifically advanced universities such as MIT and Caltech serve as mechanisms for rapid diffusion of new technical ideas. But Japan, with its lifetime employment system and its nonempirical academic traditions, needs alternate organizational contexts for technical innovation, which research cartels such as the VLSI project provide.

Like other industrialized societies, Japan finds that its private-sector firms tend to orient their research activities more toward potentially profitable product-development activities than to basic research. This tendency has been pronounced in electronics because of the nature of the firms involved. At the onset of VLSI, none of these firms—whose primary interests were telecommunications, consumer electronics, or heavy electrical machinery—had an internal constituency supportive of essentially unprofitable basic electronics research. Middle managers knowledgeable about E-beam lithography equipment and other such arcane subjects were in no position to push their views forcefully within the context of a consensus-oriented corporate decision-making structure. The VLSI project provided a means of inducing key firms to focus attention on strategically important areas of electronics research they might otherwise have neglected.

In addition to the technological innovations and the reorientation and focusing of corporate priorities produced, the VLSI project was also important as a means of ensuring the rapid exploitation of technology for commercial purposes. Both MITI and NTT purposely included rival private electronics manufacturers in their research groups, so that the fear of being preempted by rivals and of losing competitive position would induce them to seek commercial exploitation of the technical advances as rapidly as possible, to the benefit of computer users throughout the Japanese economy. The strategy seems to have worked. By June 1981, slightly more than a year after the conclusion of the VLSI project, six Japanese firms had introduced the 64-K random-access memory into mass production, with other major electronics firms following. Meanwhile, Japan's integrated-circuit, computer, and electronics-industrial capital goods markets continued to strengthen.[16]

The VLSI project dealt with what, for Japan, was a novel problem: the generation of world-class technology through indigenous research and development. The essentials of the policy response, however, typify broader patterns of business-government interaction in Japan. The private and public sectors cooperated flexibly and pragmatically, unconstrained by antitrust laws and other artificial restrictions. Government pursued an open policy of fostering oligopolistic rivalry, encouraging some firms against others, largely on the basis of size and technical capacity. Disclosure requirements were minimal, and selective access to information was used as a strategic weapon. Government provided incentives to bring strategic production technology on stream as rapidly as possible. Subsidies played a more significant role than is common in Japanese industrial relations, and the private sector was correspondingly more cooperative and less evasive than is often the case. But broadly speaking, the VLSI case is typical of government-business dynamics in other strategically important sectors in Japan.

11

The Energy Defense

IN ALL the long arc of high-growth capitalist Eastasian states stretching from Sapporo to Singapore, there is not a single major developed oil field, uranium mine, or high-grade, low-cost coal production facility. One year of oil production in Japan, the largest capitalist energy producer in the region, is equal to only one day of oil production in Texas.[1] Energy would appear to be a sword of Damocles hanging over Eastasia's economic growth prospects and even political stability. But in a striking demonstration of the Eastasia Edge, this region has moved far toward neutralizing its greatest vulnerability.

Dependence on imported energy varies from country to country throughout the region, but in no case totals less than 80 percent of total demand. Japan relies on foreign sources for 88 percent of its energy supplies; both South Korea and Taiwan have dependency ratios higher than 80 percent, and the island city-states of Hong Kong and Singapore secure virtually 100 percent of their energy from abroad.[2] The People's Republic of China is not only self-sufficient in energy but also has considerable potential as an exporter, and North Korea has great underdeveloped coal reserves. But the energy production of the Communist states is not yet available to the rest of the region, if it ever will be.

The Eastasian capitalist states appear even more vulnerable in light of their dependence for energy resources on areas outside the region. Japan in the early 1980s met nearly three-quarters of its primary energy needs with imported oil —the highest proportion of any major industrialized nation.[3] (Italy, the runner-up, imported not quite two-thirds of its oil supply.[4]) Korea meets roughly 60 percent of its basic energy needs with imported oil; the ratio for Taiwan is around 75–85 percent.[5]

Eastasian imported oil is the lifeblood of the local economy. A much higher proportion goes to industrial uses and less to personal leisure consumption than is common in the West: 70 percent in Korea, 65 percent in Taiwan and Japan.[6] Only a tenth of Japanese petroleum consumption is gasoline for motor vehicles (versus 41.2 percent in the United States during 1977), a pattern replicated elsewhere in Eastasia.[7] Only in Hong Kong, which lacks a major heavy industrial base, is a substantial proportion of energy used for consumer purposes.

The vulnerability of the Eastasian economies in the energy field is enhanced by their heavy reliance on oil imports from the politically volatile Middle East. Japan, for example, is four times more dependent on imported energy than the United States (88 percent of total requirements versus 22 percent), and more dependent on oil as a source of energy (75 percent of total energy consumption versus 50 percent in the U.S.). At the same time, Japan receives 78 percent of its oil imports from the Persian Gulf, which supplies only 30 percent of U.S. oil imports.[8] The other Eastasian states are even more heavily dependent on Middle Eastern oil. Ninety-eight percent of all Korean oil comes from the Persian Gulf, with 89 percent of total requirements from just two countries, Saudi Arabia (63 percent) and Kuwait (26 percent). Korea's next most crucial supplier is the Ayatollah Khomeini's Iran.[9] Taiwan obtains 83 percent of its oil from just two countries, Kuwait and Saudi Arabia, which provide 49 percent and 34 percent, respectively.[10]

The potential implications of Eastasian energy dependence for the region's economic performance can be seen graphically in Japan's response to the oil shocks of 1973 and 1979. The fourfold increase in oil prices in 1973 led to a $13 billion hike in Japan's oil import bill, equal to 3 percent of the GNP; oil imports rose from 17.6 to 34 percent of total imports by value. The trade deficit ballooned, and the value of the yen plummeted more than 15 percent against the dollar in a matter of weeks. By February 1974, Japan's rate of wholesale price inflation was running at 34 percent per annum, 12 percentage points above Italy's and the highest rate in the industrialized world.[11] Growth slumped sharply from 11 percent in 1973 to essentially zero in the following recession-plagued year. Taiwan's economy followed a similar pattern, and Korean growth, despite aggressive governmental pump-priming, was nearly halved from previous levels.

In 1979 the 110 percent increase in oil prices following the Iranian revolution once again sent shock waves through the economies of Eastasia, though not quite so severe (except in the case of Korea) as those of 1973. In Japan, oil bills shot up $12.5 billion, or $114 per capita (1.3 percent of GNP), while international payments went sharply into deficit. The yen once again plummeted—this time by over 20 percent within six months. Wholesale price inflation soared past 20 percent by late 1979, reflecting a 54 percent increase in electric power rates.[12] Taiwan and South Korea both absorbed staggering increases in oil bills and sustained large increases in current accounts deficits as a result.[13]

Despite the dramatic impact of this second oil shock on exchange rates, balance of payments figures, and wholesale price indexes throughout Eastasia, comparison with the effects of the 1973 price rise suggest the remarkable ability of nations in the region, particularly Japan and Taiwan, to neutralize the impact of oil price increases on their economic development. During 1979–80, Taiwan absorbed an increase in oil payments of US $3.8 billion in two years, at a time of declining world trade growth; yet Taiwan incurred a turnaround of only about $2 billion in its trade balance because of its strong trade competitiveness.[14] A similar phenomenon occurred in Japan, which was better able to minimize the impact of oil price hikes on its domestic economy than were other key industrial nations outside Eastasia.[15] By September 1980, only fifteen months after the second oil shock plunged its international payments into deficit, Japan was able to register a $938 million trade surplus.[16]

The energy problem that Eastasia confronts is twofold, involving both price and supply. The Eastasian states have, through strong industrial competitiveness and aggressive marketing efforts, largely succeeded in neutralizing the impact of oil price increases on the balance of payments and on inflation. As a consequence of their high import ratios and heavy reliance on oil for industrial purposes, however, they remain extremely vulnerable to curtailments in supply, particularly from nations such as Saudi Arabia, on which they have an extraordinary dependence. Taiwan and Korea, which lack strong diplomatic leverage or powerful private trading companies to assist in oil procurement, are especially vulnerable in this regard. Looming over their future is the prospect that energy may replace capital shortages and technology—past constraints now largely overcome—as barriers to growth.

Policies for Reducing Energy Vulnerability

The capitalist economies of Eastasia produce virtually no oil at present, and they have no major proven oil reserves. Some analysts see the prospect of offshore oil: in the East China Sea between Korea and Japan, in the Yellow

Sea between Korea and China, or near the Senkaku Islands between Taiwan and Okinawa. All of the exploration zones in which oil might prospectively be found lie in politically disputed areas, so there are international constraints which cloud their exploitation. But as economic linkages grow in intensity within Eastasia, and as a stronger sense of regionalism develops, these may become less important. Nippon Oil and Texaco have already undertaken exploratory drilling southeast of Pusan in the East China Sea, reportedly with encouraging results.[17]

Whatever the prospects for offshore drilling, oil as a commodity appears likely to be periodically in short supply during the 1980s and beyond. Sensing this reality, all the Eastasian states have sought to diversify their energy consumption patterns. Japan, for example, has set the consumption targets shown in table 11–1. The Ministry of International Trade and Industry projects that oil will remain Japan's most important energy source, but that the combined shares of coal, nuclear power, and gas will increase to 30 percent by 1985 and to nearly 38 percent by the end of the decade. Japan's Sunshine Project also proposes to make solar power a major energy source by the beginning of the twenty-first century.

TABLE 11–1

*Moving Away from Oil: MITI Long-term Energy Supply Forecasts
for Japan, 1985–95*

Energy Source	Degree of reliance (Proportion of total energy supply as a percentage)			
	1977 (actual)	1985	1990	1995
Imported Oil	74.5%	62.9%	50.0%	43.1%
Imported coal	11.6	13.6	15.6	16.5
Nuclear power	2.0	6.7	10.9	14.3
Liquid natural gas	2.9	7.2	9.0	8.7
Hydroelectric	4.8	4.7	4.6	4.6
Domestic coal	3.2	2.5	2.0	1.8
Geothermal	0.0	0.4	1.0	1.8
Domestic oil/LP gas	0.9	1.4	1.4	1.7
Other (including new energy sources such as solar power)	0.1	0.6	5.5	7.5
Totals	100	100	100	100
Million kiloliters (oil equivalent)	412	582	716	825

SOURCE: Agency of Natural Resources and Energy, ed., *Sekiyu Daigai energy binran* [Handbook on alternative energy] (Tokyo: Tsūshō Sangyō Chōsa Kai, 1980), pp. 124–25.

NOTE: These forecasts, announced by Japan's Ministry of International Trade and Industry on August 31, 1979, were the latest publicly available as of September 1981.

POLICY

Nuclear Power

In South Korea and Taiwan the projected pattern of diversification is similar
to Japan's, though with more emphasis on nuclear power and a sharper movement away from oil. During the late 1970s, Taiwan proposed a 31 percent
reliance on nuclear power by 1990, and Korea 40 percent;[18] actual construction
plans may vary moderately from these levels, depending on the rate of economic growth. Technocrats on Taiwan calculate that the cost of nuclear power
is half that of electricity produced from coal-fired plants and only 34 percent
of that from oil-fired power plants.[19] One reason for the relatively low cost of
nuclear power is that unequivocal governmental backing makes politically
induced delays in construction unlikely.

By the year 2000, Taiwan plans to have twenty-one nuclear reactors,
grouped in massive complexes, and Korea plans to have forty.[20] This commitment to the atom is without doubt the most forthright and categorical on earth.
Economic strategists in these two nations argue that the imperatives of head-
long economic growth in an era of energy shortages leave them with little
choice. And in a world disillusioned with nuclear power in the wake of Three
Mile Island, they find themselves in a buyers' market for nuclear equipment,
which has given them tremendous leverage with General Electric, Westinghouse, the U.S. Export-Import Bank, and French and German nuclear power
suppliers.

Safeguarding Oil Supplies

While downplaying oil, diversifying their energy supplies, and trying to develop additional domestic reserves, Japan, Taiwan, and Korea have also tried
to safeguard their access to the foreign petroleum they still need so badly. They
have carefully cultivated the Middle Eastern States, whose oil fields provide
over three-quarters of Eastasia's oil.

Capitalist Eastasia turned dramatically toward the Middle Eastern members
of the Organization of Petroleum Exporting Countries (OPEC) after the Arab-
Israeli war of October 1973. Japan, which had previously been thought un-
friendly to the Arab cause because of a tendency to follow U.S. foreign policy,
tilted sharply toward the Arabs after they began to embargo oil exports to
nations friendly with Israel. In 1974 the Japanese government announced $50
million in aid each for Egypt and Syria, while promising officially to "recon-
sider its position" toward Israel.[21] By 1978 more than 26 percent of total
Japanese foreign aid was directed toward OPEC, despite the massive current-
account surpluses recorded by Saudi Arabia, Iran, and Indonesia.[22] Japanese
technical assistance to OPEC in support of plant exports soared, as Japan
sought to recover part of the income forfeited to OPEC through oil price

increases by exporting whole industrial plants to the Middle East. For example, the Mitsui group sped up development of its major petrochemical complex in southern Iran; this project was virtually abandoned, though 85 percent complete, after the fall of the shah in 1979, and was gutted by Iraqi bombing in November 1980. To please the Saudis, Mitsubishi made plans for a similar complex at Jubail, a project that appears still to be under active consideration despite the sobering example of Mitsui's loss of $3 billion in Iran.

South Korea has also sought to safeguard its oil supply by aggressively offering construction contracts to the Middle East. These contracts, which totaled more than $15 billion during 1975–78 alone, both absorb large sums of petrodollar profits and cement the Arab countries into long-term dependence on Korean technology and engineering support.[23] More than 140,000 Korean workers have swarmed across South Asia from Jidda to Jakarta at the height of this construction activity.[24] Korea's total construction export effort fell to $6.3 billion in 1979 (after the Iranian revolution) and slightly less in 1980, but soared to an all-time record of nearly $10 billion in 1981.[25]

Leading the building drive into OPEC for Korea was massive Hyundai Construction, with $4 billion in OPEC contracts in 1979.[26] Hyundai made use of its many years' experience of contract construction for the U.S. military effort in Vietnam to establish its first foothold in the Middle East. But it also enjoys advantages of vertical integration not availble to American and European construction exporters: Hyundai owns its own shipping line, which allows it to transport materials cheaply, and its own heavy industry companies, which can supply construction materials at cost. The close personal relationship between Hyundai's president Chung Ju-yung and the late Republic of Korea President Park Chung-hee, who controlled the diplomatic relationship with OPEC, certainly did not hurt.

Taiwan's strategy for energy security is not so different from Korea's or Japan's, but it tends to focus heavily on one country, the Kingdom of Saudi Arabia. As the only nation in the Middle East maintaining diplomatic relations with Taiwan, and as the supplier of nearly half Taiwan's oil, Saudi Arabia is vital to the Republic of China. For the Saudis, in turn, Taiwan is a useful source of technical expertise, especially in military matters, giving the Saudis leverage against the United States, their major military provider. In addition, Taiwan supplies pilots for the Saudi air force, to buttress its operations in the Yemen Arab Republic. Joint Taiwan-Saudi ventures in materials processing are also under way: in December 1979 the Taiwan Fertilizer Company, a government enterprise, concluded an agreement for the construction of a $357 million plant in Saudi Arabia that will use surplus Saudi natural gas to provide both nations with low-cost fertilizer.[27] In this way a small Eastasian economy is proving its value to the world's petroleum giant, while hoping to establish a viable energy future.

Diversification and Conservation

To decrease the danger of heavy reliance on the Middle East, Eastasia has tried to diversify its energy sources. Japan has been the most successful, having used its trading companies and government-to-government arrangements to obtain commitments from several nations outside the Arab bloc. Japanese companies are currently joint-venturing coal and uranium exploration in Australia, liquefied natural gas production in Indonesia, and extensive natural gas exploration in Canada and Mexico. Japan offered extensive aid and excellent terms to China in the hope of obtaining Chinese oil exports, only to find that China's ability to export crude oil fell far short of its promises. In these cases, Japanese companies have been willing to advance enormous sums of investment capital for projects yet to be proven or even approved by the local governments. Taiwan and South Korea likewise have joined the energy scramble, though their officials often complain of "unfair" Japanese attempts to secure commitments. Both nations have been intensively courting African oil producers, especially Nigeria. In July 1980, Korea's Hyundai concluded a major joint-venture arrangement to mine coal in Australia, the first non-Japanese Eastasian firm to do so.

Saving is an instinctive Eastasian response to uncertainty, and the energy field is no exception. Since the oil shock of 1973, short sleeves have been the rule in government offices, with air conditioning and even elevators discontinued as economy measures in several countries. Governments in Japan, South Korea, and Taiwan have encouraged conservation by raising drastically the prices of gasoline and other oil-based consumer products. The price of gasoline in Tokyo, for example, approached $4 a gallon in 1980, nearly twice the price in Europe and three times that in the United States. In South Korea as in Japan, government has discouraged the expansion of energy-intensive industries such as copper smelting. Only in Taiwan, where such industries are particularly vital suppliers of the export sector, have these industries' energy inputs continued to receive a degree of subsidy. Not surprisingly, the conservation record of Taiwan has fallen behind that of its neighbors.

In Japan, energy expenditures have increased only half as rapidly as the GNP. Japan's framework for coordinating energy conservation is the Moonlight Project, a brainchild of the 1973 oil shock. By 1978 this set of administrative guidelines on industrial consumption laid down by the Ministry of International Trade and Industry had produced substantial savings in oil consumption per unit of production: 5.4 percent in aluminum, 9 percent in steel, 11.2 percent in petroleum refining, 18.5 percent in cement, and 20.9 percent in automobile production. In 1976 the Japanese economy was saving 10.1 percent of the energy consumed per unit of GNP in 1973; the equivalent figures for West Germany and the United States were 6 percent and 3.1 percent, respectively.[28]

Hong Kong and Singapore suffer less from the rising cost of energy than their more heavily industrial neighbors to the north. Hong Kong, which has practically no energy-intensive industry, has been affected by rising prices only through their effect on world trade levels. Singapore does have energy-related industries, including oil refining and (from 1981 on) petrochemicals, but virtually all the production of these industries is for reexport. Thus, Singapore can pass along rising energy costs to the ultimate consumer.

The Energy Outlook

Energy is potentially the Achilles' heel of industrial Eastasia. Less than a decade ago, sudden price increases shook the region to its foundations. Yet the countries of the region have neutralized many of the effects of the energy shortage by intensifying links to OPEC, developing alternate sources of energy, and diversifying sources of oil supply. They have saved energy more assiduously than any other part of the world, partly by adjusting their industrial structure and partly by patriotic appeals. They have overcome the balance-of-payments effects of each price increase by aggressively selling manufactured goods and construction services at appropriately increased prices to the oil suppliers.

This record suggests that flexible institutions and dynamic policies can continue to produce successful responses to changing factor costs, in energy as in other fields. It would be surprising if industrial Eastasia failed to weather future storms of energy uncertainty better than those industrialized nations that lack a coherent national policy. Should Japan, Korea, or Taiwan discover offshore oil in sizable quantities, they could easily outperform Britain, Norway, and the Netherlands, the North Sea oil producers. And should China's potential for energy production and export be realized, the future for Eastasia would be brighter still.

Case Study: Hyundai—Tackling the Energy Challenge

In the Korean language, "Hyundai"—the name of Korea's largest construction, engineering, and heavy industrial group—means "modernity." For Korea, and indeed for Eastasia more generally, the essence of "modernity" during the past decade has been the energy crisis. Few organizations better epitomize the complexity, the ingenuity, the vitality, and at times even the futility of the Eastasian response to that crisis than the appropriately named Hyundai Group.

In the response of Korean institutions to the energy crisis, one sees the Eastasian dilemma in microcosm, albeit in extreme form. One sees, first and foremost, vulnerability—70 percent of South Korean energy consumption is for either industrial use or electric power generation, so demand cannot easily be adjusted downward, over the short term, to compensate for reduced supply. Nearly 80 percent of total energy is imported, including 100 percent of the nation's petroleum. As noted earlier, over 97 percent of that precious commodity comes from the politically volatile Middle East.[29]

Korea imports more oil than any other Eastasian nation except Japan; in 1980, for example, Korea imported $5.64 billion of crude oil, in comparison with Taiwan's $4.10 billion.[30] In proportion to the size of its economy, Korea is affected more sharply by oil price increases than any other nation in Eastasia. In 1974, following the first oil shock, the increase in Korea's import bill over 1973 came to 5.8 percent of GNP; the analogous figure was 3 percent for Japan and much less for most other nations of the world.[31]

Korea is also profoundly affected by cutbacks in the supply of oil available on the world market. Because it has no powerful, established trading organizations to bid for scarce oil supplies on world markets as Japan does, and because it cannot command the sympathy of multinational oil firms as the United States and most European countries do, Korea not only finds itself taking disproportionate cuts in oil supply in times of world shortage but also has difficulty in building sufficient stockpiles. Thus, when the Organization of Arab Petroleum Exporting Countries (OAPEC) announced a reduction of 12 percent in oil supply to the international majors in May 1979, the majors in turn cut their supply to Korea by a whopping 24 percent.[32] While Japan casually accumulated a 110-day supply of oil during 1979–80 as a buffer against future oil shocks, Korea could not manage even half that.[33]

For South Korea, in short, energy security is an issue no less pressing than the military threat from the North Korean tank divisions poised across the demilitarized zone and the Han River, just 60 miles from downtown Seoul.

How to offset the impact of oil shocks on the domestic economy, develop alternative sources of energy supply, and decrease reliance on foreign oil is a pressing question of national survival. Although in many nations an issue of this gravity would be handled exclusively by government ministries or public corporations, in Korea there is a substantial role for private groups such as Hyundai.

The Hyundai Group is a loose association of six firms that together make up the strongest construction-oriented conglomerate in the non-Western world. The outlook of the group tends to be intensely nationalistic: Hyundai has spearheaded Korea's move into heavy industry, in direct competition with Japan. Hyundai Construction, the central firm in the group, was founded in 1947 by Chung Ju-Yung, former farm boy from Kangwon Province; for fifteen years the confidant of Park Chung-hee, Hyundai's founder has served as president of the Korean Federation of Industry since 1977. The firm thrived on barracks and airfield construction for the U.S. military during the Korean War, and grew even faster during the reconstruction boom at the end of the conflict. During the rapid national expansion of the 1960s, Hyundai undertook many of the large-scale infrastructure projects promoted by President Park, including the Soyang Dam, six major bridges over the Han River, the Chosun Hotel in Seoul, and the new National Assembly Building.[34]

Hyundai's diversification into international operations began with the outbreak of the Vietnam War. Mobilizing old contacts from the Korean War, Hyundai's Chung garnered contracts in 1966 to build the Pattani-Narathiwat Highway in northern Thailand, and subsequently to dredge the Camranh Bay, Vungtau, Mytho, and Binlong ports for the U.S. Navy. Focusing its efforts once more on Korea after the Tet Offensive, Hyundai spearheaded President Park's top-priority project for construction of a superhighway from Pusan to Seoul, with the president himself frequently hovering overhead in a helicopter to review the work as it progressed. The project, 428 kilometers long, was completed in a breakneck thirty months, at one-seventh the cost of Japan's Nagoya-Tokyo Highway, which is comparable in length.

Hyundai Construction's competitive potential has been enhanced since 1970 by the creation of numerous specialized support firms and other heavy industrial companies with which it works closely within the Hyundai Group. In addition to the long-established building-materials manufacturer, Keumkang Co., and the Hyundai Motor Co., founded in 1967, the group includes such new affiliates as Hyundai Cement (1970); Hyundai Heavy Industries (1973); Hyundai Engineering (1974); Hyundai Mipo Dockyard Co., a ship repairer (1975); the Asia Merchant Marine Co., which leases out Hyundai-built vessels (1976); Hyundai Corp., the group's international trading arm (1976); Hyundai

Precision and Industry (1977); Inchon Iron and Steel (1978); Aluminum of Korea (1978); and Hyundai Fluoro Chemical Industries (1978). By the end of 1980 there were 25 Hyundai affiliates, most of them in industries closely connected with construction.[35]

When the first oil shock plunged the Korean economy into turmoil in early 1974, Hyundai was ready to respond. The group aggressively sought construction contracts in the Middle East, organized a Korean construction work force prepared to live in the deserts of Iran, Kuwait, and Saudi Arabia for years at a time, and mobilized a vertically integrated network supplying cement, structural steel, engineering services, and even lumber on Hyundai-built ships run by Hyundai's own shipping line. To ensure adequate political leverage, Hyundai employed the son of Crown Prince Fahd, Prince Mohammed bin Fahd, as its "sponsor" in Saudi Arabia, where its most intensive efforts were focused.

The results were dramatic. During the entire 1966–75 period, all Korean firms combined had received only $1.5 billion in Middle East construction contracts; in 1976, Hyundai alone garnered $1.4 billion, as the Korean total soared to $2.5 billion.[36] Over the 1975–80 period, Hyundai built Jubail industrial harbor in Saudi Arabia, three Saudi desalinization plants, a ship repair yard in Bahrain, gas-processing plants in both Abu Dhabi and Iran, and oil refineries, power plants, and highways throughout the region. Perhaps the ultimate tribute to Hyundai capabilities was the request in early 1977 that the firm's diligent Korean workers build the private palace, complete with mosque, of Prince Abdullah bin Abdulaziz, commander of the Saudi Arabian national guard.[37] Slowly and painstakingly, Korea's construction firms, led by Hyundai, won back from the Islamic world the petrodollars that had been captured by a stroke of the OPEC pen in December 1973. As indicated in table 11–2, Korea's gross earnings from construction contracts in the Middle East by 1978 exceeded its total oil imports, having climbed nearly a hundredfold since 1974.

When Korean non-oil trade with the Middle East is also taken into consideration, Korea had nearly a $1.5 billion surplus in transactions with the Middle East in 1978, and a substantial portion of this was due to the activities of the Hyundai Group.

The Iranian revolution, the second oil shock that followed it, and the Saudi purification drive in the wake of the Mecca uprising of late 1979 all brought renewed problems to Korea and Hyundai. With the rise of the Ayatollah Khomeini, construction plans in Iran fell into chaos, and after months of confusion Hyundai's workers in Iran were finally repatriated to Seoul. Just as Korea's annual oil bill spiraled to $6 billion in 1980, turmoil in Iran and politically inspired accusations of bribery against Hyundai in Saudi Arabia threatened the firm's ability to aid Korea in offsetting the balance-of-payments

TABLE 11–2
Neutralizing the Oil Shock: Korea, 1974–78

Year	Oil imports (millions of dollars)	Gross Middle East construction earnings (millions of dollars)	Balance (millions of dollars)
1974	1,010	23	−987
1975	1,490	585	−905
1977	1,890	1,200	−690
1978	2,190	2,200	10

SOURCE: Unpublished World Bank data.

effects of the 1979 oil shock. Yet during that same year the firm was still able to garner over $850 million in construction receipts, more than 40 percent of Korea's worldwide total.[38] In mid-1980, Hyundai Construction still had $3 billion in outstanding contracts on order in the Middle East and was developing other OPEC markets, including Nigeria and Indonesia.[39] And Hyundai Construction's sister firm, Hyundai Heavy Industries, was ready to bid actively for contracts under Saudi Arabia's new five-year plan (1980–84), aided by then President Choi Kyu Hah, who flew to Riyadh and Kuwait in May 1980 on Hyundai's behalf. Despite adversity, the Korean OPEC offensive continues, spearheaded by Hyundai, which in 1979 was the world's eighth-largest construction firm and the seventy-eighth-largest industrial corporation outside the United States.[40]

Much of Hyundai's construction experience in the Middle East has related to the oil industry. In the early 1980s, Hyundai began using this expertise to garner foreign exchange closer to home. After preliminary work for Exxon on liquefied natural gas exploitation offshore from Malaysia, Hyundai in early 1981 won a major $87 million contract to build gas-extraction facilities off the eastern coast of Honshu, Japan.[41]

In addition to helping neutralize the balance-of-payments effects of oil price increases through overseas construction work and vigorous export activities, the Hyundai Group has also helped Korea develop alternate sources of energy supply. In July 1980, Hyundai Corp., the group's trading arm, signed a joint agreement with Mitsui of Japan and CSR of Australia for the extraction of coal in Australia for shipment to Korea.[42] In this, the first energy-related overseas development venture involving a Korean firm, Hyundai once again led the way.

In the early 1970s, Hyundai, at the direct request of President Park, turned a sandy beach at Ulsan into a state-of-the-art shipyard for supertankers within thirty months.[43] Just as it once strained every muscle to build supertankers to carry Korea's and the world's oil, so now is Hyundai Heavy Industries plunging heavily into coal-carrier construction. Currently the firm has several 130,000-ton coal carriers on order from major multinational oil firms and Greek shipping magnates; some undoubtedly will, in not so many years, carry Hyundai-mined coal across the South China and East China seas to help ease Korea's energy shortage.

For the government of a resource-poor nation with rapidly expanding energy needs and little fear of citizen dissent, nuclear power often looks like an attractive option. Taiwan, the Philippines, and to some extent Japan are all vigorously promoting the nuclear option, but none can match Korea, which expects nuclear plants to supply 79 percent of its electrical power by the year 2000.[44]

Once again, Hyundai, as the torchbearer of national purpose, has been at the forefront. In June 1976, Hyundai was given the green light to construct an integrated plant at Changwon capable of producing various kinds of sophisticated equipment for nuclear power plants. Korea's first nuclear power plant, a 587,000-kilowatt installation dedicated at Kori, near Pusan, in July 1978, was built by Hyundai Construction, in cooperation with Westinghouse.[45] During late 1980 a restructuring of Korean heavy industry initiated by President Chon Do Hwan led Hyundai to agree to transfer its facilities for the production of electric power equipment, including nuclear equipment, to the new state-owned Korean Heavy Industry Corporation. But Hyundai's deep involvement in providing Korea with alternatives to OPEC oil continues, as does its responsibility for building all four Korean nuclear plants under construction at the end of 1980.

The Hyundai Group is not an energy corporation in the tradition of Exxon or British Petroleum. But there is no such energy corporation native to Eastasia. Even Taiwan's China Petroleum, the only well-established energy specialist firm indigenous to the region, has no major involvement outside of oil and is involved only in importing—not extracting or refining—that resource. Multi-industry conglomerates such as Hyundai, or Mitsubishi and Mitsui in Japan, are at the heart of Eastasia's response to the energy challenge. And considering the magnitude of the challenge, it is quite a formidable response.

12

The Export Offensive

IN 1965, few Americans had ever seen a Toyota, a Datsun, or a Subaru. Fifteen years later, a quarter of the new cars on American roads were Japanese. In 1965, goods of any sort from the Chinese mainland were contraband in the United States; by 1980, Chinese textiles were flooding fashionable stores throughout the nation. Over the past decade, Eastasian exports have seized major U.S. market shares in everything from children's shoes (South Korea) to cotton socks (China), canned mushrooms (Taiwan), electronic games (Hong Kong), and advanced computer circuitry (Japan).

Seen in quantitative terms, the advance of Eastasian exports into U.S. markets has been extraordinarily rapid, particularly since the world recovery during 1975–76 from the first oil shock.[1] Japan's exports to the United States grew over twenty-three fold by value between 1963 and 1980, nearly double the growth rate of imports from France and triple that of imports from Britain.[2] Combined exports to the United States from South Korea, Taiwan, Hong Kong, and Singapore grew a spectacular forty-eight fold—from a small base, but much faster than exports from other newly industrializing nations like Brazil and Mexico, which are much closer culturally, institutionally, and geographically to the United States.[3] As figure 12–1 shows, by the mid-1970s Eastasia, led by rapid export growth outside Japan, had overtaken Europe as America's chief supplier of manufactured goods. As the 1980s began, Eastasia held a decisive and livening lead.

The United States is not alone in facing a rapidly rising tide of Eastasian exports. Even Italy, with its rigid quantitative controls on imports of Japanese and other Eastasian products, has seen those imports rise more than sixfold

FIGURE 12-1
Eastasia vs. Europe as a Supplier of Manufactured Imports to the United States,
1963–80

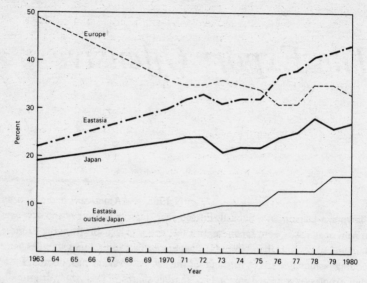

SOURCE: Organization for Economic Cooperation and Development, *The Impact of the Newly Industrializing Countries on Trade in Manufactures.* Paris: Organization for Economic Cooperation and Development, 1979, p. 72.
NOTES: (1) Figures for Europe are for the Organization for Economic Cooperation and Development member nations in Europe.
(2) Figures for Eastasia are for Japan, Republic of Korea, Taiwan, Hong Kong, Singapore, and China.
(3) All trade figures are F.O.B.

since 1963, and margins of increase have been much greater elsewhere.[4] But nowhere in the advanced world has the sheer scale of Eastasian market presence reached the levels attained in the United States. In 1977 over 37 percent of the $74.9 billion in manufactured goods this nation imported came from Eastasia (the comparable figures for Britain and France were roughly 9 percent and 5 percent, respectively).[5] And the ratio has risen substantially since then as figure 12–1 suggests.

Eastasian inroads into Western markets have come in a wide range of product lines, with Japan providing the cutting edge in the more technologically sophisticated sectors. As the bar graph (figure 12–2) shows, aggregate Eastasian shares in OECD import markets are highest in ready-made clothing, because of the extraordinary 30 percent share in this category held by Eastasian countries outside Japan. But market shares are also large, and growing rapidly, in the area of electrical machinery, on the strength both of growing Japanese competitiveness in high-technology sectors (such as computers) and the diffusion of more standard production processes (for television sets, radios, discrete device components, and so on) to South Korea, Taiwan, Hong Kong, and Singapore. Japanese industry has made inroads into traditional European domestic markets for steel and for transportation equipment, including ships and, increasingly, automobiles.

Both private business and government throughout Eastasia have been obsessed with exports at key stages in their developmental processes. In virtually all cases, a perceived sense of economic vulnerability has been a driving force behind the impressive displays of export strength. But the concrete reasons for

FIGURE 12-2
Eastasia Penetrates Western Markets

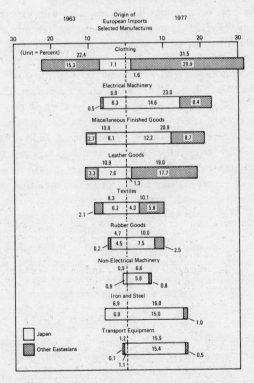

SOURCE: Organization for Economic Cooperation and Development, *Impact of Newly Industrializing Countries,* p. 24.

173

export orientation, and the nuances of export policy itself, have varied significantly from country to country. To truly understand the Eastasian export offensive, one must examine in detail both the strategic problems that induce Eastasians to export and the responses of individual nations, and firms within the nations, to these challenges.

The Export Imperative

The imperative to export is clearest in the cases of South Korea, Taiwan, Hong Kong, and Singapore—the "Gang of Four." These nations literally live by trade, with ratios of foreign trade turnover to GNP in 1979 of 54 percent, 83 percent, 160 percent, and 189 percent, respectively.[6]

Behind the impressive figures lies an obsession with export that is little appreciated in the West. Both private business and government share this obsession, which has fed on these nations' sense of economic vulnerability. Though the reasons for pursuing certain exports may vary, each country has responded to what it perceives as a threat posed by the world economy.

Each of the "Gang of Four" has a tiny domestic market. The largest had a GNP in 1979 of only $62.5 billion, or about one-fortieth that of the United States.[7] None can rely solely on a strategy of reducing import costs by emphasizing heavy industries such as steel, petrochemicals, and shipbuilding, all of which require very large-scale production, as well as the latest technology, in order to be profitable. The imperative of economic growth therefore compels these nations to export in order to pay for needed industrial goods.

Further incentive to export comes from lack of raw materials, most notably food. Population densities (which average 431 persons per square kilometer among the Eastasian "Gang of Four" but only 22 in the six most dynamic non-Eastasian NICs, with which they are often compared) are among the highest in the world,[8] and scarce arable land simply cannot meet the food requirements of the local population, particularly in an era of improving diets. Of the four, only Taiwan is self-sufficient in food production and able to turn its rich agricultural land into an exporting asset. Several of the Eastasian NICs face pressing food shortages, especially the island states of Hong Kong and Singapore, which depend heavily on neighboring agricultural states for nourishment and even in the case of Hong Kong, drinking water.

Finally, none of the exporting prodigies of the region has native energy resources. In Taiwan and especially in Korea, the lack of domestic oil and the need for imported oil and gas have triggered massive payments deficits that make exports even more critical. Korean oil imports, for example, rose from about \$2.3 billion to well over \$6 billion from 1978 to 1980, forcing the nation to find more export markets or to increase borrowing in the international credit market.[9]

Each of these national imperatives for exporting was important in producing the Japanese miracle at an earlier stage of history. During the first third of this century, Japan's domestic market was small, its population dense, and its resource base poor. Between 1883 and World War I, exports crept up from 5 percent of national income in 1883–87 to 11.8 percent in 1898–1902 and then to 20.2 percent in 1913–17.[10] Sustained by sales of textiles to Japanese colonies and to former British markets in China and Southeast Asia, exports remained at that level until the end of World War II. Only since the takeoff of the Japanese economy into postindustrial maturity have these ratios dropped to more reasonable figures (in 1978, around 11 percent).[11] By contrast, the NICs of Eastasia presently are averaging over 50 percent in their drive for economic growth, with Korea the straggler in the pack at a mere 30 percent in 1980.[12]

Like its four smaller neighbor, Japan must supply many of its basic needs through imports. More than 90 percent of Japan's consumption of oil, iron ore, copper, aluminum, nickel, wool, cotton, soybeans, corn, and wheat comes from outside the country. In fact, the only significant raw materials in domestic supply are coal and lead, with no more than one-quarter of each produced domestically.[13]

Japan's export drive has moved far beyond the immature current phase of the "Gang of Four." As the Japanese economy has grown, the importance of exports for stimulating economic growth has diminished. Japan's exports presently serve different functions: for example, they offer incremental growth for relatively mature industries such as automobile manufacturing. Whereas in 1979 domestic auto sales in Japan fell to 6.5 percent below the 1973 level, production surged by 38 percent on the strength of exports.[14] Exports have saved the Japanese automobile industry from the slow death presently being suffered by U.S. automakers. Japan now exports over half of its automobile production, as opposed to less than a third in 1973.[15]

Although the export ratio for Japan as a whole has steadily declined since World War II, there has been a consistent tendency for the export ratios of specific industries to rise as these industries mature. In 1960, for example, only 11.4 percent of Japan's steel was exported; by 1974 this ratio had risen to 30.2 percent.[16] After modest beginnings with small-scale industries during the 1960s, Japan currently exports one out of every two watches and two of every three cameras it produces. Within less than ten years (1970–78), Japanese exports of numerically controlled lathe machine tools rose from 4 percent to

53 percent of total production.[17] Whereas domestic shipments of computers have recently grown no more than 15 percent annually, the Ministry of International Trade and Industry forecasts that exports will grow at twice that rate for the 1980–85 period.[18]

Another important function served by the Japanese export offensive is that of offering markets for immature companies. In Japan, as elsewhere in Eastasia, established companies rely on their own carefully cultivated distribution systems, which are designed to shut out competition. Distributorships are exclusive, so that a marketer of Hitachi television sets has financial incentives not to sell those manufactured by Sanyo. Since a new Japanese firm experiences the same difficulty that an American television manufacturer might have in breaking into such a "locked-in" market, it is to that firm's advantage to explore export opportunities. Little wonder that the number-two and number-three firms in many Japanese industries show a higher export ratio than the top-ranked company.

Let us cite some Japanese examples of this phenomenon. In the steel industry, number-one Nippon Steel's export ratio in 1979 was 32 percent, the lowest of the top four steel firms.[19] In autos, industry leader Toyota's percentage (32) was substantially lower than Nissan's (41).[20] In electronics, top-ranked Matsushita had an exports-sales ratio of 16 percent, less than half that of its major competitors Sanyo (40 percent), Sharp (48 percent), and Sony (61 percent).[21] In general, this tendency for later-arriving companies to dominate the export markets was greater before the first oil shock of 1973, but it remains quite striking.

Yet another reason for the Japanese export offensive may be found in the unusual cost structure of Japanese companies. Firms in Japan have lifelong commitments to their employees, requiring them to pay wages even during periods of domestic economic slump. They also rely heavily on bank loans to supply capital, instead of on shareholders' contributions. Unlike stock dividends, which can wait until profits are earned, interest on loans must be paid regularly even when operations are not profitable. These pressures on management provide strong incentives to continue production throughout the domestic business cycle. Quite naturally, managers turn to markets outside Japan to fill in the gaps. This explains why Japan's export offensives seem to coincide with downturns in the Japanese economy rather than with upturns.

China, in sharp contrast to Japan and the Eastasian NICs, is more than self-sufficient in raw materials. Like present-day Japan, but unlike Meiji Japan and the current NICs, China has a massive internal market to sustain growth, as well as a large domestic economy that remains remote from international trade. Though China has been exporting more in absolute value than any of the small Eastasian NICs (about $10 billion a year), this effort represents less than 2.5 percent of China's GNP.[22]

China's incentive to export lies largely in its need to earn foreign exchange to pay for imports of foreign technology and specialized industrial equipment that China cannot yet produce. Decades of bad experience with international lenders have instilled a powerful fear of deficits and borrowing into China's leadership. While the intention of China's leaders during the "four modernizations" was originally to pay for imports with raw materials and particularly with surplus petroleum, since 1979 the Chinese have been unable to free up such primary products, largely because of declining success in petroleum exploration and development. Already China has begun to enter to a significant extent the export markets formerly dominated by the smaller Eastasian countries—cotton cloth and finished goods, common pharmaceuticals, and light industrial items.[23] China has recently passed the Philippines as America's leading source of cotton handkerchiefs, Sri Lanka as our source of tea, and India as our primary supplier of foreign floor coverings.[24] It will not be long before China, despite its inward orientation, becomes as aggressive in seeking export markets as any of its smaller Eastasian neighbors.

Honing Trade Competitiveness: The Role of Government

Despite the traditional insularity of China, Korea, and Japan, export has become a way of life in modern times. Even at the start of modernization, Eastasia exported traditional products such as silk and tea to obtain European manufactures. Industry grew on the profits from agricultural exports, even when these exports were badly needed to feed and clothe disadvantaged populations. When traditional governments isolated foreign traders in enclaves, they did so because they recognized the disruptive effect of imports on a backward economy. The earliest export operations from Eastasia took place with official sanction (despite the Confucian bias against commerce) and with direct government involvement in the revenue stream. The perception that trade policy is an integral part of national economic policy, which in turn underlies national strength and prosperity, is old and deeply rooted in this region.

Modern Eastasian governments thus follow ancient practice in recognizing the interdependence of various sectors of the economy, the strategic importance of self-reliance, and the need for national revenues to pay for national purchases. Even China, the least export-dependent country in the region, fiercely insists on maintaining a favorable balance on trading accounts to prevent becoming dependent on the outside world. The Hong Kong government, which is noted for its outdated noninterventionism, still intervenes strongly to encourage exports—as it recently has by investing several hundred million dollars of state funds in a large port to handle containerized cargo. "Japan, Inc." received its nickname largely through the Tokyo government's aggressive backing of exporters in international competition.

Lest it be thought that we exaggerate the attention given to export issues, let us cite the example of South Korea under President Park Chung-hee. In 1964, when Korean exports first topped $100 million, President Park declared November 30 as Export Day—an annual national holiday to commemorate the nation's export success.[25] In 1965, Park began holding monthly sessions of the National Expanded Trade Promotion Meeting.[26] Each month for more than fifteen years, Park and his successors have invited key ministers and economic advisers to this high-level gathering at the Blue House to discuss recent progress toward meeting the year's national export targets. The group examines Korean export progress sector by sector, nation by nation. The president himself demands solutions, and if problems arise abroad, he may even travel to the affected area to help resolve them, as then President Choi Kyu Hah did in the case of Saudi Arabia in 1980. Every ambassador is assigned a quota of exports to his mission, for which he is personally responsible. In all these ways, South Korea makes exporting a matter of top national priority.

How can governments help increase competitiveness in the dog-eat-dog world of international trade? At first glance the question appears to be foolish. Are not exports the products of businesses rather than governments? Is it not the responsibility of corporations and trading companies to meet foreign competition? Though these are important truths, the Eastasian case suggests that there is much that governments can do to enhance the growth of sales abroad.

For one thing, most Eastasian governments recognize that industry depends on energy and that low-cost output depends on the lowest possible factor or input costs. In modern, energy-intensive countries, this means that utility prices—which determine the costs of electricity, natural gas, and coal to industry—must be kept low. In Eastasia, governments owned utilities even before there were industries to use them, and this is still the case everywhere but in Hong Kong, Singapore, and postwar Japan. Even in these island states with private utilities, industrial power rates are much lower than personal rates. In 1965, at the height of Japan's growth spurt, industries paid utility rates only 38 percent as high as those paid by individuals and families; the comparable proportion in Britain was 81 percent.[27] These benefits of consumer-subsidized energy are possible because governments (and the people who elect and support them) recognize the national importance of industry.

Another example is government support for basic industry. In modern economies this means steel, petrochemicals, shipping, and even semiconductors. Meiji Japan encouraged "target" industries (so called because they were the targets of government support and subsidy for strategic reasons) by setting up factories under state ownership and then selling them to private interests once they had become viable. South Korea, Singapore, and especially Taiwan are currently developing publicly owned, efficient basic industries, though few companies have been transferred to private hands thus far. (An exception is Inchon Iron and Steel, purchased in 1978 by the Korean giant, Hyundai.) Postwar Japan continues to encourage basic industry, though now largely through tax and credit policies, since government owns relatively little. Without this kind of support—which allows Japan to produce inexpensive steel, for example—the prices of Japanese autos would be much higher abroad.

Even with cheap energy and raw materials, companies might still fail to compete because they are inefficient or greedy. To reduce this possibility, the Japanese government through the Ministry of International Trade and Industry has exercised selective control over markets. In oil refining, for example, MITI encourages furious competition by licensing more than two dozen firms to enter the industry. On the other hand, MITI selects only large firms for the petrochemical sector and insists that they build very large (and hence more efficient) factories. The government has a large menu of devices to encourage high-volume development based on low profit margins. Large facilities, which may write off their investments in as little as two years, thus enjoy enormous tax savings (accelerated depreciation schedules); they may qualify for government financing through the Bank of Japan or the Ministry of Finance; and they may receive private assurances of government support if excess capacity causes major losses. In the United States this form of support might be called a "bailout"; in Japan it is called *yamagoya,* an economic shelter built by the state to protect climbers bolder than the rest.

The opposite side of the coin is that firms and businesses which do not offer the nation an export advantage are often discouraged or even dismantled. An example is Japan's aluminum refining business, which lost its competitive edge when energy prices leaped upward in the 1970s. Whereas in the United States political pressures might have forced government to protect such an inefficient sector, in Japan government squeezed out much of its own aluminum industry by encouraging offshore preprocessing, discouraging new investment or expansion, and even encouraging cheaper imports. It is now beginning similar pressures on steel producers in the face of rising competition from Korea and elsewhere. Imagine the outcry in the United States if the Department of Commerce were actively to encourage the import of Japanese steel and the winding down of employment in inefficient American mills. Yet the result of this seemingly brutal policy is to strengthen Japan's export edge by reducing the prices of industrial imputs, even as American cars, ships, and machinery become too expensive to sell abroad because of the rising cost of protected steel.

This is not to say that Eastasian countries eschew the practice of protecting their industry with import duties and quotas. Quite the contrary: the pattern of protectionism has been loud and clear. During the early postwar period, for example, Japan, Taiwan, and South Korea all had vigorously protectionist programs, allowing most domestic industries to develop behind high tariff walls until they became viable and competitive. In the early 1970s the Japanese government resisted demands from competing nations to stop sheltering its computer industry behind a maze of bureaucratic restrictions and sweetheart purchasing arrangements. China not only restricts large-scale imports, but it also permits firms to import only those items that China cannot expect to produce within the next five years, or else only those quantities necessary to acquire the technology of production.

Eastasians see protectionism as a means rather than an end. When an industry is mature, it should be able to meet the strains of international competition or else disappear. Thus Taiwan abandoned large-scale tariff support for "import substitution" purposes in 1958–60, South Korea followed suit in 1963–65, and Japan dismantled many import barriers after joining the OECD in 1964. Japan's willingness to participate actively in free-trade talks under the General Agreement on Tariffs and Trade (GATT) and the "Tokyo round" of the Multilateral Trade Negotiations (MTN) coincided with the maturation of Japan's industrial plant in the mid-1960s and with Japan's great export surge during that decade.

Hong Kong and Singapore, with their free-port traditions, have even been more open in their commitment to the sink-or-swim strategy of exposing industry to international competition. Their governments realize that the only way to beat the competition is to be quicker and better. Lacking both a significant domestic market and the larger strategic problems of preserving basic industry, the smaller Eastasian states have made export competitiveness virtually the sole criterion of viability. They are pradigms of Eastasia's modern "outward-oriented" growth policies, which recognize that the rewards of success come to the exporter of finished goods at the highest price for the lowest cost. These policies are inherently riskier—and, if they fail, potentially more disruptive politically—but they offer the promise of rapid growth in today's dynamic markets.

To Dump or Not To Dump: The Question of Subsidies

Many critics have asserted that Eastasian nations support their exports by unfair trade practices such as export subsidies and "dumping"—the sale of products at less than cost. The American steel and automobile industries, for example, have long asserted that Japan's export prices do not reflect the true cost, since they seem so much lower than Japan's domestic prices. Over a number of years, for example, Japanese prices for steel delivered in the United States not only undercut the minimum prices American firms were capable of, but also came in substantially lower than prices quoted within Japan for the same product. This pricing strategy was termed "predatory" because it seemed aimed as much at destroying American domestic competition as at selling Japanese goods. The same charges have been laid against Taiwan in television sets, Korea in shipbuilding, and Hong Kong in textiles.

The case against "dumping" is very difficult to prove as a matter of law, although it is prohibited by several American statutes. About thirty formal charges are leveled in the United States each year against Japanese exporters alone, in sectors ranging from crude steel to microwave ovens.[28] Many of these cases are intended not so much to be proved as merely to be noted, in order to generate protectionist sentiment or to harass Japanese exporters into raising prices. Japanese steel manufacturers have been able to show, for example, that their low American prices are possible because they sell exports at or near the *marginal* cost of production. The cost of producing *one more ton* of steel once a large plant is in operation is much less than the cost of producing a ton of steel averaged over the entire production cycle.

In most cases where it can be shown that prices below marginal cost were accepted, the exporter has been able to prove that he resorted to dumping to avoid bankruptcy; several such cases involving Japanese producers of ball bearings and special steel arose after the 1973 oil shock. The Japanese electronics industry is accused of having dumped products such as color television sets during the early 1970s and semiconductors in 1978–79 in order to "gain production experience" at a loss, though the net effect of their actions was to undermine American producers. Such cases by and large do not involve government collusion.

There can be little argument about the fact that Eastasian countries have been able to sell in foreign markets in large part because they can accept lower prices than the competition—though in recent years, sophisticated consumers have been willing to pay premiums for Eastasian products such as Sony video tape recorders. Still, the major edge has been price. But the reasons for Eastasia's price advantage are far more complex than the critics recognize.

Only very rarely have Eastasian governments directly subsidized companies to allow them to price exports below cost. The closest example of such a direct subsidy is the "export credit" offered by the government export-import banks of some Eastasian countries. In South Korea, for example, a company that wishes to borrow money on its ability to export can do so at an interest rate less than half that charged on domestic sales: if it can show an export invoice to the bank, its rate for commercial credit will be less than 10 percent instead of the normal 20 percent. This preferential treatment amounts to direct encouragement of lower export prices by the South Korean government. Its effect is compounded by the preferential treatment given by the South Korean government to general trading firms that meet national export goals.

The Japanese government is constrained by its agreements under GATT and MTN not to use such indirect subsidies blatantly. Instead, it helps exporters in other ways. Japanese government support for the very large scale integration (VLSI) research consortium has important implications for Japan's future ability to export semiconductor integrated circuits, since it allows firms to cut research expenditures;[29] yet it does not constitute a direct subsidy, because private companies will ultimately be required to reimburse the state. The Japanese government's export-import bank does make inexpensive loans to promote exports to the Third World, but these are explained as a form of "foreign aid" and not as export subsidies.

Other examples of government support permitting lower prices abroad are more subtle and complex. It is true that governments sometimes inflate the prices of domestically sold products far above cost, so that the same products sold abroad may be priced more cheaply. Hyundai Pony autos, for example, sold in Korea in 1980 for $8,000 to $10,000, far above their actual cost, whereas prices for the same car delivered to Latin America ranged between $3,000 and $4,000.[30] The high domestic price is possible because the government puts steep tariffs on imported Japanese cars, which would otherwise be able to dominate the Korean market. This form of subsidy by domestic protection is widely practiced in Taiwan, Japan, and China, especially in relation to consumer goods. A Chinese one-speed bicycle selling for $120 at home can be exported for a fraction of that cost without losing money overall.

Yet another form of implicit government support for cheap exports is tax policy. Like Japan, South Korea has a system of tax reserves for overseas market development. A company with plans for future exports may set aside pretax income into a reserve fund which may later be used for such purposes as establishment of overseas offices, foreign advertising, bonuses to distributors, or even foreign-language training for employees. Both nations also offer special accelerated depreciation on plants and equipment used for export production, as well as exemptions from customs duties on export-related imports of materials and capital equipment. This last tactic has also been used in Taiwain since the 1950s, though Taiwan's tax incentives for export are less extensive than Japan's or Korea's.

In addition to material incentives, Eastasian countries also offer intangible help to companies wishing to export. Central export advisory offices have been established in virtually every country. The earliest of these was the Japanese Export Trade Organization (JETRO). Established in 1958 as an affiliate of MITI, this organization maintains a staff of more than 1,200 people and has 109 branch offices, including 7 in the United States.[31] Serving mainly smaller firms that do not have their own foreign specialists, JETRO publishes regular reports on trade conditions in the outside world, answers inquiries, and brings together businessmen with common experiences. In the late 1970s, for example, JETRO encouraged foreign businessmen desiring to trade with China to contact Japanese firms with experience in that country.

Korea and Taiwan have established similar agencies. KOTRA, the Korean Organization for Trade Advancement, established in 1962 and modeled closely after JETRO, already has 74 branch offices.[32] The China Exports Trade Development Council (CETDC), created in 1970, aims to help Taiwanese business to trade with that majority of the world's nations with which the Republic of China has no diplomatic relations. To serve this function, CETDC remains legally nongovernmental, though half its initial endowment came from the government. Even the People's Republic of China has an active body called the China Council for the Promotion of International Trade, which helps introduce Chinese manufacturers to potential buyers abroad. The contrast between these activist, export-oriented public agencies and our American bureaucracies, committed largely to regulatory tasks rather than trade promotion, could not be more striking.[33]

A final device for export promotion, first developed and now widely applied in Eastasia, is the so-called "export processing zone" (EPZ). In some ways the precursors of the modern EPZs were the foreign enclaves in premodern China and Japan. The current concept is of a small piece of real estate on which companies are permitted to build factories that operate outside the domestic economy, importing and exporting their supplies and products without duties of any kind. The first modern EPZ was created in 1966 at Kaohsiung, on the southern tip of Taiwan,[34] but the concept has spread to Korea and the People's Republic. By 1980 there were two such zones in South Korea (at Masan since 1970 and Iri since 1973). China announced in 1980 the formation of six "Special Economic Zones," four (Zhuhai, Shekou, Shenzhen, and Shantou) in Guangdong Province and two (Xinglin and Langqui) in Fujian Province. Singapore established the Jurong Industrial Estate in 1968 to perform many of the functions of an EPZ in the context of a free economy.

Of course, government policy is not the sole determinant of export potential, nor even the most important. We suggest that many other characteristics of the Eastasian political economies act to enhance export potential. A long tradition of quality control, first developed through a rich culture of handicraft production, continues to make Eastasian products attractive. Extensive private networks of the general trading companies, which for decades have been committed to expanding markets and facilitating international trade, continue to find outlets for Eastasian producers who themselves are too small or too insular to deal in foreign countries. The special international relationship between the United States and most of the Eastasian nations—with Japan as our protégé after defeat, with Taiwan and South Korea as our client states after the rise of Communism, and now with China as our newfound ally against Soviet hegemonism—has made us more tolerant of the export offensive than we might have been. We must also realize that we, too, have a stake in the Eastasian capacity to export.

Eastasia's Export Offensive: How Far Can It Go?

The American industrial plant, last refurbished in many sectors during World War II, nearly four decades ago, is chronically aging. Eastasian competitiveness, born of coherent industrial policy and efficient private-sector organization, is rapidly rising. And the Eastasian urge to export—fueled by private-sector rivalry, saturation of domestic markets, fervent desires for economic growth, and, at base, a pervasive sense of national vulnerability—is becoming ever stronger as the 1980s progress. If market forces alone are allowed to determine transpacific trade patterns, then the "semicolonial" nature of U.S.-Eastasian trade (whereby the United States exports raw materials and Eastasia provides manufactures with an ever higher value-added content) could well be intensified. How long would America be likely to tolerate such an outcome?

One of the most striking developments in international economic relations during the past fifteen years has been the rapidly rising stake of foreigners, particularly Americans, in the Eastasian export offensive. Virtually all the large U.S. electronics producers, including General Electric, RCA, and even Zenith (which led the political fight against alleged Japanese "dumping" of television sets during the 1970s) have moved the bulk of their consumer electronics production to Eastasia. These firms now use the region as their primary production base for supplying the United States and other markets with radios, television sets, and video tape recorders.

Siemens and Philips from Western Europe have done likewise. In minicomputers and mass-produced integrated circuits, such as 16K and 64K random-access memories, parallel trends have become increasingly visible. Western auto, precision-machinery, industrial-plant, and other types of manufacturers are buying larger proportions of their components from Eastasia, as well as subcontracting assembly operations to the lower-wage countries of the region and to adjacent countries such as Malaysia, Indonesia, and the Philippines.

As has been noted, retailers in the West have also relied increasingly on Eastasia, both for labor-intensive sundry goods and for more technologically intensive products such as typewriters, sewing machines, and microwave ovens. A growing proportion of the private-brand merchandise that such stores stock, including many of the smaller appliances produced under the Sears Kenmore label, is also made in Eastasia. Since the early 1970s, the purchasing by retailers has shifted from Japan to Hong Kong, Taiwan, and Singapore. But such buying remains largely within Eastasia and continues to generate substantial profits for the retail chains.

Western banks, ranging from multinational institutions such as Chase Manhattan to seemingly local operations like the New England Merchants Bank, have a strong stake in Eastasian export success. For the large multinationals, much of the commitment is to governments and government financial institutions, notably in Taiwan and especially in Korea, whose economic viability depends on their export prospects. The multinationals also have multimillion-dollar funding commitments to such export-oriented, private-sector industrial projects as the Changwon Machinery Complex in Korea or the Jurong Industrial Estate in Singapore. For the smaller Western banks, the commitment to Eastasian export success is often less direct but no less significant for their profitability. In sharp contrast to Western Europe, more than half of whose trade transactions are in local currency, Eastasia conducts over 90 percent of its rapidly growing foreign trade in U.S. dollars. Since Eastasian (principally Japanese) banks have no direct access to dollar-denominated deposits other than those entering their U.S. subsidiaries, these banks need to borrow substantial sums in interbank markets from U.S. financial institutions. For funds-surplus U.S. regional and local banks, interbank lending to Eastasian banks, or even directly to Eastasian exporters for trade finance, is often a substantial source of business. It is also one that disperses the American stake in Eastasian exports throughout the U.S. economic system in politically significant ways.

Another major form of grassroots involvement in Eastasian exports comes through the U.S. distribution system. As has been noted, nationwide retail chains have a strong stake in Eastasian exports. So do the local distributors of such consumer products as autos, stereos, and television sets. Since Eastasian exporters traditionally pass along an unusually high share (by Western standards) of total profits to distributors, these distributors have a direct interest in a continued high level of Eastasian exports to this country. And they are well placed to exert grassroots pressure on the political system to ensure that such flows continue.

Two other major pillars of support for a free-trade policy that offers Eastasian exports unimpeded access to U.S. markets are domestic raw-materials producers and the port authorities in cities such as Los Angeles, San Francisco, Portland, and (increasingly) San Diego, which handle ever larger volumes of trade with Eastasia. For the raw-materials producers in states such as Montana, Oregon, and Washington, prosperous Eastasian economies mean expanding export markets and higher prices for their products. For the port authorities, expanded trade, in both imports and exports, likewise has positive implications.

Trade with Eastasia is not, of course, an unmixed blessing, either for America or for the world's other industrialized economies. The textile belts of the Carolinas and Lancashire, together with the industrial heartlands of the U.S. Midwest and the German Ruhr, might be better off, at least over the short term, if Eastasia did not exist. Were it not for the inroads made by Japanese autos in the U.S. market, Detroit would most likely not have had 15 percent unemployment during the grim winter of 1980–81. But the domestic U.S. casualties of Eastasia's export offensive have been surprisingly few and far between, given the scale of the onslaught. And they will most likely not increase as rapidly as transpacific trade itself.

One reason for this is the relatively narrow concentration of Eastasian exports in a small number of sectors, such as autos, clothing, steel, and electronics. A second is that Eastasian exports have by design generally tended to fill gaps (*sukima* in Japanese) in the U.S. domestic supply structure, rather than meeting domestic products head-on. It was the Japanese, for example, who created the mass American leisure market for motorcycles, which until the 1960s were almost exclusively the preserve of gangs and other marginal groups. It was also the Japanese who created the video tape recorder, which has not displaced any Americans from their jobs because there have been, through 1980 at least, no American producers.

In the final analysis, the growing positive stake of Americans in the East-asian export offensive, means that the offensive will probably continue without substantial political interruption. The likelihood of this outcome is reinforced by the offensive's relatively minor negative consequences for Americans individually. As the 1980s proceed, Honda's car carriers will continue to plow eastward, over heavy seas, toward Los Angeles. But they will return to Yokohama increasingly brimming with coal.

The prospects for politically unimpeded Eastasian trade with Europe appears less sanguine. For one thing, Europe lacks the exportable raw materials and foodstuffs that the United States, Canada, Australia, and many of the less developed countries (LDCs) can use to balance their trade with Eastasia. More so than the United States, Europe has a high concentration of the heavy industries and small businesses that are most vulnerable to Eastasian competition. Finally, Europe and Eastasia do not share to the same degree the national security interests that act to cement the alliance between the United States and Eastasia. New joint-venture arrangements between European and Eastasian firms—for example, those in the auto industry between Honda and British Leyland, Nissan and Alfa Romeo, and Nissan and Volkswagen (the last involving construction of production facilities in Japan)—could be one important means of mitigating the incipient tension between Europe and Eastasia, although they may slow the growth of Eastasian exports.

In an era of economic stagnation and rising protectionist pressures in the industrialized West, particularly Europe, the brightest future for export expansion appears to lie in the developing world. Some regions, such as Latin America and Africa, are virtually virgin territory. Others, such as the Middle East, are areas where Eastasian exporters have recently become established but where rapid economic growth justifies even further efforts. Throughout the LDCs, the price-competitiveness of Eastasian products and the organizational flexibility of Eastasian marketing mechanisms will reinforce tendencies (in motion since the first oil shock) toward a closer identification of Eastasia with the developing world. Indeed, one of the major trends of the last two decades of the twentieth century may be the evolution of important new ties between Eastasia and the Third World, supplanting those of the past hundred years between the LDCs and the West. Such an evolution, should it occur, could well give new momentum, though a different geographical direction, to the Eastasian export offensive.

Case Study: Taiwan's Export Processing Zones— Offshore Production Base for the World Market

Inside the gleaming white stucco fence surrounding the Kaohsiung Export Processing Zone in southern Taiwan, General Electric, Hitachi, Philips, Canon, and 128 other companies produce goods for the world market.[35] Just as in Hong Kong, Taiwan's commercial rival 300 miles down the Formosa Strait, companies manufacturing in the Kaohsiung EPZ pay no duties on raw materials and components imported, and no taxes on finished goods exported, provided that all goods produced are sold abroad. Essentially, the government of the Republic of China has allowed these firms to create offshore manufacturing bases in which, for customs purposes, the world beyond the gleaming white stucco fence does not exist.

The EPZ concept combines the ideas of a free-trade area and an industrial park. Goods pass into the duty-free zone without being charged import fees, and factories are encouraged to locate there because they receive advantageous rates for the use of land and electric power. Many nations in Asia, Africa, and Latin America now have implemented this concept, including Taiwan's neighbors in Indonesia, the Philippines, South Korea, and even the People's Republic of China. But the world's first such zone came into being here in Kaohsiung in the early 1960s.

The Republic of China at the time was facing a serious threat to its plans to free itself from dependence on American foreign aid. Without some source of foreign-exchange earnings, the island was likely to run extensive international trade deficits. Neighboring Hong Kong was emerging as a major competitor in the growing trade linking the Eastasian countries with the United States and Europe. In September 1963 the ROC ministers of economic affairs, finance, communications, and national defense, along with other top economic officials, inspected the harbor at Kaohsiung, on the sandy southwestern shore of the island, and decided to convert an existing harbor extension project into a much larger program. The project received the highest priority from the central government. In July 1965 the preparatory office of the Kaohsiung EPZ began taking applications for investment, and in December 1966 the zone began full-scale operation with 52 factories. Most of the lessors were world-class industrial companies, many of them specializing in consumer electronics, an industry which was then discovering the advantages of using Eastasian labor.[36]

The Kaohsiung EPZ offered these firms not only low-cost labor and exemption from customs duties, but also substantial tax concessions. These included waivers on sales and commodity taxes and the choice of either a five-year corporate income tax holiday or a favorable accelerated depreciation rate on fixed assets. In addition, the EPZ supplied warehousing and transportation services, prepared building sites, and offered factory building loans in addition to export financing against letters of credit. To cut red tape, the EPZ administration was authorized to act for the ROC government in all its roles. This meant that factory owners dealt with the same people on such matters as import and export licensing, foreign-exchange settlement, company registration, construction licensing, and so on.

Not surprisingly, the response of international investors to Taiwan's investment package was strongly favorable, and industrial locations in the Kaohsiung EPZ were quickly oversubscribed. In 1970 two further EPZs, at Nantze and Taichung, were established. Ten years later, more than 70,000 workers were employed in the three zones, making products ranging from guitars (Yamaha) to sewing machines (Brother), television sets (Grundig, Philips, General Electric, Hitachi), and integrated circuits (GE).[37] As of late 1980 the EPZs had generated substantially more than $300 million in foreign investment for Taiwan and had helped boost the nation's foreign trade balance from $7.8 million in 1969 to $201.4 million in 1974 and $594.6 million in 1979.

The impact of the EPZs is greatest on the fortunes of the multinational corporations, particularly those of Japan. Seventy percent of the investment in the EPZs from 1966 through 1980 has been foreign, and 53.7 percent of that total has been Japanese, with the Japanese share rising steeply since 1973. The major target of these exports has been the United States, which received 42 percent of all the Taiwan EPZs' products by value in 1979, as opposed to only 18 percent for Japan and 10 percent for Hong Kong. The most deeply affected industry is electronics, which accounted for 57 percent of the zones' total output during the same year. In fact, at least one-third of Taiwan's entire electronics industry production takes place in the three export processing zones.

The export processing zones illustrate some key features of Taiwanese industrial and foreign trade policy. First, they demonstrate not only considerable sensitivity (perhaps greater than that of any other Eastasian political economy) to the needs of multinationals, but also the willingness of the ROC government to assist them in establishing offshore manufacturing bases for export to the U.S. and European markets, and secondarily to Japan. They also illustrate the strong commitment of the ROC government to the provision of public goods through state action, especially through the operation of public depreciation policies or fine gradations in tax schedules to influence the sort of firms that arrived. The only tool available was the ability to deny an investment application. Consequently, from the government's point of view, applicants tended to bring Taiwan export power but little new technology and know-how. The zones seemed destined to produce factory after factory taking short-term advantage of the relatively low wages of Chinese laborers, often largely untrained rural women. These were not the modern industrial plants that Taiwanese planners hoped would be built to serve the future.

During the 1970s, however, this picture began to change, as labor shortages grew and competition from cheaper-labor countries increased. The government began to conceive of a successor to the older EPZs that would attract high-technology companies. In 1980 the Hsinchu Science-based Industrial Park, modeled after the Stanford Industrial Park in California, opened amid much fanfare. This park, some 45 miles south of the capital city of Taipei, spreads across 5000 acres and includes two universities and the semigovernmental Industrial Technology Research Institute. A core of about 550 acres is set aside for private laboratories, small factories, housing, and public facilities.[38]

To this new zone the government is drawing high-technology firms through an incentive package structurally similar to those of the older EPZs, though fine-tuned to encourage sophisticated research and manufacturing. The public services offered to investors now include a computer center, a school for foreign children, and modern housing—all these in addition to the amenities offered in Kaohsiung. Moreover, new policies to encourage high technology include offers of venture capital from the Taiwan government (up to 49 percent) or free land rental for up to five years for particularly desirable tenants. They also illustrate the market-oriented bias of ROC economic authorities in matters of foreign economic policy, an approach that is curiously at variance with traditional Chinese bureaucratic approaches to regulation. In the Hsinchu Park and especially in the EPZs, most of the incentives come in the form of removal of state impediments to private action, rather than in the form of extensive government subsidies and subventions, as is more common, for example, in France and Korea. In a curious way, the EPZ concept most closely resembles a much older Eastasian institution: the "factories" that Chinese authorities permitted foreign traders to open at Canton in the 1830s. Perhaps this is why the concept has taken such deep root in the Republic of China, a country with a long memory.

Part IV

THE OUTSIDE
WORLD

13

Regional Co-prosperity

THE POLITICAL and economic systems of Eastasia, as we have noted, often benefit from the synergy they develop as a whole. Over the last decade, expanding trade, investment, and technology transfer within the region have contributed significantly to Eastasia's growing prosperity and competitiveness with the West.

Eastasia as a region of the world has at least as much economic potential as North America or Europe. That the region hangs together geographically cannot be disputed: today more than a quarter of the world's population lives within three hours' flying distance from Shanghai. This population is physically less diverse than the peoples of Europe, possesses many common cultural traditions and social characteristics, and has historically always thought of itself as a unit. Eastasians have in recent times interacted far more strongly, and often more violently, with each other than they have with other parts of the world. Eastasian countries have borrowed shamelessly from each other, recklessly invaded each other, discriminated heavily against one another, and presently trade competitively with one another. If such rivalries could block the emergence of large continental regions, we would hardly have a European Economic Community today.

The loudest opponents of the concept of Eastasian regional integration are some Eastasians themselves. A number of Japanese, in particular, are concerned that after struggling for over a century to be recognized as a member of the club of industrialized nations, Japan might suddenly be excluded from that club by virtue of her special position within Eastasia. Thus Japanese policy always stresses that, despite major commitments to investment and rapidly growing trade and aid in the region, Japan is "playing no favorites." The analogy with the American-leaning opponents of Britain's entry into the EEC is suggestive: as soon as it became apparent that building closer ties between Britain and its continental neighbors would not hamper a strong transatlantic connection with the United States and Canada, their opposition vanished. Similarly, Pan-Asian sentiment lies beneath the surface in Japan, waiting for a legitimate expression, as could be seen in the emotional welcome extended to Chinese leaders Deng and Hua at the end of the 1970s.

The major problem may come from the other side. Fears of closer relationships in Eastasia are often expressed by the smaller nations, who fear a resurgence of Japanese imperialism, at least of an economic sort. Singapore is particularly adamant, actively encouraging Western nations to stay and balance off the rising Japanese presence. Many Koreans and Taiwan Chinese today stress the importance of maintaining independent ties with America and Europe, as well as their preference for American or European products. Especially since President Park's death in 1979, South Korea has tried to diversify trade away from Japan to other nations of the region.

But since Japanese traders are the middlemen who supply these products to Eastasians, it may be a losing battle. China's leaders are determined not to lock themselves into an exclusive relationship with Japan, despite the prominence of Japanese firms in the China trade. Again, Western technology may well be imported into the People's Republic, but it is more likely to come indirectly, through representatives of Japanese trading companies or overseas Chinese, than directly through Sino-American contacts and trade.

Japan's Leadership Role

The fundamental economic fact of the region is that its nations are beautifully complementary. Japan, having mastered the skills of Western technology, continues to serve as a role model for the development of its neighbors. And its neighbors, including the People's Republic of China, continue to be excellent pupils. Forty percent of all Japan's technology exports go to other nations in Eastasia, which in turn rely on Japan for as much as two-thirds (in the case of South Korea) of their imported technology.[1] Japan runs a current surplus in intraregional trade, the others largely deficits.[2] Co-prosperity, based on Japan's dominant economic position, is becoming an ever clearer reality.

It is also inevitably a part of the future. Japan desperately needs resources and markets; the other nations will make a sizable and growing market for Japanese products, and increasing exports of Chinese raw materials can supply some of Japan's resource needs.[3] As other Eastasian nations modernize, they will spend their growing purchasing power on Japanese products, which will be cheaper and better than those imported from farther away. Japanese investment will continue to rise, as Japan finds it advantageous to offer better terms to gain access to the cheaper labor markets elsewhere in the region.[4] Even China should be no exception to this trend; Japan is already at the head of the queue seeking to enter the narrow but already opening door to trade and investment in the People's Republic.

Consider the rapid rise of Japanese manufactured imports from elsewhere in the region. These soared from only $79 million in 1968 to over $3.2 billion ten years later, by which time they made up more than 15 percent of Japan's manufactured imports. Especially important were imports with high labor content, such as textiles and footwear. But capitalist Eastasia also supplied one-seventh of Japan's iron and steel imports and nearly a fifth of its electronics (both up from near zero ten years earlier). Clearly the other nations of the region have learned quickly from their teacher in those fields where Japan was once preeminent.[5]

The electronics industry is an excellent example of the Japan-led synergism of the region. In 1970 virtually all the electronics trade, in components and assembled products, traveled across the Pacific to the United States. But the region has dramatically increased its internal trade in semiconductors, integrated circuits, and finished products, especially since 1974. In that year Japan exported one-third of its integrated circuits to other Eastasian countries; by 1978 that portion jumped to over two-thirds, or more than $200 million worth of chips. By 1980, Japan–South Korea bilateral trade in electronics reached the half-billion-dollar level, with rapidly growing trade in watches, television sets, and electronic components on both sides. Hong Kong, Taiwan, and Singapore have each targeted electronics as export specialities, even as they increase their imports of components and consumer electronics. In many ways, electronics is the leading edge of Eastasian regional integration, and the massive integrated-circuit production facilities of Japan are its new Silicon Valley.[6]

In resources, too, there is great potential for intraregional development. China is known to have the world's largest untapped coal reserves—possibly exceeding a trillion tons—which sorely need capital and infrastructure to be developed.[7] Japan is the main customer, currently taking 2 million tons a year, and China is urging it to take more—up to 10 million tons by 1985.[8] While China is eager to exploit its own natural resources for domestic development, foreign aid is essential. Japan is the natural source of this aid, and thus the natural beneficiary of China's backwardness.

An intriguing example of the possibilities of Sino-Japanese collaboration is an agreement signed in late 1978 calling for Japan to deliver up to $10 billion worth of high-quality steel and other industrial products in return for large volumes of Chinese crude petroleum.[9] This ambitious barter agreement, conducted on terms very favorable to the Chinese, has encountered difficulties because of China's inability to meet the volume requirements of the deal. After an abrupt moratorium on several key projects (including the billion-dollar Baoshan steel complex, on which construction had already begun), the two sides revived talks on $3 billion in Japanese advances to keep the deal alive. Whatever the outcome, the pattern of Sino-Japanese cooperation is now established.

Japan, for its part, clearly sees little advantage in concentrating on Chinese resources so long as the rich mineral deposits of Oceania, Latin America, and the United States are available at reasonable prices. Japanese politicians and trade strategists have been urging the formation of a Pacific trade zone, including Australia and Latin America, to minimize the likelihood of disruption in the lifelines of Japan's industrial growth. But the Japanese have also been working quietly to establish special relationships with the Chinese, just in case access to the rest of the world should be blocked by depression, war, or widespread protectionism. Eastasian regional cohesion may be hastened by anti-Eastasian threats from Europe and America.

The non-Japanese opponents of Eastasian integration likewise may be resisting an inevitable trend. The reasons they cite to justify their opposition to an expanded Japanese presence in their countries are many, and in fact have little to do with the historical experience of Japanese empire-building. The smaller or less-developed countries fear that Japanese trade and investment will not particularly benefit their own populations, since the Japanese trading companies all tend to play a self-serving game. Japanese business people outside the home islands are often clannish, showing little interest in local languages and customs. Their trading companies tend not to employ many resident nationals of the countries they penetrate. Moreover, they treat non-Japanese markets as opportunities to continue the vertical integration of the organizations they built in Japan. To be sure, Japanese often concede equity positions in local undertakings more rapidly than Western firms, but except where long-term strategic issues are at stake, the Japanese tend to strike harder bargains and to stick to them more rigidly than do Europeans or Americans.

Bitter memories of World War II continue to complicate Japan's economic ties with both North and South Korea. But even in Seoul major groups such as Samsung and Lotte make major efforts to span the most yawning psychic gap in the region. Elsewhere in Eastasia, complaints about the "ugly Japanese" do little to interfere with smooth business and political ties, and are not nearly so often heard as in less dynamic states like Thailand and Indonesia. Take the case of the China trade. Recognizing the strategic importance of the China connection to their nation's future, Japanese firms and the Japanese government have consistently offered more generous terms and more creative approaches than have Westerners. As in other strategic fields, the Japanese take the long-term view that sacrifices are necessary before the market can be established. Furthermore, the long-standing Japanese fascination with China, Korea, and Taiwan has left a large corps of experts on those countries whose skills can be tapped by business. Several Japanese trading companies maintain large staffs of China hands (many born and raised in the People's Republic) in the hope that someday trade will justify their employment. Since many hundreds of these trained specialists speak Chinese and understand Communist Chinese business practices, they offer the Japanese trading companies enormous advantage over Western corporations that have not begun to do their homework. In China, "ugly Japan" has a more beautiful image.

Forces for Regional Integration

There are many objective reasons why the nations of Eastasia should develop closer economic ties: they have complementary economies, parallel development patterns, and extensive historical ties in trade and commerce. Moreover, there is a growing organizational interest in greater intraregional cooperation.

Japanese trading companies, for example, have long had a powerful stake in trade within Eastasia. These companies, which both preceded and followed the Japanese army and navy in their expansion outward, have long-established bases in each of the other Eastasian states. Today nearly half of Taiwan's and nearly a third of Korea's entire foreign trade (import and export) is handled by Japanese trading companies. Textile and steel imports from Eastasia to Japan have been dominated by these companies, with non-Japan marketing abilities growing only slowly. Only recently have trading companies been formed by Taiwan, China, Singapore, and (notably) South Korea to compete with Japan's virtual monopoly of the sea and air lanes of the region.

In the 1970s a new set of actors with a stake in regional economic integration began to emerge. Several Tokyo department stores, such as Isetan and Matsuzakaya, entered the trade business with a flourish, aggressively importing clothing, accessories, and household goods from Hong Kong and Singapore. Japanese watchmakers and other electronics firms developed a lively direct trade in components and finished products with other countries in the region; commerce in this sector has grown explosively since 1975. Large shipping and charter companies, such as those of Y. K. Pao and C. Y. Tung of Hong Kong, expanded to handle the heavy traffic lanes between Tokyo and Singapore, using ships manufactured in various parts of Eastasia. Each of these interests benefits as intraregional ties expand, contributing to the growing domestic pressure for further economic integration.

Even before the great trading companies of Japan rose to prominence, Eastasia already possessed the beginnings of an integrated economic system. The extensive, business-oriented overseas Chinese community is still the background of much of Eastasian trade outside the trading companies. Though statistics are hard to find, it seems likely that the major share of trade among the five members of the Association of Southeast Asian Nations (ASEAN), including Singapore, is conducted through firms controlled by overseas ethnic Chinese. In this sense the Chinese already provide, through their extensive family and business connections, the means for regional integration. Unlike Japanese business, Chinese commercial activity is not highly organized into vertical systems. Instead, it follows highly complex connections, often hidden behind unimposing façades or using non-Chinese front men.

Hong Kong plays a pivotal role in these dealings, particularly since trade and contacts with both the People's Republic and the Republic of China can be conducted from the sanctuary of a nominally British colony. Hong Kong

TABLE 13–1
Intraregional Trade Expands: Percentage of Eastasian Nations' Trade With Other Eastasian Nations

	1972	1978
Japan	9.1	14.1
Singapore	21.0	25.0
Hong Kong	31.5	33.7
ROC	34.3	29.3
ROK	39.5	34.5
China	30.5	36.0
Total	18.0	20.9

SOURCE: International Monetary Fund, *Direction of Trade Yearbook, 1979,* pp. 170–71; *China Business Review,* July–August 1980, p. 35.

depends heavily on the PRC for its livelihood; in turn, the PRC depends on Hong Kong for access to foreign exchange and foreign commercial know-how. It is no surprise that the majority of early joint-venture operations established in China pursuant to the Joint Venture Law of mid-1978 were conducted by non-PRC Chinese, some from as far away as Australia. An example is the $50 million Great Wall Hotel being planned for Peking by C. B. Sung, an American-Chinese entrepreneur formerly associated with Cyrus Eaton, Jr. Overseas Chinese can speak the language, know how to make profitable deals, and are willing to take a smaller piece of the action in order to benefit the motherland.

Political Divisions and the Future of Trade

If Eastasia as a region is to meet its potential for synergistic economic development, the major political divisions of today will have to be carefully managed. The region is half-Communist and half-capitalist, part "East" and part "West" (in the global bipolar sense of the words), though as often in Eastasia, the directions are reversed. Bridging the gap will require great effort, but a beginning has been made. Hong Kong already acts as the entrepôt for the nascent China-Taiwan trade, some of it contracted for by Japanese trading companies or their "dummy" representatives. In a triangular relationship that may set the pattern for the future, North Korea exports coal to Japan, which sells electronics to China, which in turn supplies North Korea with light industrial products.

Economic integration need not imply a dramatic reorientation of political systems. Such a change does not appear likely, nor is it really necessary. China can open its economy without abandoning either its Communist goals or its Communist Party; Taiwan can trade with the motherland just as Hong Kong does today, without losing control of its political destiny. The only requirement is that all these countries pursue the pattern of mutual benefit and mutual noninterference, already laid down. As Liao and Takasaki, the founders of Sino-Japanese trade, declared in 1957, "Politics and economics are separate matters."[10]

Although the particulars are far from clear, China seems open to change in its relationship with Taiwan. Having achieved diplomatic recognition and acceptance into international councils, Beijing is now less wary of "contamination by Kuomintang elements," and imports stamped "made in Taiwan" can occasionally be seen in Chinese cities. Overseas Chinese who formerly kept close ties with Taiwan now feel comfortable visiting the motherland: among China's guests in early 1981 was Anna Chennault, the staunchly Nationalist widow of General Claire Chennault (of Flying Tigers fame), as unofficial representative of the new Republican administration in Washington. Whereas in previous years China paraded a small handful of Taiwanese exiles (including members of the minority hill tribes) as representatives of the Taiwan "liberation movement," the PRC now offers warm hospitality and even some publicity to former enemies with major standing in Taiwan who come for a visit. The public pardon in 1978 of several hundred former Nationalist generals who had been held under house arrest in Beijing did not go unnoticed in Taipei. Two-way trade, already a surreptitious reality during the 1970s, began in 1980 to approach the quarter-billion-dollar mark.

At the same time, the Beijing government must, for domestic political reasons, continue to claim its absolute right to invade Taiwan at any time. But in practice, this is the least likely option. Even a trade embargo or blockade is doubtful, since it is more likely to rally the island's population against China than to crush the island's economy or produce disaffection with the government. The most likely scenario is that of China's increasingly enticing the Taiwanese business community into ties of mutual benefit.

Of course, Taiwan sees all this as further evidence of Beijing's subversive intent, as indeed it may well be. The ROC government still prosecutes people for acting as go-betweens with the Communists, and it strictly embargoes trade items from China (though it is an open secret that for decades the mainland has been the source of many of the traditional medicines and gourmet food items imported from Hong Kong). Here the reality of increasing trade relationships will continue to be hidden beneath the impression of implacable hostility. It seems likely that over the long run the relationship between the PRC and ROC will improve, since Taiwan could supply large quantities of industrial goods, commercial products, and know-how to an acquisitive China. Though the likelihood of a sudden breakthrough does not seem great, the change should happen gradually over the next decade or two.

The future of divided Korea is more difficult to foresee. In many respects, South and North have highly complementary economies, with North Korea possessing the mineral deposits and the industrial base, and South Korea a larger population and more agricultural resources. The rapid political changes after the assassination of President Park Chung-hee in late 1979 have not changed the highly suspicious view that most South Korea businessmen take of the North's intentions. And North Korea remains, after fiercely xenophobic Kampuchea, the most intransigent of the Communist nations on the issue of

East-West trade. But anyone familiar with the tremendous energy and ability of the Korean people, as well as their competitive spirit, must recognize that should the peninsula be reunited, the result would be a close copy of Japan's success in a nation of more than 50 million.

Already we find South Korean firms looming as a major presence in the Middle East. Occasionally they play major roles in joint ventures with Japanese firms, as did Samsung in cooperating with Kobe Steel to erect a major steel mill at Misurata, Libya, beginning in 1981. More typically, the major Korean trading companies compete head-to-head with their Japanese counterparts, often unseating them through aggressive bidding and promises of rapid project completion. Korean trade with Taiwan, Hong Kong, and especially Singapore also continues to increase rapidly, particularly in the wake of President Chon Do Hwan's 1981 overtures toward Southeast Asia.[11]

Indeed, this visit suggests a possible reorientation of Korean international concerns back toward the region after years of emphasis elsewhere. Korean steel, petrochemicals, and cement compete vigorously with Japanese products in many markets within the region. Here and in the trade patterns of the other "new Japans" exchanging high-quality, low-cost manufactured goods across the region, we see growing strength in the sinews of Eastasia and an intensification of the Eastasia Edge.

14

The Rest of the World

SPEAKING from the ramparts on the Gate of Heavenly Peace in Beijing on October 1, 1949, at the founding of the People's Republic of China, Mao Zedong surveyed the fruits of his party's struggle for control of China. "China has stood up," he said simply, summing up the momentous achievements of a generation. After thirty years of revolt, his Communist movement had succeeded in "liberating" China and asserting its independence from the old economic order. Though some Chinese doubted that the break with the outside world needed to be so complete, most applauded Mao's efforts to make China "stand up" in the world of nations.

Independence, autarky, and self-determination have been goals of Eastasia since the beginning of systematic contact with the outside world in the eighteenth and nineteenth centuries. The Chinese fought several wars in a losing effort to block Westerners from penetrating the China coast with their Bibles and opium; China's "self-strengthening" movement was echoed in the slogan "Revere the Emperor, Expel the Barbarians" in Meiji Japan. Despite these profound sentiments for independence, Singapore and Hong Kong became British colonies, Taiwan and Korea became Japanese dependencies on the Western model, and Japan itself was occupied by American troops in 1945. Throughout nearly a century of Western presence in Asia, Eastasians surrendered control over important aspects of their economic and political lives to foreigners. But they never abandoned their determination to get back in control.

Eastasians perceived as humiliations many features that were common to the "civilized" Western world of the nineteenth century—most notably, the demands of foreigners for freedom of movement, for the right to own property, for the ability to trade without government interference, and for the opportunity to peddle their religion. Through "treaty ports" in China and tariff-restraining agreements in Japan, the West imposed a free-trade system that guaranteed Western access to the large markets of the Orient. From 1866 to 1911, Japan was prohibited by treaty from raising tariffs above 5 percent ad valorem; after 1858, China lost control of all its customs rules and procedures to an Imperial Maritime Customs commissioner, who was invariably British. In all the Eastasian nations the principles of most-favored-nation status and extraterritoriality for foreign residents were established early and lasted until the middle of this century.[1]

World War II brought more changes to Eastasia than it did to Europe. Japan started the Pacific war because it wanted independence from Europe and America, and thought it needed colonies and assured supplies of raw materials to achieve it. The defeat of Japan and the meteoric rise of American power in the Western Pacific between 1945 and 1950 brought a temporary halt to the growth of Eastasian independence. Despite the collapse of the old colonial order during the war, the region once again had to shape its needs to those of an outside power. The reconstruction of Japan and the strengthening of America's anti-Communist allies in Taiwan and South Korea brought further foreign involvement in the region's economies—developments matched in China and North Korea by the growth of Soviet economic influence during the 1950s.

Today, three decades after Mao's famous speech, we can begin to discern the emergence of the independent Eastasia that has long been the dream of politicians in the region. Not that the new Eastasia has or will cut itself off from world trade or from defense or political alliances with nations outside the region, but it is already making such links increasingly by choice and not by chance. It will never again limit itself to subservient relationships with the European world.

A glance at the changing patterns of world trade (table 14–1) is instructive. In 1970 nearly half of Japan's exports went to trading partners in the industrialized West. By 1980 that proportion had dropped to a little over 40 percent, and reputable forecasts suggested a reduction to little more than one-third by 1990. Conversely, the best estimates are that Japan's exports to the developing world will increase from slightly over 50 percent in 1980 to 55 percent in 1990, with the overwhelming portion going to the Middle East and to other Eastasian states. By 1990, Japan will be exporting to the developing world more than half again as much as it exports to the West. From these figures one can

TABLE 14–1

The Decline of the West in Japanese Trade

	Exports (%)			Imports (%)		
	1970	1980	1990	1970	1980	1990
Industrialized West	48.6	41.1	33.9	44.7	31.7	31.9
Developing world	43.4	50.7	55.1	41.4	56.5	55.8

SOURCE: Figures for 1980 and beyond are Japan Economic Research Center estimates. See Ministry of Finance, *Summary Report: Trade of Japan,* March 1980.

NOTE: Figures for the industrialized West include data for the United States, Western Europe, and Canada. Figures for the developing world include data for Eastasia and Southeast Asia (including China), the Middle East, Latin America, and Africa.

discern that Japan is likely to become not merely less dependent on the former centers of imperialist power, but a world power center in its own right. As trade goes, so goes the nation.

An indication of the growing independence of Eastasia from the West can be found in its expanding relationship with the Middle East. Eastasia's demand for crude oil forces it to turn to all available sources, and this means, by and large, the Arab nations. In return, Middle Eastern governments, which have been accepting large-scale turnkey plants and major engineering projects as payment for their energy, demand increasing influence in Eastasian capitals. The shift toward the Middle East is characteristic of all the capitalist Eastasian economies except Singapore's. For Taiwan the transition has been speeded up by America's rejection of Taipei in favor of Beijing. South Korea's wooing of the Saudis is all the more intense because of the former's strong rivalry with Japan for petroleum.

Access to raw materials is another area of growing Eastasian independence from the West. As late as 1978, 80 percent of Japanese oil imports were supplied by the major international oil companies; by the end of 1980 that proportion had fallen well below 50 percent.[2] Elsewhere, oil formerly supplied by the majors now comes through general trading companies and through government-owned oil firms such as South Korea's PEDCO, Japan's JNOC, and Taiwan's China Petroleum. These organizations now work with OPEC governments and national oil companies on a direct-dealing or government-to-government basis.

This new autonomy has important implications. During the Iran crisis of 1979, the Japanese government finally yielded to U.S. pressure and agreed to boycott Iranian oil. But the persuading required several months and took effect only after the price of Iranian crude drifted back up to world market levels. Eastasian nations have favored the Arab side of the Palestine dispute ever since the Japanese began to "tilt" that way following the 1973 Arab-Israeli war. As time goes on, economic diversity will inevitably lead to political self-determination.[3]

Even as the United States tries to expand its exports of raw materials like lumber, coal, and soybeans to Eastasia, the nations of the region are turning away from their single-source policies of the past. Japan, for example, is buying coal from Australia, both because the price is cheaper and because the Americans are unable to provide the railroad and harbor facilities needed to export the necessary quantities. While Eastasia's general trading companies are the largest buyers of American soybeans in the world, they still diversify to Brazil or other Third World markets whenever possible, because they fear we may embargo soybeans as we did during the summer of 1973. America is now seen as a less than reliable supplier, since in soybeans, shrimp, lumber, and other areas we have occasionally imposed sudden, inexplicable stoppages of trade. Hence Eastasia is diversifying its sources, much as we are seeking (but not yet finding) independence from the Arab oil cartel.

Symbiosis with the Third World

Behind these patterns of deepening trade relationships between Eastasia and the developing world lies a complementarity which neither group of nations shares with the developed West. This symbiotic relationship, born out of the resource shortages and industrial competitiveness of Eastasia and the development imperatives of the Third World, is mediated by the great Eastasian trading companies.

The advanced countries, particularly Japan and Singapore, import light manufactured and semiprocessed goods such as textiles, black and white television sets, and plywood from the Third World. They have made the conscious choice not to protect these industries at home, even though in former years these very products were substantial earners. Third World countries are thus the beneficiaries of advanced Eastasia's farsighted policy of allowing less sophisticated and less competitive industries to die at the hands of the market, while concentrating on the technology-intensive sectors in which advanced economies have a real comparative advantage. This attitude contrasts sharply with that of many Western countries, whose protection of dying sectors continues to frustrate newly developing nations with competing infant industries.

Trading companies are willing and able to promote the products of poorer nations elsewhere in the world. These companies profit by generating trade, whenever it may occur, so they increasingly seek third-country trade with which Eastasia may have no direct connection at all. The Mitsubishi Corporation of Japan, for instance, handles over half the nonleather footwear imports into Europe and America—most of which originate outside Eastasia.[4] The Daewoo Corporation of South Korea exports tires from the Sudan to other African countries. Such firms are becoming important to many dollar-short countries as earners of foreign exchange.

Western nations have responded to the Eastasian challenge by raising artificial barriers to imports. As recently as May 1981, the U.S. government reached an understanding with Japanese automakers limiting their exports to the United States through 1984. Since antitrust law prohibits the U.S. government from entering into restraint-of-trade agreements, this particular accord took effect without even a name of its own. But as a result, goods on which there are artificial import limits now make up 43 percent of Japan's exports to the United States.[5] Surprisingly, nearly half of Korean and a third of Taiwanese exports fall under some form of quota or treaty restriction.[6] Europe is even more dependent on import restrictions than we are. The fact is that to sustain growth and pay for raw materials, Eastasia must continue to export, and if the West is unreceptive, Eastasia must look to other parts of the world. We have driven Eastasia to seek alternate partners.

This need to diversity export markets coincides nicely with the growing hunger in the less-developed world for inexpensive capital goods. Saudi Arabia's purchase of Korean cement plants, Indonesia's acquisition of aluminum smelting equipment, and Brazil's purchase of steel mills from Japan all permit these countries to process their raw materials more cheaply—and, in turn, to supply these materials to Eastasia for a lower price. Eastasian nations are happy to export these capital goods, partly to gain access to the raw materials and partly because they are preparing their own economies for higher-technology production.

All the nations of the region except China are short of raw materials and concerned about resource security. Increasingly affluent, they can pay top prices for assured sources of supply. Again they find willing suppliers among the less-developed countries, which need stable, relatively high prices and long-term commitments for purchases of the raw materials that are often their major export.

Since the early 1970s the region has faced rapidly rising domestic wage costs.

These have been magnified by the revaluations of Eastasian currencies after the floating of the dollar in 1971. Japan particularly has sought to export labor-intensive industries. The aging of the labor force—which will reduce the number of persons supporting one retired person in Japan from 8 in 1981 to 3.3 in the year 2020—is accelerating these pressures.[7] Singapore, Hong Kong, and even Taiwan and South Korea are, with some time lag, moving along the same track. Less-developed nations, fortunately, need to build up their labor-intensive industry in the early stages of national development. Similarly, poorer countries are often happy to receive outmoded or dirty industries (such as polyvinyl chloride plants), for which they have more room than crowded Eastasia has.

Japan is one of the world's major capital-surplus nations, with an 18 percent annual savings rate and declining domestic investment. It is the one major wealthy nation that has yet to make large loan commitments to poor countries outside the oil-producing bloc. Hence the recent pattern of growing capital flows from Eastasia to the less-developed world. In 1980 the current-account deficit of the oil-poor, less-developed world was $68 billion; in 1981, nearly $80 billion.[8] Japan is beginning to step into this huge gap. During 1977–79, Japanese economic assistance rose more than 85 percent, while that of the United States climbed only 10 percent (actually a decline, considering the eroding value of the dollar).[9] Except for a small amount of humanitarian assistance, Japanese foreign aid tends to be linked to broader national objectives—like giving Japanese companies a boost in the Third World. This explains why so much Japanese aid goes to purchase telephone equipment, computers, and medical devices and supplies, since these are the products of Japanese high-technology firms seeking sales abroad.

Africa is a surprising region in which to find major Eastasian inroads. Traditionally a European preserve, African markets have been besieged since the late 1960s by Taiwan and South Korea, which used aid to try to stop Africans from siding with their Communist rivals in Pyongyang and Beijing. China made the copper-carrying railway from Zambia to Tanzania its largest foreign aid project of the 1970s for analogous reasons. Since 1979, Japan has also taken an increasing interest in Africa. In April 1981, Japan applied for membership in the African Development Bank and began stepping up its economic assistance to the continent, using this aid as a wedge for commercial penetration. Forecasts issued in 1980 by the Japan Economic Research Center in Tokyo projected that Japan's trade surplus with Africa would rise from $4.3 billion in 1980 to nearly $16.6 billion in 1990—more than 50 percent greater than Japan's surplus with the United States projected for that year.[10] Many of Japan's new inroads into Africa will undoubtedly come at the expense of

European exporters, and conceivably those of the United States. As France becomes preoccupied with domestic welfare issues in the wake of the Socialist victories in 1981, it seems likely that Eastasia may zero in on former French markets in the dark continent.

In all these ways, Eastasia is moving decisively toward a closer relationship with the non-Western world, with which it shares a fruitful symbiosis. Neither side has worldwide military capabilities, and each region poses no threat to the other. Memories of colonialism do not unsettle the relationship (except occasionally among ASEAN members who recall the old Co-prosperity Sphere). Eastasian investment—often Chinese rather than Japanese—in the Third World is undertaken by small firms, and thus is unlikely to be followed by massive imperialist intervention.

For Eastasia, the Third World offers a hedge against growing tensions with the "Trilateral" allies in America and Europe. For the Third World, liaison with Eastasia enhances possibilities for national autonomy and relative independence from the older centers of economic power. Ever since the fifteenth century, when Chinese and Japanese ships traded in porcelain and spices on the Tanzanian coast, Eastasians have been seeking their ties with the non-Western world. Maybe now their opportunity has come.

Financial Independence

A generation ago, all the nations of Eastasia apart from China and North Korea depended heavily on the West, particularly the United States, for growth capital. Japan, South Korea, and Taiwan absorbed large amounts of U.S. economic aid. The Agency for International Development financed the Kaohsiung harbor expansion in Taiwan, thus laying the groundwork for Asia's first export processing zone. AID also built roads and bridges in Japan and Korea.

Japan weaned itself from U.S. direct government aid in 1953, Taiwan in 1965, and South Korea in 1980. All these countries currently receive loans from the U.S. Export-Import Bank, as well as from European export-credit facilities, but such financing goes to support purchases of Western products that might otherwise go unbought. The World Bank, which was also a major lender in the early stages of Japanese growth, having financed Kawasaki Steel's Chiba mill in the early 1950s, stopped supporting Japanese projects in the mid-1960s and has been winding down assistance to Taiwan since the People's Republic joined the bank's governing board. Of the Eastasian countries only China still (barely) qualifies for the bank's low-interest development loans.

Eastasia now has become a region of net capital surplus, particularly since the large balance-of-payments surpluses of the 1970s. As World Bank figures show, Japan has become a strong net exporter of long-term capital and direct investment, with more than enough capital exports to balance the net imports of Eastasia's younger industrial countries. In 1977, for example, Japan had a net long-term capital outflow of $2.7 billion, versus an inflow (in substantial measure from Japan) into the Eastasian "Gang of Four" totaling $2.2 billion.[11] Excess global liquidity and stagnation in industrial investment elsewhere in the world have made the region a buyer's rather than a seller's market for funds. Western banks can no longer demand the premiums they expected less than ten years ago: the infamous "Japan rate," a penalty of several percentage points imposed on Japan's borrowings just after the first oil shock, is now a thing of the past. Of course, foreign exchange shortages (such as occurred in both Koreas in 1979–80) and the long-term financing needs of China's massive industrialization projects will doubtless soak up much of this newfound liquidity. But the pattern of an Eastasia no longer dependent on the outside world for money is rapidly emerging.

The growth of the Asiadollar market is a striking example of the new spirit. In 1968 the Monetary Authority of Singapore decided to expand the city-state's funds facilities to include U.S. dollar-denominated deposits. At the time, the government was seeking a service industry that could take advantage of the nation's excellent location and contacts with the West. The Monetary Authority offered foreign banks incentives such as reduced taxes, abolition of stamp duties, and minimal liquidity requirements for "Asian currency units" —financial institutions licensed to deal in foreign exchange. Even the Singapore government was surprised at the dramatic growth in the Asiadollar business. By mid-1981 the Asiacurrency market had grown to more than $50 billion, up from $7 billion only seven years earlier.[12] Up to 1971 the Asian market had been a net lender of dollars to the Euromarket; now it has become a net borrower, an indication that investment funds are in brisk demand throughout the region and that Eastasia's financial institutions have joined the ranks of world-class intermediaries acceptable to finicky petrodollar investors.

Overseas Chinese surpluses are another important indication of financial maturity. China currently absorbs nearly a billion dollars in remittances from overseas Chinese, mostly from Hong Kong and Singapore. Capitalist Chinese investment from overseas is rising in such countries as Indonesia and Malaysia, and makes up at least 30 percent of direct foreign investment in Taiwan.

Though often mistakenly seen as "flight capital" when it appears in the purchase, say, of Hawaiian or California real estate, these funds are the product of the recent decades of rapid growth in the Eastasian economies; for the most part, they are surpluses looking for diversification of risk, in the classical capitalist fashion.

Eastasia and Europe—The Emerging Rivalry

Since the 1950s, Western Europe has been one of the main beneficiaries of Eastasia's new prosperity. Between 1955 and 1979, as American exports to Japan were declining from 31 percent of Japan's total imports to 18 percent, Western Europe's exports grew from 7 to 9 percent.[13] More important, Europe's share of Japan's total exports expanded from 10 percent to nearly 16 percent. While this growth did not match the striking rise in Japan's new trade ties with the Middle East, it did offer Japan an alternative to the U.S. market, which had dominated the early postwar period. Japan's entry into the OECD in 1964 was a natural reward for its having joined the ranks of the rich trading nations, but it was resisted by European countries, which regarded Japan as a ward of the United States. Since then, General de Gaulle's deprecatory description of the Japanese as "traveling transistor salesmen" has rung loudly in the ears of Europeans, who are astonished at the range of products from Japan and Eastasia flooding their markets.

Europeans, who welcomed the chance to diversify their markets away from America, now find that the Eastasians are tough competitors to their own embattled and aging industries. Not only have European car manufacturers lost their edge to the Japanese in the lucrative American small-car market, but they are also in danger of losing their own domestic auto markets to the flood of Hondas and Subarus. Moreover, the expansion of Eastasian exports to Africa, South Asia, and Commonwealth countries such as Canada, Australia, and New Zealand threatens Europe's traditional upper hand in these markets. Little wonder that European governments have been under pressure to raise new protective barriers against Eastasian products.

In meeting this challenge, Europe lacks several weapons that are still available to the United States. We still to some degree have raw materials such as agricultural products and timber to barter; we have a defense relationship to use as leverage; and we have (for a few more years anyway) the mutual memories of a period of close collaboration with some of the Eastasian countries. Moreover, with the exception of such firms as Rollei (with its Singapore factory) and Philips (with facilities in Taiwan), European companies have been slow to develop global strategies for taking advantage of Eastasian growth by cooperative ventures. Europe will find it hard to meet Eastasian competition, but just as hard to exclude Eastasian products, especially in its traditional Third World markets, where protectionist weapons are of little avail. Europe may continue to be a good alternate market to the United States, should domestic political pressures within the U.S. begin to block further Eastasian penetration into our markets. Eastasia now has, in other words, the ability to play large parts of the developed world off against one another.

Curbing the Multinational Corporations

Many nationalistic commentators, particularly in Latin America, claim that foreign business is bad for national development in poorer countries. It is too tempting for poor nations to abandon autonomy to outsiders willing to pay for the privilege of controlling raw materials or access to markets. *Dependencia* —the tendency to sacrifice national interests to the almighty dollar—is far too prevalent, these critics say.

Not so in modern Eastasia. In parts of Latin America, Southeast Asia, and tropical Africa, governments have often granted economic privileges to foreigners in agribusiness, mining, and transportation. But in Eastasia, foreigners have been kept at bay, at least in recent years.

It was not always easy. Near the end of the nineteenth century, at the high noon of imperialism, foreign firms demanded and got influence over large parts of the Chinese economy, particualrly the banking system and the customs office. Major companies like British-American Tobacco in cigarettes and Texaco in kerosene captured virtually 100 percent of the large Chinese market. Foreigners became advisers to leadership—G. E. Morrison to the Manchu emperor, Professor Frank Goodnow to President Yuan Shih-kai, and a number of bankers to the various warlords that followed them. The major weakness of Chinese government before 1949—lack of tax revenues— led administrations to mortgage themselves to consortium after consortium of foreign bankers.[14]

Yet even at the peak of foreign business influence, there were still restraints in Eastasia that were absent in many other parts of the world. Foreigners never controlled agricultural land or established plantations (except, of course, on the periphery, in the colonial lands of Vietnam, Indonesia, and Malaysia). In China, foreign settlements were generally limited to the "treaty port" enclaves, since there was no legal protection for foreign residents in the hinterland. Even missionaries, intrepid pioneers bringing Western "civilization" to China, reached only a quarter of the mainland's 2,000 counties.

China closed its doors after the Communist victory: all foreign property was confiscated and all foreign companies driven out by 1952. Only a handful of trade offices representing foreign interests conducted business from 1950 until the 1970s, when foreign businessmen were once again allowed to visit (though not to reside) in China. Although today dozens of multinational corporations maintain expensive suites (paid for at daily rates) in the Peking Hotel, foreigners are kept in a small and isolated world of their own, to which they are only invited when the Chinese themselves wish to do business. Foreign participation in "joint ventures" is dangled as a promise, but laws prohibit repatriation of profits or ownership of property by foreigners. Clearly China is preparing to use foreign firms only in a limited way in its "four modernizations."

Japan, too, has made great efforts to keep foreign firms under control. Before 1945, for example, only the rubber, automobile, and electrical-engineering sectors had a significant foreign presence. Only during two short periods (1899–1914 and 1923–30) did Japan dip into foreign capital markets, and these loans were generally mediated by government bureaus. At one point in the 1920s, private foreign loans of more than a billion yen were outstanding, but these went largely to finance public works projects such as water systems, harbors, and generating plants. Most of Japan's borrowing from the outside world (60 percent in 1930) was government debt, and the government, then as now, carefully regulated financial transactions between Japanese firms and the West.[15]

The American occupation brought a high tide of foreign interest in Japan, as banks and oil companies established their footholds. But after 1952 the government once again restricted multinational activities. For example, it shelved until 1961 IBM's request for permission to build a factory in Japan, and allowed it then only on condition that IBM grant basic patent rights to Japanese competitors. Texas Instruments was allowed to manufacture integrated circuits in 1968 only under similar circumstances. Foreign personal-credit companies, including subsidiaries of Citibank and Chase Manhattan, were denied entry into Japan until the late 1970s, when the Ministry of Finance judged that the economy was sufficiently liquid to afford the luxury of personal credit.

The point is not that Japan places categorical restrictions on Western companies. Indeed, some firms have been actively aided by the Ministry of International Trade and Industry since the mid-1970s. But the entry and behavior of foreign firms is closely watched by the government to make certain that Japanese strategic purposes are being served. The contrast with American openness to easy penetration by Japanese "multinationals" is striking.

The smaller states of Eastasia have had less leverage to use against foreign corporations: indeed, the smaller the state, the more accessible its markets seem to be. Singapore and Hong Kong preserve vestiges of older colonial governments that actively promoted the interests of European and American businessmen, and their policies are the most liberal. Indeed, both countries, and to some extent South Korea, offer appealing incentives to attract foreign-technology companies. In South Korea and Taiwan, however, government financial authorities review all loans from foreign banks to ensure that such loans do not contravene national objectives or create excess liquidity. Taiwan and South Korea also try to keep the multinationals out of sensitive sectors such as defense and basic industry through the maintenance of public monopolies in these fields. Moreover, they encourage foreign firms to invest largely in labor-intensive industries, in order to raise workers' income and thus improve local income distribution. Even in these small "client states" of America, government policy ensures that there will be a minimum of *dependencia.*

Eastasia has succeeded in putting the energies of American and European businessmen to work building, not dismantling, their national systems. With its investment, its trade contacts, and its technology, multinational business has helped bring Eastasia into the modern world. In return, the multinationals have profited extensively from their openings into the rich economies of the region. We suspect that Eastasia will continue to keep these workhorses of the international economic system well in harness.

The one major respect in which Eastasia remains substantially dependent on the West is defense. The United States retains nearly 100,000 ground troops, substantial air power, and the Seventh Fleet in Eastasia to buttress its nuclear guarantee of the region's security. In the face of growing Soviet power, the continued presence of these U.S. forces is almost universally desired throughout the region, not least of all by China. The presence of U.S. forces also plays a major role in moderating latent intraregional rivalries, such as that between Japan and Korea, and in moderating pressures for Japanese remilitarization.

The extent to which the West can trade off security guarantees to gain leverage in support of a constantly weakening commercial position is problematical. Should the United States ever proceed with moves to withdraw from Korea and otherwise divorce itself from the security concerns of Eastasia, as seemed possible in the early post-Vietnam years, the prospects for the evolution of an Eastasia defiantly, perhaps even antagonistically independent of the West would be enhanced. Such moves could also induce the "Finlandization," in the direction of the Soviet Union or China, of a nation with a GNP now more than twenty times that of Finland and possibly the largest of any nation in the world by the year 2000—Japan.

One can summarize the evolving Eastasian relationship with the rest of the world by paraphrasing Mao Zedong: Asia has stood up. The region is increasingly cohesive internally, and it is also more capable of bargaining equally and independently with the West than it has been at any time in the past 200 years. In this dynamic of assertiveness, combined with efficient, innovative social organization, lies the essence of the Eastasia Edge.

15

The Uncertain
Political Future

WE have suggested that Eastasians, far from being mere "economic animals," may be the most politically sophisticated people on earth. No people builds authority structures more elaborately, or respects them, once clearly established, with as much commitment. No people so consistently subordinates individual interests to those of the group. And no people remains as loyal to the nation or the state, even in times of deep trouble. In many respects, the miracle of Eastasian economic performance is squarely based on an even more remarkable phenomenon of political coherence.

This may seem a strange assertion about a region in which the United States has fought three major wars since 1940, wars which in each case resulted from intraregional rivalries or from the collapse of political authority. Instability has been, and may continue to be, a regular part of the Eastasian scene. The important thing is to recognize the role that political instability, or the threat of instability, plays in the economic life of the region.

In the past hundred years, Eastasians have undergone more profound political changes than have affected the European world since the discovery of America. In that short span of time, ancient empires more imposing than those of Alexander the Great or the Holy Roman Emperors have crumbled, to be replaced by seemingly modern political institutions. Social, commercial, and political elites, vested for centuries with responsibility for social order, collapsed and were replaced by technicians, bureaucrats, and merchants in the modern mold. A region self-sufficient and inward-looking fell apart under foreign conquest and colonization, then reassembled as part of a complex modern world economy. Nations like China and Korea have been divided for decades or have waged war on one another, as in the case of Japan and China. With this record of rapid change, who can be confident about the future political stability of the region?

The effect of political instability on the economic performance of Eastasia is readily apparent. China grew rapidly in the 1920s and 1930s after the creation of the republic and the unification of the country under Chiang Kai-shek. That progress was destroyed by the Japanese invasion and the ensuing civil war. Even after 1949, periods of political uncertainty coincided with those of economic stagnation, as in the case of the Great Proletarian Cultural Revolution, when China's GNP fell by 3 percent.[1]

Political stability, on the other hand, has contributed strongly to dynamic growth. South Korea's remarkable recent economic resurgence dates from the restoration of authority under Park Chung-hee in 1961, while the dramatic economic setbacks of 1980 could be directly blamed on his death by assassination in October 1979. Underlying Japan's sustained performance since 1955 has been the predictability of the Liberal-Democratic coalition of conservative parliamentary forces. Any forecast about future economic performance not only cannot ignore the problem of political instability, but must begin by analyzing its dynamics.

Options for China

China is the biggest question mark of all. With the majority of Eastasia's population, land area, and resources, it holds the key to the region's future. And yet, because of its very size and complexity, it is the hardest nation of all to predict. The pattern of the last thirty years in China, with wild fluctuations between ideology and pragmatism, centralization and dispersionism, does not make the task any easier. We can begin, however, by outlining four possible patterns of development, in ascending order of probability.

Maoism

Mao Zedong, the Great Helmsman who led the Communist Party to victory in 1949 and masterminded the transformations of the 1950s and 1960s, died in September, 1976. An intellectual turned peasant leader, he commanded the Communist movement from 1935, pushing it in directions unheard of elsewhere in the international Communist movement. He based his strategy on China's backward villages instead of the industrial towns, which at the time were weak and few in number. He avoided the meaningless strikes, demonstrations, and coups d'etat that had brought only disaster to the Party before his rise. He insisted on protracted guerrilla warfare behind the lines of the enemy. He built Communist governments in base areas far from the centers of counter-revolution or foreign power. In all these ways, Mao laid out a course for China that gave the countryside priority over cities, discouraged intellectual or technocratic elitism, and relied on moral instead of material incentives in the economy. These basic Maoist concepts clashed head-on in the 1960s with rival concepts supported by several of Mao's contemporaries. Partly because Maoism resonated in some ways with traditional Chinese moral values, it continues to receive support among portions of the Chinese population and leadership.

The remarkable public trials of the "Gang of Four," beginning in 1980, mark the end of Maoism as an active ideology in China. Like the trials of Japanese "war criminals" by the Supreme Headquarters of the Allied powers in the late 1940s, the proceedings against the Maoists were designed to undermine the legitimacy of a political tradition by asserting that politically motivated acts were in fact transgressions against the law. For example, Mao's private secretary, Chen Boda, stood accused of the murder of tens of thousands of loyal officials in the province of Hebei, for which the only evidence was that he penned an editorial denouncing unnamed individuals as "spies of the Kuomintang." Chairman Mao's widow, Jiang Qing, achieved a certain dignity during the trials by asserting that she had done nothing without her late husband's explicit approval. The outcome of the trials is less important than the reason for holding them publicly: China's new leadership realized that Mao's policies had become unpopular even among the segments of the population those policies were supposed to benefit the most—the ordinary workers and peasants. The Chinese, who like other Eastasians profoundly appreciated the need for economic performance, quickly noted the organizational failures of the late Maoist years.

A resurgence of Maoism could come about only under unusual circumstances. Foreign invasion, or extensive civil warfare would produce a nationalistic reaction that might benefit "radical" interests. Widespread famine, natural disasters, or economic bungling could trigger a similar reaction. Any appreciable worsening in the living conditions of the peasantry—caused, for example, by a worsening of the urban-rural terms of trade—could produce a groundswell of Maoist opinion, though this opinion would be hard to organize without support from central authorities. The army, which played a crucial role in supporting radical causes under Lin Biao until his mutiny and death in 1971, remains crucial to any hope of a Maoist resurgence, as it does to the alternate outcomes.

Titoism

Ever since China's break with the Soviet Union in 1960, there has been much speculation about the Yugoslav model for China's development. Under Marshal Tito, Yugoslavia after 1948 carved out an independent role in the Socialist bloc that the Chinese began to emulate after 1960. The Yugoslav domestic economy developed forms of "market socialism" in which firms, controlled by committees of their own workers, created and sold their own market lines in competition with other factories.

Since 1978 there has been much talk of expanding the private or market sectors in Chinese industry as well as agriculture, and of allowing factory committees more say in the decisions of the firm. Many of China's leading economists, including Xu Dixin and Xue Muqiao, have recommended some relaxation of controls over China's planned sector. In one sense these recommendations have already taken root: to an unprecedented degree, key decisions are now being made by provinces and municipalities without central interference. Profits as much as quota fulfillment entered into the calculations of plant managers throughout the country during the "four modernizations" drive of the late 1970s.

The new blossoming of traditional Chinese competitiveness does not convince us that Titoism is here to stay. The Chinese economy still takes its orders from a central plan, with its main inputs and outputs centrally allocated. The iron and steel, transportation, petrochemical, energy, and food-grain sectors will retain their physical allocation patterns. China's economy will continue to be politically directed by the State Planning Commissions, State Technology Commissions, and State Council, which have retained the initiative in all major matters such as investment and foreign exchange. To abandon these centralized functions would run counter to general Eastasian practice as well as international Communist theory.

Stalinism

In many respects, the Chinese economy of today closely resembles that of the Soviet Union of the 1930s. Despite the careful orchestration of private markets, subsidiary production, and individualized performance criteria, the Plan is still all-important. As under Stalin, political loyalties determine who exercises economic responsibility in the government. Foreign exchange and contacts are rigidly controlled. Despite a nod toward decentralization, major decisions are still made in the ministries and councils of Beijing, just as they were in the Moscow of Stalin's day.

The Chinese Communist Party leadership has aged rapidly, despite attempts to rejuvenate it with new blood. The Maoist effort to replace disloyal older colleagues with young radicals in the 1960s failed miserably, simply arousing the determination of loyal second-generation Communists to remain in power. Many of the regional and sub-Politburo officials who were shunted aside during the Cultural Revolution have reasserted their seniority and are being placed in positions of responsibility by the post-Mao leadership.

Some of the "young" leaders in their fifties and sixties who are now assuming key positions at the center—Premier Zhao Ziyang and Communist Party leader Hu Yaobang among them—are often called "pragmatists." But they more closely resemble Stalinist *apparatchiki* than they do the young technocrats brought in to run France by François Mitterrand or America by Ronald Reagan. The silencing of democratic dissent by Deng Xiaoping after 1979 is a reminder that the Chinese Communist Party is still in control of China and will not permit its fundamental authority to be diluted.

Sun Yat-senism

The Chinese political system may be evolving toward a pattern that would be familiar to the founder of the Chinese Republic, Sun Yat-sen. Sun, who is revered by Chinese on both sides of the Taiwan Strait as the founder of modern China, developed an ideology of "Three People's Principles"—nationality, popular sovereignty, and popular welfare. Like China's current leadership, Sun subscribed to the importance of maintaining the unity of the Chinese people, whom he often referred to as "a sheet of loose sand." He abhorred class division and civil conflict among Chinese, and he believed strongly in industrial development and capital construction as the hope of China's future. Sun urged China to resist manipulation by foreign powers. His closest political allies during his rise to power were a group of farsighted Japanese Pan-Asian politicians led by Miyazaki Torazō.

The current Chinese leadership is remarkably similar to the leadership of the Republic of China on Taiwan, which adheres explicitly to the Three People's Principles. It is no accident that Taiwan's president, Chiang Ching-kuo, was educated in Moscow and has a Russian wife. Nor is it a secret that many Communists attended the Whampoa Military Academy in 1925, when it was headed by Ching-kuo's father, Chiang Kai-shek. Deng Xiaoping's concern for the people's well-being, and about Mao Zedong's failure to protect it, resonate nicely with the younger Chiang's commitment to the economic improvement of Taiwan as the first priority. Both men are cast in the mold of Dr. Sun.

Options for Japan

The political future of Japan is equally critical to the stability of the region. As Eastasia's economic center of gravity, the main source of its capital and expertise, and the prime link of its trading nexus, Japan is the fulcrum for changes in the future. Instability in Tokyo could lead to the rapid decline of Eastasia's fortunes and to serious disruptions in the region's relationships with the West and with the Third World.

Fortunately, there is little likelihood of a dramatic change in Japanese leadership that would disrupt Japan's productive orientation toward the developed world or its economically motivated attitude toward its neighbors in the region. We may nevertheless speculate about possible directions of change in Japan's political makeup, again in reverse order of probability.

A Turn to the Left

The possibility of a Japan led by left-wing forces has frightened Americans ever since the end of the Pacific war. After 1945 the Allied powers permitted the reemergence of the Communist and Socialist parties in Japan, and then in a sudden about-face attempted to purge them from the political system in 1949–50. Since then, the radical wing of the Socialist Party has maintained a strongly anti-American bias, despite indications that this is not a politically profitable view. Both the Socialists, with their massive base in the public employees' trade unions, and the Communists, who receive regular protest votes in the European fashion, have maintained a strong base in the large industrial cities, even gaining temporary control of several major city administrations during the late 1960s and early 1970s.

As Japan grew increasingly urban after World War II, the parties of the left gained consistently in popular-vote percentage at the local level, even though their representation in the Diet, Japan's national legislature, peaked in 1958.[2] In the national election of June 1980, the Socialists and Communists combined gleaned more than 30 percent of the vote and about a quarter of the seats in the Diet—a setback from their standing in the previous election, but still enough to make them a major voice in Japanese politics when added to their extensive influence in the national mass media and to the ten committee chairmanships they continued to retain in the Diet even after the 1980 election.[3] In May 1980 the left toppled the cabinet of Prime Minister Ohira Masayoshi with the first no-confidence motion to succeed in Japan since the early 1950s.[4] Some analysts suggest that the combination of rapid urbanization, conservative extremism, and Socialist successes abroad, including the victory of Mitterrand in France, may lead to a triumph of the Japanese left in the relatively near future.

This is doubtful. Despite the decline of the Liberal Democratic Party's traditional voting sectors in the countryside, the ruling party continues to adapt and to appeal to new constituencies. The LDP presently rules the government without the participation of such centrist and rightist groups as the Democratic Socialist Party, the Komei (Clean Government) Party, and its own splinter groups. Should the absolute dominance of the LDP be challenged as a result of inroads from these nonleftist groups, it would surely arrange to rule with a coalition of the right and center.

Since the conservative electoral victory of mid-1980, the demoralized left has been deeply divided, with the largest opposition group, the Japan Socialist Party, making explicit overtures toward the middle-of-the-road parties and repudiating the Communists. There is deep uncertainty as to whether the Socialist Party would wish, were it to be surprised into power, to convert Japan into a socialist or neutralist country. Despite the party's doctrinaire and parochial tradition, its leadership has grown decidedly more pragmatic in recent years, seeking to broaden the party's following. While still able to generate support on issues such as the environment, antinuclear policy, and labor relations in certain industries, neither the JSP nor the Communists find much support for their former pro-Soviet positions in foreign affairs. Even if the left were to gain power—which is not very likely unless major disaster should strike—it would not be inclined to break sharply with the United States, nor to sever Japan's growing economic relationships with Eastasia.

A Turn to the Right

Some observers detect the possibility of a militarily resurgent Japan. As the United States withdraws for financial reasons from the defense of the Western Pacific, Japan will undoubtedly play a larger role, as the Reagan-Suzuki communiqué of May 1981 suggested. A stronger defense role raises the specter of Japanese militarism, particularly since the area of maximum concern will inevitably be the same sources of raw materials and the same vital sea lanes that attracted Japanese expansionism in the 1930s. Anti-Soviet sentiment in Japan, always latent but heightened by the decades-long dispute over the Russian-occupied northern islands, might be used as an excuse to increase Japan's military presence in northwestern Asia. There are even groups such as the militant Seirankai (Blue Wave Society), with a substantial following among young Diet members, who feel that the former colonies of Japan, such as Taiwan and Korea, belong in a special relationship with the home islands. These groups oppose the dominant view that Japan should seek closer ties with Communist China.[5] The right presumably stands to gain from the rapid aging of Japanese society in the same way that the left ostensibly gains from its increasing urbanization.

While all these phenomena may continue to bubble to the surface, it seems unlikely that the world need fear a resurgence of fascism or organized militarism, in Japan. If there is one principle which unites all politicians and which appears in all the polls, it is that Japan must never again walk the path of arrogant military power. As the only nation ever to suffer atomic attack, the Japanese are extremely unlikely to support the nuclear capability that superpower status requires. The Japanese people are too sophisticated to fall for the simple martial virtues of fascism, as the pathetic response to the suicide in 1970 of neo-fascist novelist Yukio Mishima showed.

A Softening in the Middle

The most likely outcome of future changes in the Japanese political scene is continued rule by the same parties in the same political and administrative setting. However, the quality of political life seems likely to change as Japanese society matures. It seems likely that the long-suffering Japanese workers will increasingly claim compensation in the form of higher wages, greater leisure, and fewer demands on their time and energy by their employers. Welfare costs, heretofore minimal to the government because they were borne largely by families and the private sector, are likely to rise rapidly, particularly in view of a "graying" of Japanese society much more rapid than anywhere else in the industrialized world.[6] The steady increases in productivity that have made Japanese goods increasingly competitive will be difficult to sustain without larger and larger inputs from the public sector, thus bringing to an end the era of minimalist government that has made Japan the cutting edge of the Eastasian economic miracle. These changes—all signs of the maturing of the region's most advanced country—will not in all likelihood produce instability, but they may shift the dynamic center of change in the region away from the Japanese islands.

Ironically, the graying of Japan will, if anything, strengthen Japan's ties with the rest of Eastasia, in the same way that the maturing of England in the early twentieth century strengthened its ties with America and the Commonwealth. We can visualize Japanese in the future wearing inexpensive clothing, using consumer products, and even driving automobiles manufactured by the younger neighboring economies.[7] In turn, the Japan of the future will export higher-technology items—computers, communications equipment, airplanes —to its neighbors and to the United States, which will in all likelihood still be supplying Eastasia with large quantities of food and raw materials, our main earners of foreign exchange from across the Pacific.

Peripheral Eastasia

A surprise-free projection of the two Eastasian giants suggests little major change in their political orientation and a mellowing in their relations with each other. But what about the peripheral Eastasian countries? To them the future may not be so kind.

Taiwan and Hong Kong are part of the larger political sphere of the People's Republic of China, whether they like it or not. Hong Kong is regarded by China as a part of Guangdong Province presently under British administration. The question is not whether China will take over the colony but when. The treaty which leased a large part of Hong Kong—the New Territories— to the British crown expires in 1997, a date which some regard as the dooms- day for foreign enterprise.

In fact, the Chinese government is not particularly swayed by legal niceties in its acquiescence in British control, any more than it accepts the British and Portuguese absolute legal claim to the original portions of Hong Kong and Macao. Deng Xiaoping went out of his way during 1980–81 to assure both Chinese and foreigners that their investments in Hong Kong plant and real estate would remain "safe" for the indefinite future—long beyond 1997, he implied. That China does not intend to dismantle and destroy foreign invest- ment in Hong Kong as it did in Shanghai after 1949 is suggested by the growing Communist official presence—in personnel and investment alike—in the colony. Were China's intention to plunder the colony in 1997, it would hardly be prudent to build expensive factories and high-rise buildings now, as China is doing.

Hong Kong's great virtue in Chinese eyes is precisely that it has no legitimate claim to independence from China, for who could maintain that its 5 million Chinese citizens are truly British subjects? The colony is independent of China only in reality, not in the sacred realm of "name." Taiwan, on the other hand, presents China with a different problem. Since the Nationalist government on the island still maintains its pretense of power over all of China, Taiwan's independence is a thorn in the side of the People's Republic. Chiang Ching-kuo has the audacity to claim the name of China as his own—hence, the PRC must treat him and his government as anathema. This does not, however, prevent China from wooing the population of Taiwan by every means, nor from planning the overthrow of the Taiwan authorities by force if necessary. Indeed, China will continue to insist on the right to "liberate" the province of Taiwan so long as the Nationalist government maintains its rivalry in name. Moreover, any attempt now by the Nationalists to abandon the claim of Taiwan to be the Republic of China and to seek recognition as a Republic of Taiwan would be vehemently opposed within Taiwan itself (though some in Japan and elsewhere would heartily support the move). This impasse lies at the core of one of Eastasia's most intractable problems: how to resolve the Taiwan question without destabilizing the region.

The U.S. government has wisely opted to leave this question to "Chinese on both sides of the Taiwan Strait," as stated in the Shanghai communiqué signed by Mao Zedong and Richard Nixon in February 1972. Japan, which sought recognition from China shortly after the Nixon move, came one step closer to accepting China's claim to the island province by breaking off all official government contact with Taiwan in 1974. The Carter administration, which recognized the People's Republic on January 1, 1979, accepted the Japanese pattern, but by special act of Congress maintained in full force all the nonmilitary treaties between Taiwan and the United States. Taiwan's diplomatic isolation has deepened since then, though economically Taiwan's relations with the outside world have grown strikingly since 1979.

While Taiwan continues to ask for, and occasionally obtains, military help from the United States, Chinese forces would doubtless prevail should the People's Republic follow through on the threat to invade. For several reasons, however, China seems unlikely to risk such a move. To do so would automatically isolate China from its main ally against the Soviet Union, namely the United States. Moreover, China's new leaders may find a separately developing Taiwan useful in the future as a supplier of western technology and skilled manpower—though there are few current signs that this is a consideration. It seems likely that China's best move is to continue to isolate Taiwan politically and to assume that the future will take care of itself. After all, if Taiwan continues to grow at its recent rate, all China needs to do is wait to capture an even riper plum.

Instability on the Korean Peninsula may be an even more intractable problem. Taiwan and Hong Kong are so much smaller than their giant motherland that over the long run there can be no contest. But the two Koreas are so evenly balanced that the likelihood of warfare to test the balance of power on the peninsula is not negligible. Each regime is committed to the other's extermination; their populations are constantly on alert, their armies poised for attack or defense. The fact that the capital of South Korea is only twenty-five miles from enemy territory makes the demilitarized zone a hair trigger that could set off armed conflict almost instantly. While border incidents have occurred with decreasing regularity in recent years, they still take place, and occasionally even involve U.S. troops. Left alone, North Korea and South Korea would probably have been at each other's throats long ago.

In fact, both regimes are partially restrained by their allies: the United States in the case of the South, the Soviet Union and China in the case of the North. North Korea is in a delicate position between the Chinese and the Soviets, each of whom would doubtless insist on greater influence in return for supporting military action. The Chinese have acted privately to restrain Kim Il-sung's more drastic gestures, and Kim has so far resisted Soviet requests for a greater Russian military presence on Korean soil. The South Korean government, led in 1981 by former colonels turned politicians, recognizes the need to keep the American army friendly—even though the coup d'état of October 1979 for the first time violated an explicit rule about the use of front-line troops without American permission.

The Korean national unity drive is currently frustrated by the artificial division of the country and by the standoff in the balance of power. Both sides have committed themselves verbally to "unification" talks, though to date these have mostly been unproductive harangues. The fact of the matter is that it is not in the interest of any of the four major powers concerned—China, Russia, America, and particularly Japan—to see a strong, unified Korea. A unified Korea with current military budgets would rank high on the list of the world's military powers and might provoke Japan's own remilitarization. It seems likely that the current division may last into the next century unless international agreement to resolve the issue can be reached. Even then, the two Koreas would face the same standoff that divides China and Taiwan.

One prospect that could severely complicate the overall stability of Eastasia would be major domestic political unrest on the Korean Penninsula. Occasional student demonstrations and military coups d'etat may result in periodic personnel changes at the top in South Korean society. Regional cleavages may continue to be more serious than elsewhere in Eastasia, sometimes resulting in isolated outbursts such as that at Kwangju in early 1980. Intellectuals in the cities may well continue, in unison with colleagues abroad, to decry perceived human rights violations. In the North, the changing of the guard to a new generation of leaders may suggest dangers.

But the strong basic underpinnings of South Korean stability—a conservative peasantry, a powerful bureaucracy, and a massive military obsessed with the threat from the North—will most likely continue to hold that nation on an even keel. The transition to affluence during the 1980s is even creating interest-group pluralism, which could ultimately serve as the underpinning for democracy in the Western sense. The vested interests of established military and bureaucratic groups should augur well for stability in the North.

Perhaps the gravest threat to the stability of Eastasia is the Soviet Union, which maintains an army of more than a million men in Asia and the most potent fleet in the region. Currently, virtually all the nations of Eastasia agree on this threat, and to a degree the Soviet presence is a unifying factor. Japan's claim for its tiny northern islands is matched by China's irredentist hope for a million square miles of Soviet-occupied territory. No Eastasian nation relishes the thought of Soviet domination of the sea lanes, especially of the oil convoy lanes through the Strait of Malacca. That Eastasian nations tend to find the Russians generally unattractive is a fortunate accident for Eastasian unity. Japan has many cultural and emotional reasons to prefer Chinese crude oil to Siberian natural gas, just as China can absorb Japanese technicians without fearing a repeat of the Soviet pullout of experts in 1960.

The Soviet presence is more destabilizing in Southeast Asia than in the northeast. Vietnamese acceptance of Soviet support, first against China during the border war of 1979 and then against the Khmer Rouge of Kampuchea in 1980 and 1981, has brought Soviet influence into the heart of the old co-prosperity sphere. Russian soldiers parade at the American-built navy base at Camranh Bay, Russian advisers fight alongside Vietnamese against Chinese and Cambodians, and Russian fighting ships lie off the coast of Southeast Asia, where formerly Japanese and then American navies once dominated the seas.

Singapore's attitude toward this development is predictable: as the creature of European business and Chinese immigrants, Singapore has little sympathy for increased Soviet penetration in the region. While the other four members of ASEAN—Thailand, Indonesia, Malaysia, and the Philippines—hedge their bets, hoping at least to neutralize their neighbor Vietnam, Singapore continues to urge a firm anti-Soviet stance. But since Japan is little inclined to stand up to Soviet expansion, and because the United States, fresh from its land-war debacle in Vietnam, is unable to increase its presence, the region seems destined for more turmoil.

Singapore, together with its hinterlands of Malaysia and Indonesia, is remote from the heartland of Eastasia, and thus most vulnerable to forces outside our purview. Fortunately, Singapore no longer must face both a hostile Indonesia, bent on *konfrontasi* under Sukarno, and an indifferent Malaysia, miffed at the island republic's declaration of independence. Nevertheless, without a navy or army to speak of, and without the kinds of formal allies that back Taiwan or the two Koreas, Prime Minister Lee Kuan Yew is a lonely international figure. He can take heart at the fact that Vietnam's armies would have to pass through three nations to reach his island overland. He may also feel relieved that ASEAN, after a shaky start, has begun to grow teeth and to coordinate its security efforts (as in the Indonesian guerrilla operation that overwhelmed Muslim hijackers in the Bangkok airport in early 1981). If there is any part of the Eastasian region where political forces may produce sudden and dramatic change in the future, it is in the environs of Singapore—though the possibility is strong that the island's government would weather most storms.

In Southeast Asia, as opposed to the northeast, Eastasian peoples are in the minority. In Indonesia and Malaysia, the domestic economies are dominated by the few million ethnic Chinese who populate the cities and towns, surrounded by a sea of predominantly Muslim ethnic Malays. Singapore dominates the economies of these regions from outside the Muslim-Malay political sphere. But its economy depends in part on the prosperity of Chinese ethnics in the larger countries. The potential for political instability in all the ASEAN countries is greater than in Eastasia, but particularly over the issue of Chinese domination of the native economies. This issue flared up in bloody communal riots in Malaysia in 1969 and in Indonesia in 1965 and 1980.

There are those who forecast that this southern tier of nations from Malaysia to the Philippines will show an even faster growth rate than Eastasia in the coming decade. Indeed, the potential for growth among the resource-rich countries of the archipelago is great, if only because the world will continue to need their oil, minerals, and timber. We can discern, however, many reasons to expect an inconsistent performance from these countries, despite the importance of Eastasians in their economies. The Philippines seems ripe for instability should the high-handed Marcos regime falter in the face of widespread opposition from Muslims in the south, peasants in the north, and clergy and intellectuals throughout the islands. In Indonesia, economic growth may be hampered by the lack of political wisdom needed to restrain expectations of higher standards of living—as witness the continuing wasteful subsidies to domestic petroleum consumption, which eat into the nation's foreign exchange earnings. That the tropical populations of Southeast Asia have the discipline and political skills needed to create and sustain growth is yet to be proved—a charge that cannot be made convincingly about the people of Eastasia.

16

Eastern Challenge: Western Response?

AMERICA continues to be Eastasia's largest trading partner, the home of the most active international companies doing business in the region, and the superpower most interested in the security of the area. The Eastasia Edge is not likely to shake these fundamental commitments. But the need for rethinking the transpacific relationship is already upon us.

We are already primarily a raw-materials exporter to Eastasia, regardless of our view of ourselves as the most advanced industrial nation. Our four leading exports (by value) to Japan in 1980 were corn, lumber, coal and soybeans.[1] Only about one-tenth of that export trade was in high-technology products such as aircraft, nuclear reactors, or computers.[2] Even China, the least developed of the Eastasian countries, imports mostly raw materials from the United States. Programs to increase manufactured exports to Eastasia will require sustained effort to penetrate tough markets such as Japan, or highly creative financing and pricing to gain an edge on Eastasia's own manufacturers. Regaining our own competitive edge means moving to higher levels of technology and delaying the spread of that technology to potential competitors.

The effects of the Eastasian challenge upon the United States have varied from region to region and sector to sector. Eastasians have had a strong and positive impact on the growing Sunbelt, for example, which absorbs investment and provides a willing, nonunionized labor force for the manufacture and assembly of Eastasian components. Certain multinational firms, including IBM and General Electric, have benefited more than other American companies (notably the automakers and their parts suppliers) from Eastasian growth. California and Oregon now draw large revenues from the expanding trade relationship, with incomes derived mainly from transshipment in western ports and from raw-materials exports. The American consumer has certainly benefited from the cheaper, better, safer products marketed by Taiwan, South Korea, Japan, and China. And there are large fortunes being made by the distributors of Eastasian products. So far the challenge has not ruined us, at least not all of us.

But clearly something must be done. Our trade deficit with Eastasia spiraled eightfold during the 1970s to exceed $10 billion.[3] OPEC industrial investment dollars are being recycled with Japan and Singapore, and not adequately into the shares of American firms where they are so badly needed. World commodity prices fluctuate with Asian demand for soybeans, lumber, or shrimp, leaving our producers and consumers helpless. American workers are out of jobs in industry (or working for foreign bosses), and American businessmen fail to invest from fear of the competition. Are we destined to be, in George Meany's phrase, "A land of investment banks and hamburger stands"?

Protectionism Doesn't Work

The most obvious response is not necessarily the best. Many shortsighted politicians and lobbyists are already clamoring for protection of American industry through higher tariffs, quotas, and other restrictions against Eastasian products. The temptation is strong to isolate our domestic economy from the impact of other nations' aggressive export policies, hoping thereby to increase domestic employment, make our corporate environment more predictable, and improve our balance of payments. The trouble is that protectionism will have none of these effects, and will harm us even more in the long run.

Take, for example, the "voluntary restraint agreements" that have recently been used to protect American steel, television, and now auto manufacturers. In 1969, Japan curtailed its steel exports to the United States to a level agreed upon by the two governments. But the Japanese simply began sending higher-quality (and higher-priced) steel products to this country, so that the U.S. trade deficit in steel actually increased in 1970 and 1971.[4] Again, when we revised our arrangements with Japan in 1972 to meet this new challenge,

Japanese trading companies arranged with German steelmakers to sell Japanese steel by proxy in the United States. Japanese steel producers found that U.S. quotas helped them to keep prices artificially high in American markets, thus passing on higher costs to steel consumers. U.S. auto makers, the largest such consumers, were forced to raise prices and then compelled to compete against cheaper Japanese cars built with cheap Japanese steel in Japan. The import quotas on special steels of 1976 had a similar snowball effect on the ball-bearing industry, by increasing prices to American bearing manufacturers and driving them to import cheap bearings from Korea and Japan to replace the American product with its expensive domestic steel content.

The television restraint agreement of 1977 did cut Japanese imports from nearly 3 million to less than 1 million sets a year.[5] But it did not stop the steady decline in jobs available within the industry. Zenith soon moved its main production facilities to Taiwan, and Japanese firms, to get around the agreement, began assembly operations in the United States, though few parts other than the wooden cabinets were actually made in America.

In a nutshell, protectionism without exception has been inflationary, has increased unemployment in related sectors, and has weakened the ability of an industry to compete in foreign markets. But for our friends across the Pacific, it has not been such a bad experience, despite a few disruptions and "shocks."

Contrasting sharply to the debilitating effects of protectionism on our own economy and diplomatic ties, are the stimulative commercial consequences for our Eastasian competitors. Western protection, of course, introduces uncertainty into their own commercial calculations, and some short-term economic pain. They cannot be expected to like it. Nevertheless, our restrictions have forced them to adapt, to innovate, and to move into higher-value-added sectors where their profitability in trade with us is even better. Export restraints in cotton textiles and apparel during the 1960's for example, moved Eastasian exporters toward leadership in synthetic fibers. Restrictions on shoes galvanized Taiwan and Korea to challenge American supremacy in middle-priced footwear. The 1981 restraint "nonagreement" on autos nudged the Japanese to send us more of their exotic (and expensive) electronic-gadgeted sports cars, and to save their Toyotas and Hondas for the Third World markets, where they easily displace the European mini-cars, including those of Ford and General Motors affiliates. Datsun's catchy slogan "We are driven" has an unspoken predicate: "to greater heights by your harassment."

It would be foolish to assert that political restrictions should never be applied to the operations of markets. Under certain conditions they may be the only solution to a particularly urgent structural adjustment problem. Since trade has become such an important part of our diplomatic activities, the option of applying quotas or embargoes must be left open. Eastasian nations maintain their own protective restrictions, often in such indirect forms as discriminatory buying practices of governments, arbitrary customs valuation practices, or monopolistic distribution systems. The weapons of retaliation must be kept ready. But the important point to recognize is that we harm only ourselves by protecting inefficient industries and hoping their problems will go away. We must think in terms of global markets and the consequences of protection for our global competitiveness. And then we must take the competitive struggle to Eastasia's own home markets with all the commercial vigor they have shown in our own.

Don't Borrow Blindly from Eastasia

A sizable number of commentators currently recommend remedial measures that range from copying the great Eastasian trading companies in their large-scale buying and selling practices to imitating the "quality circle" used to improve performance in Japanese companies. One author, proposing a "Theory Z," urges American companies to improve their employee relations to get the most out of their workers.[6] Another suggests a New American Ideology, modeled on the New England town meeting as a functional substitute for the Eastasian concept of village solidarity.[7] Yet another author recommends that the U.S. government form an agency that would promote industry as effectively as does Japan's Ministry of International Trade and Industry (MITI).[8] As the world progresses, we will undoubtedly hear proponents of one-party systems, large industrial groups, and even street committees of citizens.

Absorbing "lessons from Eastasia" is becoming a national fad. But copying Japan and other nations of the region is not the key to our national economic renaissance, as the passage of time will make ever more clear. Many of Eastasia's most prominent qualities, such as rigid hierarchies and secrecy, are traits we would not want to imitate even if we could. Stressing conformity at the expense of individualism could also alter the course of our democracy in morally as well as practically repugnant ways.

Copying Eastasia uncritically would also be frustrating as well as potentially dangerous, since the most fundamental reasons for Eastasian economic success are not transferable. Eastasian society from Japan to China to Singapore took centuries to evolve and works together only in the aggregate. The bureaucracy is strong because society respects it and because private information flows are faulty. Policies are predictable because leadership is too; land reforms and industrial developments profoundly different from our own have played vital roles in shaping the stable coalitions that rule. To believe that we can extract parts of the Japanese or Chinese pattern and leave out the others is as misleading as the old arguments of counterinsurgency experts that we could beat guerilla rebels with their own tactics. As we learned in Vietnam, when it comes to entire nations and societies, one cannot fight fire with fire.

This is not to say that we can learn nothing from Eastasia. We can, but our lessons inevitably will be piecemeal. We will gain from studying Japanese quality control techniques, Korean worker motivation, or even some aspects of Chinese technology borrowing. We can likewise profit by promoting expanded government-business-labor communication, and encouraging efforts at consensus building rather than confrontation by both Left and Right or national leadership. But putting these lessons into practice in our own society will not be easy. While we clearly have much to gain from knowing our adversaries well, what we learn from them directly will be less important than what we learn about ourselves in the process.

Let's Play the Game—Our Way

The fact is that America, too, is a unique sociey, with its own historical and cultural imperatives. A MITI-like government agency which tried to "guide" industrial investment or even to develop "visions" of appropriate industrial structures would be suspected as one more new, unsympathetic form of government regulation. Americans distrust their government too much for the Eastasian pattern to work. Those who recommend a rejuvenated work ethic in American corporations run into several similar problems. Americans are fiercely individulistic about their work and find it hard to be loyal for a lifetime to a single company, unless it is their own; they find Asian attitudes toward the community, with its lack of privacy and its leveling tendencies, to be deeply intrusive; and they strongly dislike any hint of regimentation and imposed discipline. Perhaps some companies with unusual leadership and work styles can make new forms of management work, but it is doubtful that this microeconomic approach is the solution for the nation as a whole.

More consistent with American character is the pattern of vibrant growth which California's Silicon Valley epitomizes. A sunny, sleepy land of vineyards in the early 1950s, this region just south of San Francisco more than quadrupled its population between 1950 and 1980 and is now a principal home to a U. S. semiconductor industry with annual sales well over $5 billion. Furious competition among entrepreneurs moving rapidly from firm to firm is even now spawning vigorous new industries such as laser applications and biotechnology—in which government plays little role. Although defense contracts were important in the area's early development during the 1950s, government procurements currently represent less than 10 percent of total semiconductor sales and a similarly meager portion in most of the newer industries of the Valley. Indeed, the firms of the region tend to be highly suspicious of state intervention, and prefer to live and die throgh the play of market forces.

Silicon Valley relies for defense against Eastasian challenge on shrewd product development and creativity—a key variable in markets such as microprocessors and software, which have growing importance in the electronics industry overall. Although the Valley is losing to Japan in production of commodity devices such as random-access memories, it retains strong positions in higher value-added custom-made product lines, and it grows more than four times as fast as the U.S. economy overall. Silicon Valley has learned how to play the game our way and should be supported. What it needs is not a centralized semiconductor policy but better opportunities to raise capital and more aggressive defense of market access abroad. Through such measures we can give special priority to this region's creative firms, without curbing their dynamism.

A second example of how we could play the game our own way lies in the successful story of some American corporations abroad, regarded with awe even by the Eastasians. Companies such as General Motors, IBM, General Electric, and Mobil Oil mesh the efforts of employees throughout the globe in complex production systems with few parallels in Eastasia. Their weakness from the American standpoint is that they undertake a growing share of sophisticated manufacturing processes abroad. Such firms should be encouraged to use their financial and marketing strength to promote American exports rather than imports, and to undertake more research and development at home. This could be accomplished by offering tax benefits to high value-added manufacturing, by making domestic research and development more financially attractive than foreign, and by more vigorously supporting export activities in general. In this way, instead of funneling technically sophisticated foreign products into America and leaving us producing TV cabinets rather than circuitry, our multinationals could be turned into an effective export machine—working for us rather than against us. As the skilled linebacker uses his opponents momentum to his own advantage, our multinational corporations could moblize Eastasian strength to our own benefit. They could undertake portions of complex manufacturing processes in which Eastasia excels abroad, but concentrate increasingly the high value-added operations here at home.

Americans mobilize well for war, and under wartime conditions can pull together in teamwork that would make and nation proud. We have been at war in Eastasia before, but our military fortunes there depended on the extent to which we felt genuinely threatened. Against Japan we had little doubt, since the Japanese militarists made the mistake of attempting a stab in the back at Pearl Harbor; against China in Korea we fought to a standstill because (in part) we had just emerged from a war where China was one of our most loyal allies; and against Vietnam we fought poorly (as a nation, though served by a valiant army) because we were not convinced that vital interests were at stake. In this sense the Eastasians are much more sophisticated than we: they realize that their nation is always at war, in economic terms if not political, and always requires a mobilized society. But we are capable of equal commitment when we sense the need for it.

Cohesion in External Policy

Clearly if we are in a national crisis, the time has come to act in concert. But we do not act as though we appreciated the dangers at hand. Our Congress passes laws making it difficult for businesses to close deals overseas without expensive paperwork, proving that no government official has been "bribed" in the process. The Japanese trading companies are subject to no such rules. Indeed, they are encouraged by their expense-account and slush-fund policies to make negotiations extremely pleasant down to the signing table. American tax authorities impose double taxation on our companies' employees who live abroad and pay taxes to foreign governments. Our antitrust laws (as they have been interpreted) make it difficult for American firms to put together large packages, to collaborate in contracts abroad, or to form integrated finance and trading companies that can move swiftly in the world of international trade. Our natural bias against bigness, translated to the international sphere, makes it difficult for our nation to concert its economic strategy against an outside world where bigness rules.

By cohesion we mean more than just allowing large companies to trade aggressively and at will. We mean more sharing of information between companies and within the government about Eastasian strategies and practices. We mean more serious use of the little expertise we have on Eastasia—in universities, government, and business—for research, intelligence work, and analysis. (The amount of English-language material generated by Eastasian governments, banks, and trading and securities companies is astonishing, and yet we seem to have few people equipped to read it.) We mean the education of a new generation of students—experts for the future—who can speak the languages of the area but who are not tied to its special interests. We continue to be at the mercy of foreign companies and governments who speak our language much better than we do theirs. We mean a government with diplomats and officials who have studied economics and dealt with commercial problems in the kind of detail with which Korean or Taiwanese commercial officials deal routinely. Above all, we mean a perception that any American official, trader, soldier, diplomat, politician, or academic must consider the national interest first in his or her dealings with nations where national interest is not just first but almost everything.

If we have a lesson to learn from Eastasia in this vein, it is that all sectors of public policy must be integrated with one another and not compartmentalized. We tend to treat social welfare policy, with its concern for the unemployed and underprivileged, as though it were in conflict with industrial policy, with its concern for profits and investments. Industrial strength is the basis upon which rests a nation's ability to provide for its needy. Cohesion of policymaking allows Singapore and Japan to use social security and postal insurance payments to fund steel mills without stimulating inflation or scaring off private investors. The same cohesion of policy allows Hong Kong to manage its public debt by selling land to private buyers. Americans do not permit such freewheeling policies because they have little confidence that government will act in a cohesive and rational way.

National defense stands to gain most from the integrated approach we recommend. From ancient times the Chinese and Japanese have thought of economic policy and national defense policy as one; during the late nineteenth century, Chinese reformers and Meiji oligarchs both harked back to those classical origins to draw their rationale for industrialization in the face of foreign threat. The ancient Chinese classical expression *Fuguo qiangbing* ("Bountiful country—strong military"), or *Fukoku kyōhei* in Japanese, became the rallying cry of groups bent on modernization in both lands. America must now realize that a potent national defense can only be built on strong economic foundations. If we do not grow, and if we commit our public resources to nonproductive uses, we cannot compete with the Soviet Union. Conversely, military development will undoubtedly sharpen our technological edge, as it already has in advanced electronics. Raw-material supply is critical to our national security as well as to our economic well-being, as Eastasian countries have seen clearly.

Lean and Decisive Government

The U.S. government cannot be evenhanded but must exercise choice about directions for the future. For Americans, with a political system devoted to equality, this concept often raises profound philosophical problems in the abstract. But for a people devoted to efficiency, it also has appeal on pragmatic grounds. A nation that tacitly treats shoes and semiconductors as strategically coequal is simply avoiding choices and courting disaster. Industries must be treated differently by encouraging those that contribute more to the wealth of the society as a whole. This calculation may be made in terms of value added, technological leadership, or relative contribution of inputs to other industries. Growth sectors deserve some priority over those that are stable or declining; export industries need encouragement in an increasingly politicized international trading environment.

Of course, choices of this sort are painful. For Americans who cherish equality before the law, equal treatment by government has become almost a constitutional right. Political forces, particularly regional interests in our federal system, will often slow down the process of choice (as they have in Eastasia itself). Social "safety nets" will have to be fashioned to offset the human consequences of an open trade policy. And government must avoid the pitfall of trying to pick winners before the market has spoken. But whatever the difficulties, American government can no longer avoid making decisions.

Eastasian governments operate with low budgets but manage entire economies. They succeed because they know how to focus on narrow, strategic target sectors whose production serves as a crucial input to many other industries. Governments watch carefully such industries as steel, energy, shipping, and, most recently, semiconductors; insist that these sectors introduce efficient production facilities; and require them to adopt low-margin, high-volume production strategies that benefit sectors further downstream. In present-day Taiwan, as in Meiji Japan a century ago, the vehicle for government guidance of industry is the public corporation. In postwar Japan and South Korea, government aid has come mainly through assistance to dynamic private sectors such as steel and electronics parts manufacturing. Finished and consumer goods industries such as autos and consumer electronics have received, in most cases, relatively little direct government guidance or aid, although they have often been assisted indirectly by protectionist barriers in home markets, as in the case of the Korean auto industry during the 1970s. American government must have the courage to single out critical new sectors for help instead of supporting lost causes.

Nowhere are the contrasts between Eastasian and American approaches to economic management more strikingly different than in attitudes toward basic industry. American presidents have tacitly recognized the strategic importance of steel in affecting inflation rates—for example, when they have singled the industry out for "jawboning," as John F. Kennedy did in 1962. But both they and the Congress have failed to give industry incentives to create efficient new capacity, without which the auto, machinery, shibuilding, construction, and electric-appliance industries cannot acquire the low-cost steel they need. Rapidly rising capital costs, import competition, and increasing volatility of demand all discourage basic sectors such as steel, petrochemicals, and aluminum from expanding capacity; the firms in these areas recoup their investments through the high profit margins produced by inflationary supply shortages. These industries receive few special tax or credit benefits; their costs are often significantly raised by government regulatory policy. The result is declining competitiveness for finished-goods sectors, and cost-push inflationary pressures throughout the economy.

Eastasian public policy, in sharp contrast, tends to look at basic industries as public utilities, to be nurtured for the common good. Government encourages them to keep the prices they charge to downstream clients low, but it tries to do so by reducing the production costs for these industries, rather than by unduly depressing their profit levels. Basic industries, for example, often get preferential access to credit or raw materials. Favorable accelerated-depreciation tax provisions encourage them to introduce the most modern equipment. The certainty of government support (in the form of recession cartels or aid in scrapping excess equipment, should expansion plans prove overly optimistic) encourages firms to be aggressive in expanding capacity.

Clearly there are serious philosophical and practical problems involved in abridging this nation's traditional free-enterprise system. But some systematic form of differentiation among industries is critical for policy purposes. So long as it does not involve creation of a cumbersome, intrusive state bureaucracy, such an arrangement does not represent a radical departure in our traditional conception of the role of the state in economic life. The Commerce Department's current practice of lumping integrated circuits, shoes, and textiles together as primary objects of attention in the newly created Office of Industrial Policy leaves much to be desired.

Targeting should be carried from the sectoral level to the level of specific technology, just as it is in Eastasia, particularly in Japan. (The Taiwanese and Singaporeans use broader-gauge weapons of industrial policy, such as fixed-period tax holidays, at the microeconomic level.) In Japan, rates of accelerated depreciation are fine-tuned down to the level of specific machinery; the rate varies, depending on how strategic a specific machine is to the development of a particular industry, and on how much MITI wants to see it introduced. The Japanese system is extremely flexible, with adjustment of depreciation schedules lying largely in the hands of working-level engineers and administrative functionaries within MITI, and the Ministry of Finance, and subject to change when changing technological circumstances demand. Because this sytem operates through the tax mechanism, it does not require the creation of a large, cumbersome government bureaucracy. Some variant of the Japanese system might well be considered for introduction here. Representatives Jim Jones (D-Oklahoma) and Barber Conable (R-New York) made a positive start with the accelerated depreciation proposal they introduced into Congress during 1980, and the concept was advanced in the Reagan administration tax legislation of 1981.

In many respects the experience of Japan, as the most sophisticated of the Eastasian economies, has the greatest relevance to the United States. The key element in its successful "lean government" approach to industrial policy has been its astute use of market forces to achieve policy goals, even as it has provided an underlying cushion of support for basic industry. In textiles, for example, MITI has forced domestic producers out of labor-intensive, low-value-added product lines, or out of the industry altogether, by allowing a growing flood of imports from Korea and Southeast Asia over the past decade. The United States has for over twenty years followed the path of protection instead. In petroleum, MITI has simultaneously discouraged nonessential consumption and encouraged expanded supply from the international majors by allowing gasoline prices to rise with world market prices. The United States, by contrast, long had price controls that encouraged consumption. In high-technology industry, MITI has made a point of including multiple competing firms in key government-business research projects, such as the recent effort to build state-of-the-art VLSI electronic circuitry. Five major electronics firms were involved in that effort, and MITI distributed information to all of them.

U.S. government research contracts, by contrast, have tended to be with individual firms, thus restraining the incentives to develop technology for the market that exists when rival firms have access to it.

MITI is careful in shaping markets and offering access to them. It controls industrial standards and licenses production capacity in newly opening sectors. But once a market has been established with certain strategic specifications, MITI does not intervene directly. Government only rarely tells industry what equipment to buy or what technology to introduce, although it routinely varies rates of depreciation in order to shape these decisions. During the early 1970s, for example, Japanese firms were allowed to depreciate pollution-control investments 60 percent in the first year. Later, as pollution subsided as a problem in Japan, this rate was reduced to only 27 percent. Instead of ordering industries to relocate, MITI deliberately encourages them to move by offering them attractive facilities such as harbors, water hookups, and railway terminals. By using prices and costs rather than rules to change policies, Japan does not need to hire large numbers of bureaucrats. This notion is gradually even spreading into China, where the Soviet bureaucratic mentality still prevails.

Even in the relatively small range of cases where the Japanese bureaucracy seems to depart from its reliance on market forces to interfere with business decisions, it generally does so to speed up the operation of those market forces. For example, the Japanese government created a cartel in shipbuilding under special depressed-industries legislation passed in 1977, several years after the first oil shock. In consultation with industry, MITI decided to scrap over 40 percent of existing capacity and designated the facilities to be scrapped. But this action, like the scrapping of much open-hearth steel and fertilizer production capacity after 1973, assumed that market forces would in any case ultimately move Japanese industrial structure in that direction.

Lean government has succeeded so well in coordinating the trillion-dollar Japanese economy because it has been able to rely extensively on initiative and information from the private sector. In each major sector, an industry association *(gyōkai)* representing the major firms provides MITI with current data on the industry's condition, makes policy proposals to MITI, and helps administer depressed-industry cartels and capacity-reduction and voluntary-restraint agreements. Major business federations like Keidanren also maintain substantial staffs to draft policy proposals and to orchestrate Japan's increasingly complex resource-oriented diplomacy.

The United States, which lacks such influential business institutes as Mitsubishi or Nomura Research, also tends to distrust industry policy-development bodies such as Keidanren or the *gyōkai.* But we might learn from their example and make more use of our Conference Board or our existing "think tanks," such as the Brookings Institution or the American Enterprise Institute. Such institutions will be more widely respected if they make every effort to represent the national interest and not some set of special interests.

Lean government in the Eastasian style preserves the freedom to fail for most industries, while at the same time reducing the uncertainties of major capital investment. The number of Japanese bankruptcies in 1978, for example, was more than double that in the much larger United States, and the average liabilities per bankruptcy were twice as great as in this country.[9] Even one of the top-ten general trading companies, Ataka Sangyō, was recently on the list of failures; losses to Ataka's principal bank alone exceeded $800 million. At the same time, government encourages the kind of close ties between firms and banks, especially the long-term credit banks, that permit massive investments with long-term payout. These ties have been especially important in the evolution of basic industries with heavy capital requirements, such as steel and petrochemicals.

The U.S. government will have to walk a tight line between callous unconcern for business failure and excessive favoritism for particular industries, exercising special caution when the market verdict on such sectors is not clear. It might try loan guarantees in order to develop new technology in strategic sectors such as semiconductors, where the high cost of capital is currently eating away at our competitive edge; but it must also be prepared to tolerate high failure rates in less competitive fields such as clothing and shoe manufacturing, or even precision machinery. It can try to implement special tax credits for basic research and development expenditures in high-technology fields, but it also must be prepared to resist the general clamor for such largesse from all sectors of the economy. Here again the Eastasians have the edge because their governments and corporations are subject to less public scrutiny and skepticism. The American public may be too jealous of the concentration of power in large industries and too sensitive to the use of financial strength by bankers to permit this kind of careful screening of the economy.

Encouraging Savings and Investment

We have singled out the government-sponsored savings systems—such as Japan's postal savings system and Singapore's Central Provident Fund—as examples of how Eastasian governments encourage their citizens to save rather than consume the fruits of growth, and thus foster growth without inflation. If our country were interested (as we think it should be) in encouraging savings, it would need to take certain basic steps far beyond the temporary introduction of the All-Savers Certificate. Eastasian governments employ many gimmicks to increase the savings rates, from rank propaganda to special tax treatment of savings, including some interesting loopholes we have already examined. But the most important first step must be to reduce the rate of inflation to a point where savings accounts can keep pace, or to permit the interest rates on government and thrift investments to rise in order to accomplish the same goal. To ask Americans to put money into a postal savings system (which, incidentally, was abolished in 1958) or into thrift institutions at a statutory 5 percent instead of into moneymarket instruments or current consumption is stretching patriotism too far, as we have increasingly come to realize. The new certificate, introduced in October 1981, is a step in the right direction. But whether this program will substantially increase the overall national savings rate, as opposed to merely attracting funds formerly invested in other types of assets, is open to question. More fundamental efforts at drawing savings from the grassroots—for example, through improved tax incentives to company savings and profit-sharing programs for ordinary employees—should be considered. Private savings would also be fostered by a more realistic debate on the future prospects of our social security system, which political pressure, demographics, and low economic growth are pushing slowly but surely toward bankruptcy.

Encouraging investment adequately may involve some reorganization of our banking system, which historically has been too fragmented and decentralized effectively to support capital-intensive basic industry, or the organization of general trading companies on the Japanese pattern. Already there are signs that the restrictions on interstate banking and on offshore involvement of domestic banks, which date from the early part of this century, will be modified in order to meet the needs of modern international competition and domestic capital investment, a development we wholeheartedly support. Given the current crisis of American capital markets in the face of volatile inflation and exchange rates, we might consider establishing specialized long-term credit banks in the United States. In Eastasia these institutions borrow short-term funds and assume the risk of converting them into massive, quickly available long-term loans for basic industry. American capital markets cannot now readily perform this function except at unacceptable cost to the borrower.[10] A Federal Development Bank, with legislative authorization to raise capital and invest in strategically important long-range projects, could provide to America's reindustrialization the kind of long-term security that the Federal National Mortgage Association has given to the thrift institutions, or the Federal Land Bank to agriculture.[11] Such an institution, supplemented with appropriate changes in tax-credit and capital-gains legislation, could be especially useful for financing capacity expansion and research expenditures relating to alternate-energy sources and high-technology electronics, sectors in which capital shortages appear likely to be among the most important constraints on growth over the course of this decade.

Creative Destruction

Tax policy is a favorite political football in American politics, so much so that entire presidential campaigns are waged on reform of the system. Not surprisingly, most of this political rhetoric misses the point: that the tax structure of a nation is a key to its future growth. Tax incentives built the oil industry, the highway system, our sprawling suburbia, and many other hallmarks of modern America. They could be used to reindustrialize this country. In Eastasia tax systems promote savings, as we have seen. They are also used to encourage what we have called "creative destruction" of the industrial economy, to encourage rapid renewal of capital equipment and innovation in producing higher-value-added production. The United States badly needs to reexamine its investment credit tax provisions to encourage more productive use of taxpayer dollars. The price of poor tax policy is not, as politicians hint, that one part of society will benefit at the expense of another, but that all sectors will lose out to more efficient outsiders.

In an America where a heavy portion of the basic industrial plant dates from World War II and is now nearly forty years old, the dynamics of "creative destruction" in Japan have considerable relevance. Despite the fact that the average age of Japanese capital stock is less than ten years, capital spending increased 16 percent in 1979 and included substantial replacement expenditures, or expenditures for newer equipment capable of producing higher-value-added products. In high-technology sectors, such frequent renewal is facilitated by extensive leasing programs with favorable equipment-return provisions; both computers and, since 1980, industrial robots have been offered to Japanese industry under such programs. In other sectors, such as shipbuilding and textiles, government subsidies for the scrapping of equipment have been a factor. Additionally, of course, there is normally special accelerated depreciation for the introduction of new equipment, especially when it is technologically advanced.

An American Version of the General Trading Company?

Much of the competitive edge of Eastasia, we have argued throughout this book, stems from the sophistication of its private institutions, including its industrial groups, industry associations, and general trading companies. Also important have been the various consultative bodies or government-business-labor deliberative councils. These help not only to break down tension among various groups with divergent interests but also to legitimate a consensus once it has been achieved behind the scenes. Behind all these organizations stand the primary groups of society—the extended family in China and the corporation in Japan. They are the real bedrock on which the intense dynamism of the region rests.

Despite the differences in social structure between East and West, this nation might try encouraging the "togetherness" that seems to give Eastasian firms such vitality. We could, for example, offer tax credits to individual firms that undertake job retraining within the firm rather than precipitously firing workers. Other support could also be provided to encourage companies to form closer links to the communities in which they are situated. The unit of people willing to work together as a group needs to be encouraged. Only on this basis can productivity, low inflation, and economic growth ultimately be built. This will be a hard pill for some rugged individualists to swallow, unless it is given a sweet coating.

Perhaps the Eastasian private-sector organizational form with greatest potential application in the West is the general trading company.[12] Such firms could provide specialized expertise on foreign trade to the huge number of small firms in the United States with promising products to sell abroad, but without a knowledge of foreign markets or commercial procedures. They could also help coordinate the complex process of building necessary infrastructure and exporting commodities such as coal. North America has these in abundance, but often in hard-to-get-at locations. They could help promote trade in new products for which no established marketing infrastructure exists. Finally, American-based general trading companies might be unusually aggressive promoters of American exports, especially in Japan and neighboring states, because they would not have the conflicting ties with domestic producers in Eastasia which often constrain the marketing efforts of Japanese companies.

Perhaps the major obstacle to introducing the general trading company into the United States is cultural. There is no guarantee that Americans, entrusted with complex, difficult, and potentially lucrative transactions in which personal ties and personally obtained information are a crucial element, would use such information and personal ties exclusively on behalf of their firm. In the absence of strong personal incentives, especially financial ones, they might well be inclined to leave the firm at a critical juncture and try their luck elsewhere, leaving the organization in chaos. Complex human networks such as trading companies demand, like diamond-trading syndicates, strong organizational loyalty as a prerequisite. There is some question as to whether such qualities are available in America, except in families and in ethnic subgroups with exceptionally strong bonds of interpersonal trust.

The problem of transferring the concept of the general trading company to the United States is in many respects the problem of "lessons from Eastasia" in microcosm. Given their sharply divergent cultural backgrounds and conceptions of the relationship between business and government, the United States and Eastasia in many ways find it difficult to learn from one another. To be sure, there are numerous technical dimensions, such as blast furnace technology or quality control methods, in which the West can learn from the East, just as the reverse was true a century ago. The general philosophy of Eastasian public policy can also be instructive, as in its emphasis on an integrated approach to all aspects of economic policy. But whether the sophisticated private-sector organizational forms and cultural expectations of a people of scarcity, living and working together in crowded lands for millennia, can be transferred to an individualistic people of plenty is more questionable. The Eastasia Edge represents a spiritual and organizational challenge that will be difficult, but not impossible, for this nation to meet.

17

The Edge of the Future

AFTER examining in detail a wide range of policies and strategies, we are now in a position to return to the fundamental question we raised in our first chapter. What is the best way for us, as outsiders, to understand the strengths and weaknesses of the Eastasian nations and to explain their success to date?

As we suggested, the key to the answer is to pass through the looking glass and to see the nations as a whole, for their success is more than the sum of the individual parts. Looked at in this way, China, Japan, and Korea display political systems that seem better geared to economic competition than our own. Let us review some of the high points of our argument before venturing to speculate about the future.

First, we have argued that Eastasian political systems are admirably flexible in dealing with the uncertainties of the modern world. Flexibility stems from Eastasia's sophisticated and resilient private-sector organization, which even in the Communist societies is encouraged in the guise of families, farms, and firms. Flexibility is an advantage enjoyed by governments and organizations that can maintain secrecy and a tight elitism of the sort that characterizes the Japanese cabinet or the Chinese Politburo. Flexibility enables Eastasian nations to meet unexpected shocks with bold and unusual strategies—as the South Koreans did with their construction drive after the oil shock of 1973, as Japan did in gearing for peaceful economic competition after losing the Pacific war, and as China did in its sudden switch from Maoism to pragmatic modernization. Such dramatic changes in policy are more likely in societies such as Eastasia, where ultimate power is closely held and where authority is respected and followed even when it proves wrong—until it can be replaced by alternate authority. Eastasian political and economic leaders enjoy powers —and responsibilities—that in the Western world are normally exercised only by naval commanders of isolated warships.

Second, Eastasian political systems are inherently stable and work to maintain stability for their countries. Stability in Eastasia is a hard-earned condition, resulting from a long series of struggles in the last century. Land reform, whether Communist or capitalist, has contributed to this political stability by isolating and coopting a potentially destabilizing force, wealthy landlords in the countryside. (In Latin America, the Philippines, and elsewhere, such groups have played a central role in frustrating the process of economic growth.) Bureaucratic leadership by government ministers or by managers of industrial and financial groups gives Eastasian societies a central rudder, providing continuous and responsible direction. Stability is also enhanced by the tendency of Eastasian societies toward one-party rule. Government consequently is able to resist radical changes in fiscal or monetary policy and can therefore make the business environment much more predictable than in the West. It is also able to pursue taxation, welfare, and labor policies clearly favorable toward business, even when these run counter to the apparent interests of intellectuals and urban working classes to a degree that would be untenable elsewhere in the world. This stable, business-oriented pattern of economic policy is a result of the peculiar coalition of bureaucrats, businessmen, and rural freeholders that brought Eastasia into the modern world.

As a result of this underlying political stability, governments in Eastasia can undertake long-range policies and maintain credibility. They can guarantee to heavy industry billions for future investment, which in turn allows the private sector to make aggressive, audacious international commitments and honor them. This stability creates, in short, the kind of political economy that permitted Korea's Hyundai in 1972 to make contracts to deliver supertankers in thirty months from a shipyard which was a sandy beach at the time the contracts were signed. The Eastasian kind of long-range commitment to economic goals has been possible in the United States only in the case of projects with military implications, such as the Manhattan Project or the Apollo program.

Finally, Eastasian political systems are characterized by a high degree of respect for hierarchy and for order from top to bottom. Lean government is possible because government receives more respect than in most countries of the West. Dual rule by public and private interests occurs in Eastasia because all realize that the alternative is chaos. A situation in which there is no central authority is quite intolerable in Eastasian political culture. In response to the deference which its citizens confer, the state in Eastasia generates policies much as the Pope grants blessings to the loyal and faithful of the Catholic Church. Even in "private" life, hierarchy often rules, as industries defer to the largest among them, private and public power coalesce, and ordinary citizens defer to whoever may be shown to possess authority. The striking discipline and obedience of the Chinese citizens of Hong Kong to the British colonial government is surely a rare occurrence in the history of the British Empire. And where but in Eastasia can governments deploy nuclear power plants often without a whimper of resistance?

Flexibility, predictability, and hierarchy are a rare combination of virtues in the nations of the 1980s. This decade presents the world with greater challenges than ever before: a heightening energy crisis, increasing population pressures, a widening gap between rich and poor nations, dramatic new industrial technologies. All these challenges require not just one of these virtues, but a combination of them.

The remarkable fact about all these growth-promoting facets of the Eastasian scene is that they are in the final analysis primarily structural, not cultural, as is commonly believed. Eastasian culture has remained largely constant over hundreds of years, yet the region's explosive economic growth is a matter of the past few decades. Culture provides a background of values reinforcing respect for authority, promoting education, and rewarding diligence. But without the appropriate political structures, such a background will not produce the desired economic results, as the disastrous experience of Republican China demonstrated before 1949.

It is this structural advantage of Eastasian political systems which leads us to conclude that it is impossible to beat the Eastasians at their own game. We could no more copy the leading role of Japan's Ministry of International Trade and Industry—cajoling, appealing to deference, playing the haughty Tokyo University graduate-bureaucrat role, planning strategy for the rest of the country—than we could expect a Japanese to join gaily in the apparent chaos of a Democratic Party national convention or to understand the American penchant for empty moralism in its political leaders. And the gulf between our politics and those of the Chinese and North Koreans is even wider.

This conclusion does not mean that there is nothing to be gained from a careful study of the Eastasian pattern of economic growth. On the contrary, we have suggested a number of important lessons we should by now have learned, and even a few experiments that might be worth trying. The important thing to learn is that, whatever the political inputs required, it is in our best interests to create an environment for success. That environment must include provisions for more stability of policy, more predictability of economic conditions, more flexibility of bureaucratic response, more integrated development strategies, and a greater consciousness of the national interest in our economy. It must also include those same guarantees of freedom for enterprise, of open markets, and of lively competition that put us on top in the first place.

The bottom line of our recommendations about how to regain our competitive edge is that we must learn the name of the game, but not play it their way. The name of the game played by China, Japan, Korea, and the smaller Eastasian states is national survival in a world where production and marketing are as important as weaponry and firepower in keeping one's country in the running. We ignore this fundamental rule only at our own peril.

What does the future hold? Will Eastasia continue to increase its edge on us into the indefinite future? The last twenty-five years have been exceptional in many ways. The balance of military power, maintained stably between the two superpowers, the United States and the Soviet Union, has permitted the rest of the world to develop economically. The regime of free trade has remained surprisingly strong, despite setbacks in the world monetary order and occasional minor trade wars, thus giving opportunity to new entrants to the world market. The vanquished nations of World War II have been set free to enter the economic arena on the coattails of the victors. But these unusual conditions may be coming to an end.

The next quarter century will be more difficult for Eastasia. Already many are asking whether it is in our interest, regardless of our desire to frustrate the Soviet Union, to continue to develop China's science and technology in the way we did Japan's in the 1950s. We are surely likely to get even less for it than in the case of Japan, both in the short and in the long run. Many are asking whether Japan should continue to be allowed a free ride on the merry-go-round of world rearmament, particularly since an increasing portion of the burden of maintaining U.S. forces abroad goes for the defense of Eastasia. The maturing of our competitive relationship with Eastasia has put many American companies on their guard about future commitments to develop further the economies across the Pacific—and so on.

But it is one thing to doubt whether Eastasia can continue to grow at the same phenomenal rate, and quite another to believe that its fortunes will be reversed. Short of a world war or some other cataclysmic event that interrupts the flow of commerce and raw materials, it is hard to conceive of a dramatic decline in Eastasian growth and performance, and the possibility exists of a considerable and sustained upward thrust. Given the deep-seated ills of Western societies, Eastasia may gain against the West even if, in comparison with past performance, it only stands still.

Again the major unknown is China, and particularly the Sino-Japanese relationship. We have speculated that China's political future will remain in the hands of men and women who are moderate, pragmatic, and determined to walk in the successful path of modern Japan. Others will disagree with this assertion, either by suggesting the possibility of a more radical outcome in China or by doubting that Japan will benefit from China's modernization more than will other nations. We remain convinced that the world has seen only the beginning of a long and remarkable relationship between these two giants, a relationship that may transform Eastasia from a mere challenger to Western leadership into the dominant region of the world in the twenty-first century.

One thing seems certain, almost reassuring, about our findings: there is little likelihood that the peculiar combination of long-term political and economic strengths that has given Eastasia the edge over us today can be duplicated elsewhere or actively exported from Asia to other continents. The non-Confucian countries of South and Southeast Asia, where overseas Chinese business-men still play a major economic role, have perhaps the best chance for rapid growth. But their political stability and managerial capability over the long run remain seriously in question.

Since the economic performance of Eastasia rests heavily on political conditions so unique as to be unreproducible, other nations will have to be inventive in order to compete. Sadly, this prescription also applies to ourselves, for we are likely only to be frustrated by recommendations that we change our political systems to resemble more those of our competition. The challenge is to find in ourselves a uniquely American response, turning on our sense of creativity and initiative, which can steady us in the stormy years of economic confrontation ahead.

APPENDICES

APPENDIX A
Vital Statistics of Eastasia

Year	DPRK	China	Hong Kong	Japan	ROK	Singapore	ROC
			(a) Real Growth Rate of GNP				
1956	—	7.8	6.7	9.4	0.5	4.8	3.8
1965	—	8.0	15.1	4.1	6.1	7.5	6.7
1974	6.5	3.0	2.2	-1.0	8.6	0.4	0.4
1978	—	10.0	10.1	5.7	12.5	10.8	13.9
1980	—	—	9.0	3.8	-3.4	10.2	6.7
			(b) Investment Share of GNP				
1955	—	14.6	12.1	17.2	12.0	—	14.4
1965	—	24.2	24.7	24.8	12.9	14.7	28.2
1974	—	26.8	19.6	28.0	28.8	27.2	40.0
1978	35.0	26.8	24.1	30.2	31.4	34.1	31.5
1980	—	—	27.5 (1979)	34.4*	31.0	[43.6]	36.3
			(c) Savings Share of GNP				
1955	—	—	5.1	25.5	4.9	—	10.6
1965	—	—	10.3	34.2	7.5	12.0	25.0
1974	—	—	10.7	33.0	18.0	20.8	35.3
1978	25–35	—	13.0	20.0	27.2	26.1	30.1
1980	–-	—	—	18.1*	16.5 (1979)	28.4	33.4
			(d) Export Share of GNP				
1955	—	1.3	25.7	8.4	0.7	—	12.0
1965	—	1.2	41.4	9.5	5.9	26.4	23.9
1974	4.9	1.0	56.4	12.1	27.5	43.5	58.9
1978	5.0	2.2	78.0	11.1	35.1	31.9	52.7
1980	—	—	92.0	11.4	32.1	174.2	49.1
			(e) Exports-Imports GNP				
1955	—	-0.2	-30.8	-0.1	-14.1	—	-3.0
1965	—	1.0	-20.-	2.3	-9.7	-31.3	0.2
1974	-6.0	-1.2	-11.2	3.8	-5.7	-75.9	2.5
1978	0.0	-2.5	-13.5	1.7	-4.9	-38.0	6.9
1980	—	—	-15.5	0.6	-8.9	-41.6	0.1
			(f) Manufactured Share of Exports				
1955	36.8	11.4	87.5	81.7	10.9	—	8.4
1965	55.9	30.7	92.2	85.5	60.6	21.3	41.6
1974	58.4	50.6	95.0	87.1	82.8	41.2	76.6
1978	—	51.0 (1977)	96.2	91.5	88.7	46.0	89.1
1980	—	—	96.0	96.2	95.8	44.7	90.8
			(g) Capital Goods Share of Imports				
1955	33.0	23.0	8.3	7.6	22.1	—	23.4
1965	21.2	15.9	16.0	12.1	18.7	14.7	38.6
1974	34.2	22.2	18.7	9.6	31.4	18.1	47.4
1978	37.0	18.0 (1977)	19.8	8.2	33.0	29.1	30.7
1980	—	—	22.5	6.5	22.3	29.8	28.2

APPENDIX A (continued)
Vital Statistics of Eastasia

Year	DPRK	China	Hong Kong	Japan	ROK	Singapore	ROC
			(h) Growth Rate of Population				
1956	—	2.4	4.2	1.0	2.1	—	3.4
1965	—	2.2	2.6	1.1	2.8	2.5	3.0
1974	—	2.4	2.1	1.2	1.7	1.6	1.8
1978	3.1	2.0	2.1	0.9	1.6	1.2	1.9
1980	—	—	3.4	0.7	1.6	1.4	1.9

SOURCES: For 1955, 1965, 1974 (all except China): Edward K. Y. Chen, *Hyper-Growth in Asian Economies: A Comparative Study of Hong Kong, Japan, Korea, Singapore and Taiwan* (New York: Holmes and Meyer, 1979), Appendix A. For China: R. M. Field, "Real Capital Formation in the People's Republic of China, 1952–1973," in Alexander Eckstein, ed., *Quantitative Measures of China's Economic Output;* U.S. Congress, Joint Economic Committee, *China: A Reassessment of the Economy* (Washington, D.C.: U.S. Government Printing Office, 1975): Mah Feng-hwa, *The Foreign Trade of Mainland China,* Appendix B; U.S., Congress, Joint Economic Committee, *China: An Economic Assessment* (Washington, D.C.: U.S. Government Printing Office, 1975); National Foreign Assessment Center, *China: A Statistical Compendium* (July 1979). Republic of Korea. Economic Planning Board, *Major Statistics of Korean Economy,* 1979 (Seoul; 1980); Republic of China, Executive Yuan, Council for Economic Planning and Development, *Taiwan Statistical Data Book* (Taipei: 1980, 1981); Republic of Singapore, Ministry of Trade and Industry, *Economic Survey of Singapore 1979* (Singapore: Singapore National Printers, 1980); Bank of Japan, Statistics Department, *Keizai Tōkei Nenpō 1979* [Economic statistics annual] (Tokyo; 1980).

For Democratic People's Republic of Korea: Joseph Sang-hoon Chung, *The North Korean Economy: Structure and Development;* (Stanford: Hoover Institution Press, 1974); National Foreign Assessment Center, *Korea: The Economic Race Between the North and the South* (January, 1978); Donald Wise, ed., *Asia Yearbook 1981* (Hong Kong: Far Eastern Economic Review, 1981). For Hong Kong: Hong Kong, Census and Statistics Department, *Estimates of Gross Domestic Product, 1966–1979* (1981); *Hong Kong Monthly Digest of Statistics,* April 1981; Hong Kong, Trade Industry of Customs Dept., *1980 Annual Statistical Review.*

*For the first quarter.

APPENDIX B

Key Actors in Eastasian Economic Policy Formation

	JAPAN	CHINA	S. KOREA	N. KOREA	TAIWAN	HONG KONG	SINGAPORE
Government Ministries							
Trade	Min of Intntl Trade & Ind	Min of Foreign Trade	Min of Commerce & Ind	Min of Trade	Min of Econ Affairs	Trade, Ind & Customs Affairs	Min of Trade & Industry
Fiscal Affairs Central Bank	Min of Finance Bank of Japan	Min of Finance People's Bank of China	Min of Finance Bank of Korea	Min of Finance Bank of Korea	Min of Finance Central Bank of China	Financial Branch HK-Shanghai Bank (informal)	Min of Finance Monetary Auth of Singapore
Development Bank	Japan Dev Bank	—	Korea Dev Bank	—	—	—	Singapore Dev Bank
Planning	Econ Plng Agcy	State Plng Commiss	Econ Plng Board	State Plng Commiss	Coun for Econ Plng & Dev	—	Econ Dev Board
Political Actors							
Head of Government	Prime Minister	Premier	President	Premier	President	Governor	Prime Minister

APPENDIX B (continued)

Key Actors in Eastasian Economic Policy Formation

	JAPAN	CHINA	S. KOREA	N. KOREA	TAIWAN	HONG KONG	SINGAPORE
Chief of State	Emperor	Premier	President	President	President	Queen of UK	President
Executive	Cabinet	State Council	Blue House (Pres House)	Admin Council	Exec Yuan	Exec Council	Cabinet
Ruling Party	LDP	Communist	Dem Justice	Korean Workers	KMT	—	People's Action
Typical Business Organizations							
Cross-industry Federations	Fed of Econ Organizations (Keidanren)	—	Fed of Korean Industry	—	Chinese Fed of Industry	Chinese Chamber of Commerce	Chamber of Commerce
Industry Associations	Japan Iron & Steel Fed.	Chinese Council for Promoting Intnl Trade	Korean Traders Assn	—	Retired Servicemen Assn	Assn of Banks	Singapore Manufacturers Assn
Groups	Mitsubishi Mitsui Sumitomo	Shanghai bureaus; Industrial trusts	Daewoo Hyundai Samsung	—	Tatung Formosa Plastics	Jardine-Matheson Cheung Kong Hutchison-Whampoa Swire-Pacific	Inchcape

APPENDIX C
Major Industrial Enterprises of Capitalist Eastasia (1980)
Units—US $(000)

Firm	Major Business	Sales Turnover	Assets	Net Income	Int'l Ranking*
Japan					
Toyota Motor	Motor vehicles	14,233,779	7,842,615	616,051	22
Nissan Motor	Motor vehicles	13,853,503	9,293,328	461,647	23
Nippon Steel	Steel	13,104,996	13,793,676	496,205	25
Hitachi	Electronics, appliances	12,871,328	12,422,812	503,385	26
Matsushita Electric	Electronics, appliances	12,684,404	11,599,230	541,923	27
South Korea					
Hyundai	Shipbuilding, industrial equipment, motor vehicles	5,540,543	4,415,363	97,164	72
Lucky Group	Petroleum, electronics	4,452,461	2,761,487	25,490	101
Samsung Group	Appliances, food, textiles	3,798,093	3,273,225	17,756	125
Korea Oil	Petroleum	3,321,064	1,271,798	(54,589)	139
Hyosung Group	Textiles, industrial equipment	1,950,220	1,593,454	3,651	237
Taiwan					
China Petroleum	Petroleum	5,373,416	3,475,029	8,657	75
Nan Ya Plastics	Plastics	495,356	427,031	36,263	—
Formosa Plastics	Chemicals	390,334	359,177	38,975	284
Yue Long Motor	Motor vehicles	367,573	256,568	20,308	—
Tatung Co.	Electronics	360,806	425,258	15,950	—

APPENDIX C (*continued*)
Major Industrial Enterprises of Capitalist Eastasia (1980)
Units—US $(000)

Firm	Major Business	Sales Turnover	Assets	Net Income	Int'l Ranking*
Hong Kong					
Winsor International	Textiles, clothing	203,471	137,846	21,506	
Textile Alliance	Textiles, clothing	123,243	113,903	(1,942)	
Nan Fung	Textiles, clothing	94,274	87,554	12,120	
Stelux	Watches	75,122	139,555	2,654	
Jan Sing Mee	Clothing	70,551	39,339	2,459	
Singapore					
Inchcape Berhad	Motor vehicles, shipping	475,604	358,650	22,157	
Cycle and Carriage	Motor vehicles	223,346	125,178	15,671	
Malaysia Breweries	Brewery	196,803	107,715	11,946	
Wearne Brothers	Machinery	165,046	168,468	6,500	
Nat'l, Iron and Steel Mills	Steel	119,558	116,571	13,463	

Sources: *Fortune,* 10, August 1981, P. 207–12; T. K. Seshadri, ed., *Asia 1981: Measures and Magnitudes* (Hong Kong: Asian Finance Publications, 1981).

*Ranking in *Fortune*'s list of largest industrial corporations outside the United States.

Notes

1 Challenge from Eastasia

1. In 1975, U.S. trade with Asia was $55.3 billion, just barely greater than the U.S. trade of $54.2 billion with Europe. By 1980, this gap had widened to nearly $20 billion: U.S. trade with Asia was $139 billion, while that with Europe was $119.2 billion. See International Monetary Fund, *Direction of Trade Statistics,* 1976 (annual) and April 1981.

2. In 1980, U.S. exports to Eastasia (Japan, South Korea, Taiwan, Hong Kong, Singapore, and Mainland China) were $38 billion, while imports from the region exceeded $52 billion; see ibid., April 1981. See also Republic of China, Executive Yuan, Council for Economic Planning and Development, *Taiwan Statistical Data Book 1981* (Taipei, 1981), p. 191.

3. See U.S. Congress, House Committee on Ways and Means, SubCommittee on Trade, *World Auto Trade: Current Trends and Structural Problems* (Washington, D.C.: U.S. Government Printing Office, 1980), esp. pp. 99–127, 186–99. On Eastasian penetration of the European auto market, see, for example, "Automobile: pourquoi les petites japonaises?," *L'Express,* 4 October 1980, pp. 55–56.

4. European production of integrated circuits in 1979 was valued at roughly $500 million, while that of Eastasia was worth well over $1 billion. See U.S. International Trade Commission, *Competitive Factors Influencing World Trade in Integrated Circuits* (Washington, D.C.: U.S. Government Printing Office, 1979), and Kent E. Calder, "High-Technology Electronics Trade and the U.S.-Japan Relationship," *Fletcher Forum,* Winter 1980–81, pp. 30–31.

5. *Fortune,* 14 December 1981, p. 55.

6. *Business Week,* 9 June 1980, pp. 62–73.

7. Ibid.

8. On Eastasian advances in the aerospace sector, see, for example, "Survey on Aerospace," *The Economist,* 30 August 1980, after p. 42.

9. Both Italy and South Korea had nine firms on *Fortune*'s list of the 500 largest non-U.S. industrial corporations for 1979. See *Fortune,* 11 August 1980, pp. 190–204.

10. World Bank, *World Development Indicators,* June 1979.

11. Ibid.

12. Japan's total international trade volume in 1979 was 10 percent larger than Canada's entire GNP and nearly double that of Australia. See Nishiyama Takeshi, *Nihon kokusei zue* [Japan national almanac] (Tokyo: Kokusei Sha, 1980), pp. 87, 140.

13. Chen Kao-tang, ed., *China Yearbook 1979* (Taipei: China Publishing Co., 1979), pp. 15–16.

14. Ibid.

15. For details on the evolution of China's foreign trade and investment policy, see Vembar K. Ranganathan, *China Trade: Review and Prospects* (New York: Citibank Economics Department, August 1980), esp. pp. 63–169.

16. Donald Wise, ed., *Asia Yearbook 1981* (Hong Kong: Far Eastern Review, 1981), p. 10.

17. See Lester Thurow, *The Zero-Sum Society* (New York: Basic Books, 1980), pp. 3–25.

2 Perceiving the Edge

1. During 1975, Japanese auto exports to the United States totaled 2,190 per day. This figure rose to about 1,900,000 vehicles, or 5,200 a day, in 1980. See U.S. Congress, House Committee

on Ways and Means, Subcommittee on Trade, *World Auto Trade: Current Trends and Structural Problems* (Washington, D.C.: U.S. Government Printing Office, 1980), p. 103; and Edward Lincoln, ed., *Yearbook of U.S.-Japan Economic Relations in 1980* (Washington, D.C.: Japan Economic Institute of America, 1981), p. 47.

2. See Transportation Systems Center, *The U.S. Automobile Industry, 1980* (Washington, D.C.: U.S. Department of Transportation, 1981), pp. 40–44; also William J. Albernathy, Kim B. Clark, and Alan M. Kantrow, "The New Industrial Competition," *Harvard Business Review,* September–October 1981, pp. 80–81.

3. At exchange rates of around ¥231.60 to US $1 prevailing in mid-September 1981, U.S. cold-rolled sheet steel production costs were 22.1 percent higher than Japanese, while hot-rolled sheet production costs were 27.2 percent higher. See *World Steel Digest,* various issues, 1981.

4. See F. Knickerbocker, *Notes on the Watch Industries in Switzerland, Japan, and the United States,* abr. (Cambridge: Harvard Business School, 1975), p. 10, for 1970 figure of 89,500 Swiss watchmakers. According to unpublished data from the Watchmakers' of Switzerland Information Center, New York, in September 1980 there were 46,998 watchmakers continuing to reside and work in Switzerland.

5. Singapore's per capita income in 1979 was $4,150, while that of the United Kingdom was $7,054. See Donald Wise, ed., *Asia Yearbook 1981* (Hong Kong: *Far Eastern Economic Review,* 1981), p. 10, and U.S. Bureau of the Census, *Statistical Abstract of the United States, 1980* (Washington, D.C.; U.S. Government Printing Office, 1980), p. 910. At average rates of growth for the two nations over the 1974–79 period, Singapore would pass Britain around 1986–87 in per capita GNP. But accelerating growth in Singapore, combined with the short-term negative effects of the conservative austerity program on British growth, appear likely to bring the day Singapore passes Britain much closer.

6. South Korean per capita income in 1979 was $1,636, while that of India was $204 and Bangladesh $110. See Wise, *Asia Yearbook 1981,* p. 10.

7. During the 1977–80 period, for example, U.S. unit labor costs rose 22.7 percent and British costs by 57.1 percent. See Bank of Japan, *Kokusai hikaku tōkei* [International comparative statistics] (Tokyo: Nihon Ginkō Chōsa Tōkei Kyoku, 1981), pp. 19–20.

8. Koo Chian Kim, *Yearbook of Statistics: Singapore 1979/80* (Singapore: Department of Statistics, 1980), pp. 50–51, 81.

9. James C. Abegglen, "The Economic Growth of Japan," *Scientific American,* March 1970, pp. 33–35. It should be noted that Abegglen, one of the foremost U.S. authorities on Japanese business, has substantially revised his views of Japanese business-government relations since 1970, taking into account the growing pluralism of Japanese society.

10. See A. D. Barnett, *China's Economy in Global Perspective* (Washington, D.C.: Brookings Institution, 1981), chap. 1, for a sober account of the prospects for change in this direction. The "market socialism" toward which China seems headed will not "restore capitalism" but will be "distinctly Chinese," in Barnett's view.

11. *Far Eastern Economic Review,* 20 March, 1981, p. 36.

12. Many observers of the Chinese scene in the 1950s adopted a "corporatist" interpretation of Chinese behavior similar to that presently in vogue with respect to Japan. They noted the appearance of new forms of organization and structure in Chinese society: as villages became communes, companies became committee-run enterprises, and warlord bands became disciplined units of the People's Liberation Army. H. F. Schurmann, for example, noted the resemblance between Chinese factory organization and the traditional management practices of General Motors, which preferred committee votes to decisions by individual managers. See H. F. Schurmann, *Ideology and Organization in Communist China* (Berkeley: University of California Press, 1966).

13. See Richard Tanner Pascale and Anthony G. Athos, *The Art of Japanese Management* (New York: Simon & Schuster, 1981), esp. pp. 29–57.

14. Excluding China, which is only beginning to build its national infrastructure, Eastasian nations rank highest in the world in percentage of GNP spent by national governments on such projects.

15. It should be noted that the Japanese in particular have a strong sense of how their culture diverges from that of China. They tend to treat Chinese culture as a foreign entity to a greater degree than do other Eastasians.

16. See John K. Fairbank, "Why Peking Casts Us as the Villain," *New York Times Magazine,* 22 May 1966, pp. 30ff.

17. This situation contrasts strongly with the political situation in the United States, where power is so decentralized and the governing political coalition at any point so unstable that formulation of systematic, long-range policies becomes extremely difficult. The meanderings of U.S. depreciation policy from 1962 to the present are a case in point.

3 The Puzzle of Growth

1. See, for example, Cynthia Kerr Rao, ed., *Hong Kong 1981* (Hong Kong: Government Press, 1981), p. 266; Republic of China, Executive Yuan, Council for Economic Planning and Development, *Taiwan Statistical Data Book 1981* (Taipei, 1981), pp. 154–55.

2. Hollis Chenery, Montek S. Ahluwalia, C. L. G. Bell, John H. Duloy, and Richard Jolly, *Redistribution with Growth* (New York: Oxford University Press, 1974), p. 8.

3. Ibid.

4 Common Sources of Strength

1. For a concise introduction to the essentials of Confucian thought, see Arthur Waley, ed. and trans., *The Analects of Confucius* (London: George Allen & Unwin, 1938).

2. On the sharp contrasts between the United States and Japan in the social and political roles of litigation, see Hideo Tanaka, ed., *The Japanese Legal System* (Tokyo: University of Tokyo Press, 1976). For a recent application of the term to modern Eastasian systems, see Roderick Mac Farquhar, "The Post-Confucian Challenge," *The Economist*, February 9, 1980.

3. On the relationship between nationalism and modernization in late-developing states, see, among others, Alexander Gerschenkron, *Economic Backwardness in Historical Perspective* (Cambridge: Harvard University Press, 1962); Henry Rosovsky et al., *The Modernization of Japan and Russia: A Comparative Study* (New York: Free Press, 1975); and Dankwart A. Rustow and Robert E. Ward, eds., *Political Modernization in Japan and Turkey* (Princeton: Princeton University Press, 1964).

4. For details on U.S.-Japanese encounters shortly after Perry's initial landing, see Edwin O. Reischauer, *The United States and Japan,* 3d ed. (Cambridge: Harvard University Press, 1965), pp. 8–11; and William L. Neumann, *America Encounters Japan* (Baltimore: Johns Hopkins Press, 1963), pp. 19–50.

5. On the early industrial development of China and the role of reformers in furthering it, see Albert Feuerwerker, *China's Early Industrialization: Sheng Hsuan-huai, 1844–1916, and Mandarin Enterprise* (Cambridge: Harvard University Press, 1958).

6. Chie Nakane, *Japanese Society* (Berkeley: University of California Press, 1970).

7. Eastasian patterns of intra-organizational contact, which normally involve highly flexible communication between superiors and inferiors, contrast sharply with the European patterns described by Michel Crozier in *The Bureaucratic Phenomenon* (Chicago: University of Chicago Press, 1964).

8. For details see Kent E. Calder, "Shomin vs. Kanryō: Contrasting Dynamics of Conservative Leadership in Postwar Japan," in *Leadership in Contemporary Japan,* edited by Terry E. Mac-Dougall (Ann Arbor: University of Michigan, Center for Japanese Studies), forthcoming.

9. See Neil H. Jacoby, *U.S. Aid to Taiwan: A Study of Foreign Aid, Self-help, and Development* (New York: Praeger, 1966).

10. One of the key members of the group was Huang Hua, China's foreign minister during the early 1980s. For details on the group, see John Israel and Donald W. Klein, *Rebels and Bureaucrats: China's December 9ers* (Berkeley: University of California Press, 1976).

11. See Nai-yan Shih, *Water Margin* (Shanghai: Commercial Press, 1937).

5. Structural Diversity: A Major Asset

1. On the role of the Japanese business community in policy formation, see Gerald R. Curtis, "Big Business and Political Influence," in Ezra E. Vogel, *Modern Japanese Organization and Decisionmaking* (Berkeley: University of California Press, 1975), pp. 33–70; and *Far Eastern Economic Review,* 24 April 1981, pp. 76–80.

2. For a detailed breakdown by industry, together with an analysis of accounting complications associated with U.S.-Japan comparisons of debt-equity ratios, see Kent E. Calder, "Politics and the Market: The Dynamics of Japanese Credit Allocation, 1946–1978" (Ph.D. dissertation, Harvard University, 1979), esp. pp. 421–26. See also Mitsubishi Research Institute, *Kigyō keiei no bunseki* [An analysis of enterprise management], various issues.

3. For an overall view, see Kent E. Calder, "Japan's Minimalist Government," *Wall Street Journal,* 13 February 1981.

4. On Korea's industrial groups, see Leroy P. Jones and Il Sakong, *Government, Business, and Entrepreneurship in Economic Development: The Korean Case* (Cambridge: Harvard University, Council on East Asian Studies, 1980).

5. For details, see Jae Yoon Kim, ed., *The Korean Financial System,* (Seoul: Bank of Korea, 1978), pp. 20–22.

6. Calder, "Politics and the Market," pp. 347–48.

7. The autonomy of Korean industrial groups reached a high point in the late 1970s, around the time of the assassination of President Park. It declined somewhat after the accession to power of President Chon Do Hwan, who moved vigorously to curb their autonomy during 1980.

8. On *Fortune's* list of the largest non-U.S. corporations for 1979, China Petroleum ranked 119th, up from 125th in 1978. See *Fortune,* 11 August 1980, p. 192.

9. Watanabe Toshio, ed., *Azia kōgyōka no shin jidai* [The new age of Asian industrialization] (Tokyo: Nihon Bōeki Shinkō Kai, 1979), p. 201.

10. Goh Chok Tong, *1980 Budget Statement,* p. 10.

11. Republic of Singapore, Ministry of Trade and Industry, *Economic Survey of Singapore 1980* (Singapore: Singapore National Printers, 1981), p. 12.

12. Interview with top-level Singapore government official, July 1980.

13. Republic of Singapore, Ministry of Culture, Information Division, *Singapore Facts and Pictures 1979* (Singapore, 1980), p. 117.

14. See Koo Chian Kim, *Yearbook of Statistics: Singapore 1979/80* (Singapore. Department of Statistics, 1980) p. 54. During the entire 1969–81 period, Singapore had only 44 industrial work stoppages.

15. Hong Kong and Shanghai Bank Group assets totaled HK$242.95 billion in 1980, while the GNP of Hong Kong itself was slightly over HK$100 billion. See Hong Kong and Shanghai Bank, *Annual Report 1980,* (Hong Kong, 1980), p. 9.

16. Long-time Hong Kong Financial Secretary Philip Haddon-Cave, for example, stressed this point strongly. See Alvin Rabushka, *Hong Kong: A Study in Economic Freedom* (Chicago: University of Chicago, Graduate School of Business, 1979), p. 123. Rabushka's work, although provocative, ignores the important elite-level private coordination within the Hong Kong political economy, and thus overstresses its market orientation.

17. For a thorough description of the workings of Hong Kong politics, see N. J. Miners, *The Government and Politics of Hong Kong,* 3d ed. (Hong Kong: Oxford University Press, 1981).

18. See Joseph Sang-hoon Chung, *The North Korean Economy: Structure and Development* (Stanford: Hoover Institution Press, 1974).

19. Arthur G. Ashbrook, Jr., "China: Economic Overview, 1975," in U.S. Congress, Joint Economic Committee, *China: A Reassessment of the Economy* (Washington, D.C.: U.S. Government Printing Office, 1975), p. 23.

20. See Parks M. Coble, *The Shanghai Capitalists and the Nationalist Government, 1927–1937* (Cambridge: Harvard University Press, 1980).

21. For details on the evolution of monetary policy in the People's Republic since 1949, see Katharine Huang Hsiao, *Money and Monetary Policy in Communist China* (New York: Columbia University Press, 1971).

6 The Dual Rule of Public and Private Power

1. See A. D. Barnett, *Cadres, Bureaucracy, and Political Power in Communist China* (New York: Columbia University Press, 1967), pp. 6–9.

2. Hong Kong and Shanghai Banking Corp., *The People's Republic of China,* Business Profile Series (July 1980), p. 14.

3. For an engrossing history of a *zaibatsu*'s development and an assessment of its functions, see John G. Roberts, *Mitsui: Three Centuries of Japanese Business* (New York: Weatherhill, 1973).

4. See Dwight Perkins, "Industrial Planning and Management," in Alexander Eckstein, Walter Galenson, and Ta-chung Liu, eds., *Economic Trends in Communist China* (Chicago: Aldine, 1968), p. 604.

5. On the industrial development of Shanghai, see Christopher Howe, ed., *Shanghai: Revolution and Development in an Asian Metropolis* (Cambridge: Cambridge University Press, 1981).

6. Japan's largest trading company, Mitsubishi, had sales in fiscal 1980 of ¥13.9 trillion (US $68.5 billion). See Oriental Economist, *Japan Company Handbook: Second Half, 1981* (Tokyo: Tōyō Keizai Shinpōsha, 1981), p. 768. On U.S.-Japan trade volume, see Edward Lincoln, ed., *Yearbook of U.S.-Japan Economic Relations in 1980* (Washington, D.C.: Japan Economic Institute of America, 1981), pp. 121–22.

7. See Inoue Munemichi, *The Economics of the Japanese Trading Company* (fellow's dissertation, Harvard University, Center for International Affairs, 1980), p. 21, on the shares of Japan's total foreign trade and of trade with specific regions that are handled by the general trading companies.

8. On this subject see Keneth I. Juster, "Foreign Policymaking During the Oil Crisis," *Japan Interpreter,* Winter 1977, pp. 293–312.

9. On Japan's "scrap and build" programs, (including the shipbuilding program) since the first oil shock, see Gary R. Saxonhouse, "Industrial Restructuring in Japan," *Journal of Japanese Studies,* Summer 1979, pp. 289–95.

10. See Walter Galenson, ed., *Economic Growth and Structural Change in Taiwan* (Ithaca: Cornell University Press, 1979), p. 345.

11. See Kent E. Calder, "Shomin vs. Kanryō: Contrasting Dynamics of Conservative Leadership in Postwar Japan," in *Leadership in Contemporary Japan,* edited by Terry E. MacDougall (Ann Arbor: University of Michigan, Center for Japanese Studies), forthcoming.

7 Agriculture: Root of the Nation

1. For introductions to some of the peasant movement literature, see Henry A. Landsberger, ed., *Rural Protest: Peasant Movements and Social Change.* (London: Macmillan, 1974); Lo Kuan-chung, *Three Kingdoms: China's Epic Drama,* trans. Moss Roberts (New York: Pantheon, 1976); and David Mitrany, *Marx Against the Peasant: A Study in Social Dogmatism* (Chapel Hill: University of North Carolina Press, 1951).

2. See Clifford Geertz, *Agricultural Involution: The Processes of Ecological Change in Indonesia* (Berkeley: University of California Press, 1963).

3. See John D. Powell, *Political Mobilization of the Venezuelan Peasant* (Cambridge: Harvard University Press, 1971).

4. The corresponding values for the United States and Russia would be larger by a factor of ten to twenty. See J. Lossing Buck, *Land Utilization in China* (Nanking, 1937), pp. 268–69; and R. P. Dore, *Land Reform in Japan* (London: Oxford University Press, 1959), pp. 26–27.

5. Thomas C. Smith, *The Agrarian Origins of Modern Japan* (Stanford: Stanford University Press, 1959), describes in a wealth of detail the sophisticated relationships between villagers and their *daimyō,* or feudal chieftains.

6. Hayami Yūjirō et al., eds., *Agricultural Growth in Japan, Taiwan, Korea, and the Philippines* (Honolulu: University Press of Hawaii, 1979), p. 9.

7. Ibid.; the estimate for China is the authors' own.

8. National Foreign Assessment Center, *China: Economic Indicators,* December 1978; and People's Republic of China, State Statistical Bureau, "Communiqué on Fulfillment of China's 1978 National Economic Plan."

9. A. D. Barnett, *China's Economy in Global Perspective* (Washington, D.C.: Brookings Institution, 1981), p. 280.

10. Benedict Stavis, *The Politics of Agricultural Mechanization in China.* (Ithaca: Cornell University Press, 1978), p. 238.

8 Cities of Industry and Commerce

1. World Bank, *World Development Indicators,* June 1979.

2. Even the London of Samuel Johnson and Charles Dickens was not so large as seventeenth-century Tokyo, or Edo as it was known until the Meiji Restoration in 1868. Edo grew large at a very early date because of the *sankin kōtai* system, which required all feudal lords to spend every other year at the shogun's court and to leave retainers and close members of their families in Edo when they were not personally in residence.

3. See Hong Kong, Government Information Services, *Hong Kong 1980* (Hong Kong: Government Press, 1980), chap. 1.

4. Japan, Office of the Prime Minister, Bureau of Statistics, *1970 Population Census of Japan* (1971), vol. 1, pp. 2, 4–6.

5. This figure is drawn from unpublished World Bank calculations. See also Edwin S. Mills and Byung-Nak Song, *Urbanization and Urban Problems* (Cambridge: Harvard University, Council on East Asian Studies, 1979). South Korea, as Mills and Song point out, has urbanized extremely rapidly by international standards. In 1950, 18.4 percent of its population was urban; in 1975, 50.9 percent. For the developing world as a whole, the comparable figures were 16.5 and 28.3 percent (ibid., p. 9).

6. Government Information Services, *Hong Kong 1980,* chap. 1.

7. See Economic Planning Board, *Handbook of Korean Economy 1980* (Seoul, 1981), pp. 397–98.

8. Edwin Mills and Katsutoshi Ohta, "Urbanization and Urban Problems," in *Asia's New Giant,* edited by Hugh Patrick and Henry Rosovsky (Washington, D.C.: Brookings Institution, 1976), p. 718.

9. Ibid., p. 701.

10. In January 1981, land in central Shinjuku, Tokyo, was valued at ¥3.71 million per square meter. See *Asahi Shimbun,* 17 January, 1981, p. 1.

11. Sales prices in 1981 for prime commercial space in Central District, Hong Kong, were over US $850 per square foot—by far the highest in the world. See *Far Eastern Economic Review,* 16 January, 1981, p. 37. For a detailed discussion of land policy in Hong Kong, see the case study at the end of this chapter.

12. Unpublished World Bank data.

13. Ibid.

14. Japan, Ministry of Justice, Research and Training Institute, *White Paper on Crime 1980* (Tokyo: Foreign Press Center, 1980), p. 4.

15. Ibid.

16. See Kishida Junnosuke, ed., *Toward the 21st Century* (Tokyo: Gakuyō Shobō, 1978), pp. 494–504.

17. On industrial stoppages see, for example, Republic of Singapore, Department of Statistics, *Singapore Statistical Charts, 1978* (Singapore, 1979), p. 27.

18. See Sato Takashi, ed., *Kokusai hikaku tōkei* [International comparative statistics] (Tokyo: Nihon Ginko Tokei Kyoku, 1981), pp. 135–36.

19. Yoshi Tsurumi, *Sōgōshōsha* (Montreal: Institute for Research on Public Policy, 1980), p. 16.

20. Japan, Office of the Prime Minister, Bureau of Statistics, *Kokusai tōkei yōran 1980* [International statistical handbook] (Tokyo: Ōkurashō Insatsu Kyoku, 1980), p. 228.

21. In 1980, when there were 12,000 lawyers in all of Japan, there were almost 600,000 in the United States as a whole, and 64,000 in New York State alone. In Japan, nonlawyers handle many tasks, including real-estate transfers and the drafting of wills, that are handled by lawyers in the United States. Even so, the differences in the overall role of law and litigation in the two societies—as well as the trends—are striking. See *Wall Street Journal,* 9 February 1981, p. 16.

22. Interviews with political analysts in Seoul, August 1979.

23. In 1980 it was officially 5,067,900. See Cynthia Kerr Rao, ed., *Hong Kong 1981* (Hong Kong: Government Press, 1981), p. 281.
24. Government Information Services, *Hong Kong 1980*, chap. 1.
25. Cheng Tong Yung, *The Economy of Hong Kong* (Kowloon: Far East Publications, 1977), p. 345.

9   Capital for Growth

1. See Bank of Japan, *Kokusai hikaku tōkei 1981* [International comparative statistics] (Tokyo: Nihon Ginkō Chōsa Tōkei Kyoku, 1981), pp. 39–42.
2. Ibid.
3. See Republic of China, Executive Yuan, Council for Economic Planning and Development, *Taiwan Statistical Data Book 1981*, (Taipei, 1981), p. 49.
4. Japan's savings rate rose, from 19.9 percent in 1973 to 22.9 percent in 1974, despite the deflationary effects of the first oil shock. See Bank of Japan, *Kokusai hikaku tōkei 1981*, pp. 39–42.
5. This figure is for nonhousing credit provided to consumers to cover purchases such as automobiles, electric appliances, and furniture. Credit extended in Japan to cover these items in 1980 totaled about $6.9 billion; in the United States, with a GNP slightly more than double Japan's, total consumer credit was more than 15 times as much. See Bank of Japan, *Kokusai hikaku tōkei 1981*, p. 67.
6. For details of Japanese taxation see, for example, Hayashi Taizō, *Guide to Japanese Taxes* (Tokyo: Zaikei Shōhō Sha), various years.
7. Sakakibara Eisuke, Robert Feldman, and Harada Yūzō, *The Japanese Financial System in Comparative Perspective* (Cambridge: Harvard University, Center for International Affairs, Program on U.S.-Japan Relations, 1981), table ii, after p. 8.
8. Neil H. Jacoby, *U.S. Aid to Taiwan* (New York: Praeger, 1966), p. 38.
9. Ibid., p. 118.
10. K. T. Li, *The Experience of Dynamic Economic Growth on Taiwan* (Taipei: Mei Ya Publications, 1976), p. 123.
11. See *Nihon Keizai Shimbun*, 4 August 1979; and Watanabe Toshio, *Azia kōgyōka no shin jidai* [The new age of Asian industrialization] (Tokyo: Nihon Bōeki Shinkō Kai, 1979), p. 201.
12. Republic of Singapore, Ministry of Trade and Industry, *Economic Survey of Singapore 1980* (Singapore: Singapore National Printers, 1981), p. 12.
13. Mah Feng-hwa, *The Foreign Trade of Mainland China* (Chicago: Aldine, 1971)
14. See Mah Feng-hwa, "Foreign Trade," in Alexander Eckstein, Walter Galenson, and Tachung Liu, eds., *Economic Trends in Communist China*. (Chicago: Aldine, 1968), pp. 671–738.
15. Cheng Tong Yung, *The Economy of Hong Kong* (Hong Kong: Far East Publications, 1977), pp. 61ff.
16. Sakakibara, Feldman, and Harada, *Japanese Financial System* table xxiv–3, after p. 54.
17. Ibid., p. 148.
18. Ibid. Japanese financial markets began to develop extremely rapidly during the early 1980s, however, especially in the foreign-exchange-related area. Their growth was facilitated greatly by the introduction in December 1980 of a new Japanese foreign-exchange law. On the details of this law, see Bank of Tokyo, *Tokyo Financial Review*, March 1981, pp. 1–4.
19. For details on the development of Mitsui Aluminum see, among others, Kent E. Calder, *The Japanese Aluminum Industry: Problems and Prospects, 1976–1980* (Tokyo: International Business Information), ERS vol. 2, no. 33.
20. Sakakibara, Feldman, and Harada, *Japanese Financial System*, p. 46.
21. See Industrial Bank of Japan, *Annual Report 1980*, various sections.
22. Sakakibara, Feldman, and Harada, *Japanese Financial System*, table xxiv–3, after p. 54.
23. See Jae Yoon Kim, ed., *The Korean Financial System* (Seoul: Bank of Korea, 1978), p. 53.
24. On the loan portfolio of the Korean Development Bank, see Bank of Korea, *Economic Statistics Yearbook 1981* (Seoul, 1981), pp. 60–61.
25. On the Development Bank of Singapore, see *Annual Reports* from 1969. See also Tan Chwee

Huat, *Financial Institutions in Singapore* (Singapore: University of of Singapore Press, 1978), pp. 182–94.

26. Republic of Singapore, Ministry of Culture, Information Division, *Singapore Facts and Pictures 1979* (Singapore, 1980), p. 86–87.

27. Development Bank of Singapore, *Annual Reports,* various issues.

28. For a detailed study on this point, see Kent E. Calder, "Politics and the Market: The Dynamics of Japanese Credit Allocation, 1946–1978" (Ph.D. dissertation, Harvard University, 1979), esp. pp. 184–98.

29. Bank of Korea, *Economic Statistics Yearbook 1981,* p. 19.

30. See Ishikawa Itoru and Gyōten Tōyō, eds., *Zaisei tōyūshi* [Fiscal investment and loans program] (Tokyo: Kinyu Zaisei Iijo Kenkyu Kai, 1977), p. 86; and Bank of Japan, *Keizai tōkei nenpō 1980* [Economic statistics annual] (Tokyo-Nihon Ginkō Chosa Tōkei Kyoku, 1980), p. 214.

31. For a good general introduction to Japan's postal savings system and the uses to which its income is put, see Ishikawa and Gyōten, *Zaisei tōyūshi.*

32. Sakakibara, Feldman, and Harada, *Japanese Financial System,* table xx-4, following p. 52.

33. *Business Week,* 13 April 1981, p. 127.

34. On the Singapore Asiadollar market, see Tan Chwee Huat, *Financial Institutions in Singapore* (Singapore: Singapore University Press, 1978), pp. 51–72.

35. *Business Week,* 13 April 1981, p. 127.

36. Ibid. The Japanese government restricts holdings by foreign residents in "strategic" stocks to 30 percent of total common shares outstanding.

37. Ibid.

38. Indeed, Toyota and Matsushita are so liquid, and lend so actively to affiliated firms and to the repurchase *(gensaki)* market, that they themselves are sometimes known in Japan as banks. See Kondō Hiroshi, *Toyota shōhō Matsushita shōhō* [Toyotaism vs. Matsushita-ism] (Tokyo: Nihon Jitsugyō Shuppan Sha, 1977), pp. 65–80.

39. Sakakibara, Feldman, and Harada, *Japanese Financial System,* table ix after p. 21.

40. See special survey on money and finance, *The Economist,* 29 November 1980, pp. 46ff.

41. Bank of Korea, *Monthly Economic Statistics,* July 1981, p. 22.

42. Ibid., p. 23.

43. See Bank of Japan, *Keizai tōkei nenkan* [Economic statistics annual] (Tokyo), various issues.

44. Ministry of Culture, *Singapore Facts and Pictures 1979,* p. 164.

45. Koo Chian Kim, *Yearbook of Statistics: Singapore 1979/80* (Singapore: Department of Statistics, 1980), p. 41.

46. Drawn from interviews with Singapore government officials, July, 1980.

47. Ministry of Trade and Industry, *Economic Survey of Singapore 1980,* pp. viii, 66.

48. See Huat, *Financial Institutions in Singapore,* p. 178.

49. See Republic of Singapore, Ministry of Trade and Industry, *Economic Survey of Singapore 1979* (Singapore: Singapore National Printers, 1980), p. viii.

50. Koo Chian Kim, *Yearbook of Statistics: Singapore 1979/80,* p. 199.

51. Ministry of Trade and Industry, *Economic Survey of Singapore 1980,* p. 12.

10. Technology for Competition

1. From 1.6 percent of all U.S. patents in 1966, Japan's share grew to 9.3 percent in 1976. See James Abegglen and Akio Etori, "Japanese Technology Today," *Scientific American,* October 1980, p. 12.

2. Ibid.

3. Interview with KIST officials, Seoul, July 1980.

4. *Financial Times,* 2 July 1979, p. 5.

5. Japan, Science and Technology Agency, *A Summary of the 1979 White Paper on Science and Technology* (Tokyo, 1980), p. 19.

6. Japan, Science and Technology Agency, Planning Office, *Kagaku gijutsu yōran 1981* [Indicators of science and technology] (Tokyo 1981), p. 22.

7. *Financial Times,* 2 July 1979, p. 5. In 1979, Japan's overall technology trade surplus in steel

reached ¥11.9 billion, with exports nearly three times imports. See Science and Technology Agency, *Kagaku gijutsu yōran 1981,* pp. 120–23.

8. Science and Technology Agency, *Summary of the 1979 White Paper,* p. 15.

9. In 1969 the United States graduated 16,282 electrical engineers from its universities, while Japan graduated 11,848. But in 1979 the United States graduated only 16,093 electrical engineers, whereas Japan graduated 21,435. See *Engineering Manpower Bulletin,* various issues.

10. Interview with KIST officials, Seoul, July 1980.

11. See Science and Technology Agency, *Kagaku gijutsu yōran 1981,* pp. 10–11.

12. On MITI efforts to encourage technological innovation in Japan during the 1980s, see Ministry of International Trade and Industry, *The Industrial Structure of Japan in the 1980s: Future Outlook and Tasks* (Tokyo, 1981), pp. 42–63.

13. On the early history of government assistance for the Japanese computer industry, see Eugene Kaplan, *Japan: The Government-Business Relationship* (Washington, D.C.: U.S. Department of Commerce, 1972), pp. 79–95.

14. Comptroller General of the United States, *U.S.-Japan Trade: Issues and Problems* (Washington, D.C.: U.S. Government Printing Office, 1979), p. 29. Japanese government subsidies over the duration of the VLSI project amounted to roughly ¥29 billion.

15. Ibid.

16. In June 1981 the six Japanese producers of 64-K RAMs (random access memories) had a production capacity of roughly 500,000 chips a month, well over one-half the total world capacity. Announced plans called for a fivefold increase in this capacity to 2,500,000 chips a month by early 1982, making Japan the virtually unchallenged 64-K RAM production base for the entire world. See *Japan Economic Journal,* 30 June 1981.

11. The Energy Defense

1. Japan's total oil production in 1978 was only 640,000 kiloliters. See Nishiyama Takeshi, ed. *Nihon Kokusei zue* [Japan national almanac] (Tokyo Kokusei Sha, 1980), p. 303.

2. Japan Economic Journal, *Industrial Review of Japan 1980* (Tokyo: Nihon Keizai Shimbun Sha, 1980), p. 6.

3. Bank of Japan, *Kokusai hikaku tōkei 1981* [International Comparative Statistics] (Tokyo: Nihon Ginkō Chōsa Tōkei Kyoku, 1981), pp. 158–93.

4. Ibid., pp. 163–64, 187.

5. Republic of Korea, Economic Planning Board, *Handbook of Korean Economy 1980* (Seoul, 1981), pp. 313, 321; Republic of China, Executive Yuan, Council for Economic Planning and Development, *Taiwan Statistical Data Book 1981* (Taipei, 1981), p. 88.

6. See ibid., pp. 91–92; Economic Planning Board, *Handbook of Korean Economy 1980,* p. 329.

7. The proportion of gasoline consumption to total oil consumption in Japan is lower than in any other major industrial nation. Percentages for other major nations in 1977 were: Britain, 21.5; West Germany, 18.1; Italy, 12.4; and France, 12. See Keizai Kōhō Center, *Rising to the Energy Challenge: The Case of Japanese Industries* (Tokyo: Keidanren, 1980), p. 7.

8. David H. Deese and Joseph S. Nye, eds., *Energy and Security* (Cambridge, Mass.: Ballinger Publishing Co., 1981), p. 211.

9. Iran in 1980 supplied 9.1 percent of South Korea's total crude oil imports. See Economic Planning Board, *Handbook of Korean Economy 1980,* p. 321.

10. Council for Economic Planning and Development, *Taiwan Statistical Data Book 1981,* p. 216.

11. For details of the Japanese economy's reaction to the oil shock of 1973, see Yoshi Tsurumi, "Japan," in *The Oil Crisis,* Raymond Vernon ed., (New York: W. W. Norton, 1976), pp. 113–27.

12. For details of the Japanese economy's reaction to the oil shock of 1979, see Japan Economic Journal, *Industrial Review of Japan 1980,* chap. 1.

13. South Korea's foreign exchange payments for imported crude oil rose from $2.17 billion in 1978 to $3.33 billion in 1979, an increase amounting to roughly 2 percent of GNP. Taiwan's crude oil imports rose from $1.59 billion in 1978 to $2.18 billion in 1979. See Economic Planning Board, *Handbook of Korean Economy 1980,* p. 322; Council for Economic Planning and Development, *Taiwan Statistical Data Book 1981,* p. 213.

14. *Far Eastern Economic Review,* 8 August 1980, p. 41. The $3.7 billion increase in oil payments that South Korea incurred during 1979–80 led to a commensurate increase in the nation's trade deficit, however.

15. See *Far Eastern Economic Review,* 8 August 1980, pp. 40–41.

16. Adjusted for seasonal trade fluctuations, this surplus actually amounted to $1.5 billion in September 1980. See Sanwa Bank, *Ltd., Economic Letter,* November 1980, p. 2.

17. When Shikoku businessman Hisao Tsubouchi was considering taking the presidency of Sasebo Heavy Industries in early 1978, Minister of International Trade and Industry Toshio Komoto reportedly showed him confidential MITI seismological surveys of the ocean bottom near Sasebo, on the East China Sea, which suggested the possibility of substantial oil reserves in the area. See Nihon Keizai Shimbun, *Sasebo Jūkō* [Sasebo Heavy Industries] (Tokyo: Nihon Keizai Shimbun Sha, 1978).

18. *Far Eastern Economic Review,* 8 August 1980. Korean planners anticipate that by the year 2000, nuclear power will provide 70 percent of the nation's electricity.

19. Ibid.

20. Ibid.

21. On Japan's policy shift toward the Arabs, see Kenneth I. Juster, "Foreign Policymaking During the Oil Crisis," *Japan Interpreter,* Winter 1977, pp. 293–312.

22. See Japan, Ministry of International Trade and Industry, *Keizai kyōryoku no genjō to mondaiten* [The reality and problem areas relating to economic cooperation] (Tokyo: Tsūshō Sangyō Shō, 1979), pp. 724–33.

23. World Bank unpublished data.

24. Ibid.

25. Ibid.

26. See the case study at the end of this chapter, which considers in detail Hyundai's Middle East construction operations.

27. The agreement stipulated that the fertilizer plant would start production around the end of 1982, with an annual output of 500,000 metric tons of urea. See Chen Kao-tang, ed., *China Yearbook 1980* (Taipei: China Publishing Co., 1981), p. 338.

28. Kaya Yōichi, "Japan's Energy Consumption Structure and the Direction of Energy Conservation," *The Wheel Extended,* Autumn 1979, p. 5.

29. In 1980, Saudi Arabia provided 62.6 percent, Kuwait 25.9 percent, and Iran 9.1 percent of South Korea's oil imports. See Economic Planning Board, *Handbook of Korean Economy 1980,* p. 321.

30. See ibid.; and Council for Economic Planning and Development, *Taiwan Statistical Data Book 1981,* p. 213.

31. *Far Eastern Economic Review,* 8 August 1980, p. 41.

32. Tong Whan Park, *Problems of Petroleum Supply to Korea: Analysis from the Perspective of International Political Economy* (Seoul: Institute of Foreign Affairs and National Security, 1979), p. 55.

33. Background interviews with economic analysts in Seoul, July 1980.

34. On the history of the Hyundai Group, see Leroy P. Jones and Il Sakong, *Government, Business, and Entrepreneurship in Economic Development: The Korean Case* (Cambridge: Harvard University, Council on East Asian Studies, 1980), pp. 354–58.

35. Included, for example, are producers of cement, finished lumber, steel, and refined aluminum. See Hyundai Construction Co., Ltd., *Hyundai* (Seoul, 1980), pp. 82–83.

36. Drawn from unpublished World Bank data.

37. For details on these Hyundai projects in the Middle East, see Hyundai Construction Co., Ltd., *Hyundai Civil Engineering and Construction* (Seoul, n.d.), esp. pp. 30–35.

38. Drawn from interview data, Seoul, July 1980.

39. Drawn from interview data, Seoul, July 1980.

40. By 1980, Hyundai had risen to 72d on *Fortune's* list of the top 500 non-U.S. corporations. See *Fortune,* 10 August 1981, p. 208.

41. *Hyundai News,* May 1981, p. 1.

42. See *Hyundai News,* August 1980, p. 1.

43. Jones and Sakong, *Government, Business, and Entrepreneurship in Economic Development: The Korean Case,* pp. 357–58.

44. Drawn from World Bank unpublished data.
45. Hyundai Construction, *Hyundai,* pp. 20–21.

12   The Export Offensive

1. See Organization for Economic Cooperation and Development, *The Impact of the Newly Industrialising Countries on Trade in Manufactures* (Paris: OECD, 1979), p. 72.
2. Ibid. See also Edward Lincoln, ed., *Yearbook of U.S.-Japan Economic Relations in 1980* (Washington, D.C.: Japan Economic Institute of America, 1981), p. 120.
3. OECD, *Impact of the Newly Industrialising Countries,* p. 72.
4. Ibid., p. 74.
5. Ibid., pp. 72, 73, 75.
6. Donald Wise, ed., *Asia Yearbook 1981* (Hong Kong: Far Eastern Economic Review, 1981), p. 10.
7. South Korea's 1979 GNP was $61.5 billion, while Taiwan's was $26.9 billion, Hong Kong's $11.8 billion, and Singapore's $8.3 billion. See ibid., p. 10 .
8. OECD, *Impact of the Newly Industrialising Countries,* p. 47.
9. Bank of Korea, *Economic Statistics Yearbook 1981* (Seoul, 1981), pp. 224–25.
10. Yoshihara Kunio, *Japanese Economic Development* (Tokyo: Oxford University Press, 1979), p. 55.
11. Bank of Japan, *Keizai tōkei nenpō 1979* [Economic Statistics Annual] (Tokyo, 1980), pp. 223, 323.
12. See T. K. Seshadri, ed., *Asia 1981: Measures and Magnitudes* (Hong Kong: Asia Finance Publications, 1981), pp. 96–97.
13. See Nishiyama Takeshi, ed., *Nihon Kokusei zue 1981* [Japanese national almanac] (Tokyo: Kokusei Sha, 1981), p. 128.
14. See U.S. Congress, House, Committee on Ways and Means, Subcommittee on Trade, *Auto Situation 1980* (Washington, D. C.: U.S. Government Printing Office, 1980), p. 30.
15. Ibid.
16. Tsuru Shigeto, *The Mainsprings of Japanese Growth: A Turning Point?* (Paris: Atlantic Institute, 1977), p. 25.
17. James Abegglen, "Japan, the United States, and Asia's Newly Industrializing Countries," *Roundtable Reports* (New York: Columbia University, East Asian Institute, 1980), no. 1, p. 51.
18. See Japan, Ministry of International Trade and Industry, *Sangyō Kōzō no chōki vision* [A long-range view of industrial structure] (Tokyo: Tsūshō Sangyō Sha), various issues.
19. See Oriental Economist, *Japan Company Handbook: First Half, 1980* (Tokyo: Tōyō Keizai Shinpōsha, 1980), p. 397.
20. Ibid., pp. 648, 650.
21. Ibid., pp. 577, 578, 582, 587.
22. Wise, *Asia Yearbook 1981,* p. 10.
23. See Paul Balaran, "China: A Competitor for World Markets?" *Wall Street Journal,* 4 December 1980, p. 30.
24. Ibid.
25. See Sangjin Chyun, "Economic Diplomacy of the Republic of Korea, 1948–1980" (fellow's dissertation, Harvard University, Center for International Affairs, 1980).
26. Ibid., pp. 43–44. This paper, written by a seasoned insider, provides an excellent introduction to the dynamics of Korean economic diplomacy.
27. Tsuru, *Mainsprings of Japanese Growth,* p. 51.
28. For details concerning specific cases, see U.S.-Japan Trade Council, *U.S.-Japan Economic Handbook* (Washington, D.C., annual).
29. See the case study on the VLSI project at the end of chap. 10.
30. Based on discussions with businessmen and economic analysts, Seoul, July 1980.
31. See Japan, Ministry of International Trade and Industry, Information Office, *MITI Handbook 1979–1980* (Tokyo: Japan Trade and Industry Publicity, Inc., 1979), pp. 255–67.
32. See Korean Exchange Bank, *Businessman's Guide to Korea* (Seoul, 1978), pp. 171–75.

33. Even laissez-faire Hong Kong has established the government-supported Hong Kong Trade Development Council, which coordinates trade missions and overseas exhibitions of the colony's wares. For a description of Hong Kong's governmental trade-promotion activities, see Tzong-biau Lin and Victor Mok, *Trade Barriers and the Promotion of Hong Kong Exports* (Hong Kong: Chinese University Press), pp. 65–79.

34. See the case study at the end of this chapter.

35. Kaohsiung EPZ unpublished data, July 1980.

36. For further details on the establishment of the Kaohsiung EPZ, see K. T. Li, *The Experience of Dynamic Economic Growth on Taiwan* (Taipei: Mei Ya Publications, 1976), pp. 352–58.

37. The discussion here and subsequently relies on unpublished figures from the Republic of China, Foreign Trade Section, Export Processing Zone.

38. On the development of science and technology in Taiwan see, *inter alia,* Chen Kao-tang, ed., *China Yearbook 1980* (Taipei: China Publishing Co., 1981), pp. 266–74.

13   Regional Co-prosperity

1. *Financial Times,* 2 July 1979.

2. Ibid., p. iii. Bilateral deficits of Asia's "Gang of Four" totaled $21.7 billion in 1978.

3. James Abegglen, "Japan, the United States, and Asia's Newly Industrializing Countries," *Roundtable Reports* (New York: Columbia University, East Asian Institute, 1980), no. 1, p. 43.

4. Japan Economic Research Center projections suggest that Japanese investment in Asia will rise from $7.7 billion in 1978 to $23.7 billion in 1985 and $49.4 billion in 1990. See Kanamori Hisao et al., *The World Economy and Japan in 1990* (Tokyo: Japan Economic Research Center, 1980), p. 68.

5. Abegglen, "Japan," p. 40.

6. Ibid.

7. See Christopher Howe, *China's Economy: A Basic Guide* (New York: Basic Books, 1978), pp. 107–8, on Chinese coal reserves.

8. Donald Wise, ed., *Asia Yearbook 1981* (Hong Kong: Far Eastern Economic Review, 1981), pp. 128–29.

9. On the details of the 1978 agreement and the negotiating process leading up to its conclusion see, among others, Hong N. Kim, "The Fukuda Government and the Politics of the Sino-Japanese Peace Treaty." *Asian Survey,* March 1979, pp. 297–313.

10. A "private" memorandum, signed in 1962 by Liao Chengzhi and Takasaki Tatsunosuke, created the basis for what was called "L-T trade." This trade averaged $100 million annually between 1962–67. A. D. Barnett, *China and the Major Powers in East Asia* (Washington, D. C.: The Brookings Institution, 1977), p. 106.

11. On the potential of the Korean overtures and on the details of President Chon's 1981 visit to the ASEAN nations, see *Far Eastern Economic Review,* 26 June 1981, pp. 28–32.

14   The Rest of the World

1. For a provocative assessment of the consequences of Western imperialism for Eastasian economic and political development, see Frances V. Moulder, *Japan, China, and the Modern World Economy* (Cambridge: Cambridge University Press, 1977). For a more descriptive and highly scholarly treatment, see G. C. Allen and Audrey Donnithorne, *Western Enterprise in Far Eastern Economic Development* (London: George Allen & Unwin, 1954).

2. At the end of 1979, the majors supplied roughly 52 percent of Japan's crude oil; by the end of 1980 this figure had fallen to 46 percent. See *Petroleum Intelligence Weekly,* 1980, various issues.

3. For an elaboration of this theme with respect to Japan, see Isaac Shapiro, "The Risen Sun: Japanese Gaullism?" *Foreign Policy,* Winter 1980–81, pp. 62–81.

4. See Peter F. Drucker, "Japan Gets Ready for Tougher Times," *Fortune,* 3 November 1980, p. 112.

5. Among the key restricted items are steel (subject in 1981 to the so-called "trigger price" import restraint mechanism), textiles (subject to the provisions of the multilateral Multi-Fiber Agreement), and automobiles.

6. Textiles were the most important Korean and Taiwanese export to the U.S. under restraint as of late 1981. Others included color television sets and, in the case of Taiwan, canned mushrooms.

7. See Kishida Junnosuke, ed., *Toward the 21st Century* (Tokyo: Gakuyō Shobō, 1978), pp. 502–04.

8. Morgan Guaranty Trust Co., *World Financial Markets,* May 1981, p. 5.

9. Calculations based on figures for net official development assistance. See Organization for Economic Cooperation and Development, *Development Cooperation* (Paris: OECD, 1979), various sections.

10. Kanamori Hisao et al., *The World Economy and Japan in 1990* (Tokyo: Japan Economic Research Center, 1980), p. 72.

11. International Bank for Reconstruction and Development, *1980 World Tables* (Washington, D.C., 1980), pp. 411, 413. By March 1980 all the Asian developing nations, including Indonesia, Malaysia, the Philippines, Thailand, India, and Pakistan, as well as the four Eastasian developing states, had a combined net liability position to Bank of International Settlements member banks (including major Japanese banks) of only $7.1 billion. Deducting loans to Japanese banks, these nations as a group were in surplus. Latin America, by contrast, had a $69.3 billion net liability position with the BIS banks, and Eastern Europe a deficit of $40.5 billion.

12. Tan Chwee Huat, *Financial Institutions in Singapore* (Singapore: Singapore University Press, 1978), p. 57, updated with unpublished data from Citibank.

13. Kanamori Hisao, *World Economy and Japan in 1990,* p. 72.

14. On the details of nineteenth-century Western economic involvement in China, see Allen and Donnithorne, *Western Enterprise,* pp. 13–181.

15. On the prewar involvement of Western enterprises with the Japanese economy, see G. C. Allen, *Japan's Economic Policy* (London: Macmillan, 1980), pp. 90–94. See also Allen and Donnithorne, *Western Enterprise,* pp. 185–237.

15   The Uncertain Political Future

1. Arthur G. Ashbrook, Jr., "China: Economic Overview, 1975," in U.S. Congress, Joint Economic Committee, *China: A Reassessment of the Economy* (Washington, D.C.: U.S. Government Printing Office, 1975), p. 23.

2. In 1958 the Socialists and Communists together gained 35.7 percent of the total seats in the most-crucial Lower House of the Diet. This proportion fell to 26.6 percent in 1980. See Asahi Shimbun Sha, *Asahi nenkan* [Asahi yearbook], various editions, 1959–81.

3. See *Asahi Shimbun,* 24 June 1981; Takechi Teruhiko, ed., *Kokusei shikihō* [National politics quarterly], Spring 1981, pp. 207–21.

4. This motion succeeded because key opponents of Prime Minister Ōhira within the ruling Liberal Democratic Party—mainly in the Fukuda and Miki factions—abstained on the crucial no-confidence vote.

5. Former Prime Minister Kishi Nobusuke, a key figure in rightist circles, has openly suggested the importance of reviving the "special relationships" with Japan's former colonies in Southeast Asia.

6. Between 1980 and 2000 the proportion of the Japanese population over 65 is expected to nearly double, to 14.3 percent of the national total. In Britain, Germany, and Sweden, by contrast, the proportion of the aged is expected to decline, while in the U.S. it will only rise from 10.7 to 10.9 percent. See Kishida Junnosuke, ed., *Toward the 21st Century* (Tokyo: Gakuyō Shobō, 1978), p. 518.

7. Indeed, these changes are already occurring. Between 1976 and 1978, for example, Japan's footwear imports, over two-thirds of them from elsewhere in Eastasia, grew by more than 93

percent. Trends were similar in many textile and electronics product areas. See James Abegglen, "Japan, the United States, and Asia's Newly Industrializing Countries," *Roundtable Reports* (New York: Columbia University, East Asian Institute, 1980), no. 1, p. 45.

16 Eastern Challenge: Western Response?

1. Edward Lincoln, ed., *Yearbook of U.S.-Japan Economic Relations in 1980.* (Washington, D.C.: Japan Economic Institute of America, 1981), p. 121.

2. Aircraft, computers, medical devices, and telecommunications equipment, the major high-technology categories, together comprised only 11 percent of U.S. exports to Japan in 1980. See ibid., p. 121.

3. In 1969 the U.S. trade deficit with Eastasia was $1.3 billion; in 1979, $10.8 billion. In 1980 the U.S. deficit with all of Eastasia fell to $10.2 billion because of sharply expanded U.S. exports to the People's Republic of China. With China excluded from the calculations, the U.S. deficit continued to expand, from $12.1 billion in 1979 to $13.2 billion in 1980. See International Monetary Fund, *Direction of Trade Statistics,* 1969–81, selected issues.

4. The U.S. iron and steel trade deficit decreased following the imposition of import restrictions, from $1.44 billion in 1968 to $738 million in 1970. But it increased again sharply to $1.9 billion in 1971 and $2.1 billion in 1972, as the import product mix moved to higher-value-added products. See U.S. Department of Commerce, *Survey of Current Business,* 1968–72, various issues.

5. In 1976 more than half of the 5.5 million color television sets Japan exported went to the United States. See *The Economist* 23 April 1977, p. 83.

6. See William Ouchi, *Theory Z* (Reading, Mass.: Addison-Wesley, 1981).

7. See George Lodge, *The New American Ideology* (New York: Knopf, 1976).

8. Ezra Vogel suggests tentatively that Lodge's concept of communitarianism may provide the answer to the problems of community consciousness that plague the American political economy. See Ezra F. Vogel, *Japan as Number One* (Cambridge: Harvard University Press, 1979), pp. 254–56.

9. Gary R. Saxonhouse, "Industrial Restructuring in Japan," *Journal of Japanese Studies,* Summer 1979, pp. 289–95.

10. On the functions of the largest long-term credit bank (the Industrial Bank of Japan) in the Japanese political economy, see Kent E. Calder, "Politics and the Market: The Dynamics of Japanese Credit Allocation, 1946–1978" (Ph.D. dissertation, Harvard University, 1979), pp. 238–56.

11. Various versions of such an institution have, of course, been suggested. Former President Jimmy Carter, among others, supported the idea of a National Urban Bank. Felix Rohatyn also promoted a similar urban redevelopment scheme. But most of the government financial institutions proposed would have, as their major objective, support for the obsolete, uncompetitive sectors of American industry, rather than for the sectors with real competitive potential. Eastasian government financial institutions occasionally give substantial aid to noncompetitive sectors such as coal and shipping. But their overall strategic priority is, in sharp contrast to most of the recent U.S. proposals for industrial banks, clearly to promote sectors of the future rather than attend to welfare needs.

12. On the organization and functions of the Japanese general trading company, as well as the possibility of adapting it to American circumstances, see Yoshi Tsurumi, *Sōgōshōsha: Engines of Export-Based Growth* (Montreal: Institute for Research on Public Policy, 1980).

NOTE: The rear endpaper map shows the disparities in industrial production per person across the Eastasian region. This map plots isoproduct contours between data points, which are (1) provincial capitals in the case of China, (2) geographical centers of the major home islands in Japan, and (3) national capitals elsewhere in the region.

Data sources for the rear endpaper map include the following references. China: *Zhongguo Jingjian 1981* [Chinese Economic Yearbook 1981] (Beijing: Journal of Economic Management, 1981); Japan: *Min Ryoku 1981* [Popular Forces 1981] (Toyko: Asahi Shimbun Sha, 1981); and other nations: Donald Wise, ed., *Asia Yearbook 1981* (Hong Kong: Far Eastern Economic Review, 1981).

Index

Index

"think tanks," in Eastasia, 150–51

Third World, 153, 207–10; auto industry competition in, 233; Eastasia, and relationship with, 187–88; as European market, 213; exports of, 207; and Hyundai Pony, 153; and Japanese export credit, 182; market expansion to, 212; *see also* Africa; Latin America

thought reform, of Chinese intellectuals, *viii*

"Three People's Principles," of Sun Yat-sen, 221

Thurow, Lester, 13

tianming (Mandate of Heaven), 44–45

Titoism, and options for PRC, 220; possibility of in China's future, 22

Tokyo, 103–4, 246*n*2; crime rate in, 108; department stores in, 200; education in, 113, 150; and Japan Economic Research Center, 50, 209; land value in, 105; securities exchange in, 134; stock prices in, 136

Tokyo Stock Exchange, 134

Tokyo University, and space exploration, 150

Toshiba, and joint computer research, 155

toxic chemicals, and industrial pollution, 107, 166

Toyota, 5, 20, 54, 176

trade: opening of Eastasia, 47; transatlantic and transpacific, compared, 3

trade associations, 80–82; characteristics of in Eastasia, 80–82

trade deficit, 29, 159–60, 232

trade unions, *see* unions

trading companies, 74, 76–78, 198, 199, 246; buying and selling practices, 234; and commercial banks, in Japan, 128; and diversification of energy sources, 164; and economic growth, 26; in Eastasian economies, 54, 76–78, 246; and export growth, 184; and foreign exchange, 208; and intraregional trade, 56, 201; in the Third World, 207, 208; U.S. and difficulty establishing, 247; Western countries, and need for, 237, 246; and Western technology, 147

tradition, in Eastasia, 43, 45; and ethics vs. written law, 45

training subsidies, 141

transportation, 55, 64, 102–4 passim

transportation equipment, 30, 173

treaty ports, 5, 65, 205, 214

Troeltsch, Ernst, 121

trust banks, in Taiwan, 129

Tsubouchi, Hisao, and influence of MITI, 270 *n*17

Tsukuba Science and Industrial Park, 141, 151

Tung, C.Y., 200

two-tier pricing, 182

type, moveable, and early invention of in Eastasia, 5, 145

typewriters, and Eastasian production for Western companies, 185

Ulsan shipyard (ROK), and Hyundai, 170

unemployment, 13, 35, table 3–2 (p. 35), 233

unemployment compensation, 36

Union of Soviet Socialist Republics (USSR), 75, 228, 229; and collectivization, 95, 100; and Japan 8, 224; Korean conflict and, 227; PRC, and influence of, 95; research and development budget in, 148; scissor program, 92; and U.S. armed forces in Eastasia, 215

unions, 53, 59, 110, 112, 232

United Nations, and PRC, 97–98

United States, 15, 23, 46, 73, 196, 207, 235, 236, 237, 263*n*17; and agriculture, 13, 98; and aluminum industry, 240; and antitrust legislation, 4, 73, 237; and automobile production costs, 15; "bailout" of industry, 179; business style in, 198; and capital for industry, 236; and competition, 13, 238, 251; and corporate responsibility, 112, 246; and defending international markets, 236; depreciation provisions in, 241, 263*n*17; diplomatic relations with PRC, 226; and dumping prohibition, 182; Eastasian development, and effect on, 12–14, 184–85, 186, 187, 205, 210, 212, 231, 232; and Eastasian EPZs, 189; education in Eastasian language, 238; education of Eastasians in, 146; education for lawyers in, 114; and European market, 213; and exports to Eastasia, 100, 101, 171, 186, 207, 212, 231, 261*n*2, 274*n*2; and export industries, 189; and foreign investments, 13; and free enterprise, 251; as fuel source for Eastasia, 198; government of, 20, 234, 239, 242–43; growth and inflation compared, 31, figure 3–1 (p. 32); and immigration laws, 42; and imports from Eastasia, 4, 148, 171, figure 12–1 (p. 172), 172, 177, 273*n*6; and intelligence network in Eastasia, 238; international trade and policies of, 237; and Iranian oil boycott, 206–7; and Japanese quality control techniques, 5, 16; Japanese steel industry and, 4,

Index

16, 148, 240, 262n3, 274n4; and Korean conflict, 226; and land reform in Japan, 91; and licensing in China, 251; loan guarantees for new technology in, 243; and long-term credit, 244; and military aid to Taiwan, 226; as military arms supplier to Saudi Arabia, 163; and multinational corporations, 78, 147, 153, 215, 236; and Office of Industrial Policy, 241; OPEC petrodollars, 232; and open markets, 251; per capita income, 19; and petrochemicals, 240; and population distribution, 13; port authorities of and profit from Eastasian trade, 186; and postal savings plan, 244; and postwar occupation of Japan, 139, 204, 205, 214; and power redistribution, 13; pragmatism and, 239; price control effect on fuel consumption, 241; protectionism in, 233, 241; recognition of PRC and effect on Taiwan, 206; research and development in, 148, 243; and restraint-of-trade agreements, 208; retail chains in, and Eastasian imports, 186; and savings in, 244; and Shanghai communiqué, 226; and Silicon Valley, 236; and steel industry, 240, 274n4; and strategic aerospace control, 146; supply structure of, and Eastasian imports, 187; and support of declining industries, 240; Taiwan's relationship with, under Carter administration, 226; tax credits, 243, 246; tax-GNP ratio, 33, table 3–1 (p. 34); and technology, 156, 243, 274n2 (*see also* Western technology); trade deficit of, 232, 274n3, 274n4; and trade with Europe and Asia, 261n1; and trade relations with Japan, 81, 232–33; and trading companies, 246; and treatment of growth industries, 239; and unemployment in automobile industry, 13: and USSR, 238; and wartime solidarity, 237; and welfare-orientation of social security, 143; and worker motivation, 235
United States aid to Eastasia, 3, 29, 209, 210–12
United States armed forces: defense spending of, and Japan compared, 149; in Eastasia, 3, 215; and effect of withdrawal from Eastasia, 216, 223; Japan's reliance on, 207; role in Korean conflict, 227, wages of, in Japan, 111
United States Department of Commerce, 241
United States Department of Defense, and research and development, 156, 249
United States Department of Transportation, and study on automobile imports, 15
United States Export-Impot Bank, 162, 210

United States Marines, and opening of Korea to trade, 47
United States Navy, and Hyundai dredging operations, 161
unit labor costs, 19, 262n7
uranium, and Japanese joint ventures in Australia, 164
urban American, and effect of Eastasian economic growth on, 13
urbanization, limit on, in PRC, 96
urban street patterns in Eastasia, 104–5
utility rates, for industry, 178–79

vertical integration: and Hyundai, 163, 168; and Japanese trading companies, 198
Very Large-Scale Integration microelectronic circuitry (VLSI): research project on, 153–57, 241; and effect on export prices, 182
video tape recorders, 153, 187
Vietnam, language of, 43
Vietnam War, 43, 228
village collective, and PRC, 95, 96
VLSI, *see* Very Large Scale Integration microelectronic circuitry
VLSI Technology Research Corporation, 155
Volkswagen joint venture with Nissan, 187
voluntary restraint agreements, 232, 233

Wang Laboratories, and research in Taiwan, 153
watchmaking industry, 17–18; in Hong Kong, 5; in Japan, 175; in Switzerland, 262n4
water: and agricultural importance in PRC, 94, 99, table 7–1 (p. 99); and industrial pollution in Japan, 107
wealth, distribution of, in Singapore, 59
Weber, Max, 121
welfare, *see* social welfare
welfare state, absence of in Eastasia, 37
Western banks, and Eastasian exports, 185
Western Electric, research in Taiwan, 153
Western European trade, 3, 185–86
Western import-export firms, and GTCs compared, 78
Western markets for Eastasia, 172–73, figure 12–2 (p. 173), 176

295